family **fh** handyman

DIY TRADE SECRETS

Chief Content Officer Jason Burhmester
Content Director Mark Hagen
Creative Director Raeann Thompson
Senior Editor Julie Kuczynski
Editor Sara Strauss
Associate Creative Director Kristen Stecklein
Manager, Production Design Satyandra Raghav
Senior Print Publication Designer Sweta Chandra
Deputy Editor, Copy Desk Ann M. Walter
Associate Assigning Editor Mary Flanagan

A FAMILY HANDYMAN BOOK

Hardcover: 978-1-62145-698-8
Paperback: 979-8-88977-058-9

Component number 118300127H

We are committed to both the quality of our products
and the service we provide to our customers. We value
your comments, so please feel free to contact us at
TMBBookTeam@TrustedMediaBrands.com.

For more Family Handyman products and information,
visit our website: *www.familyhandyman.com*

Printed in China
10 9 8 7 6 5 4 3 2 1

Text, photography and illustrations for *DIY Trade Secrets*
are based on articles previously published in *Family
Handyman* magazine (*familyhandyman.com*).

WARNING

All do-it-yourself activities involve a degree of risk. Skills,
materials, tools and site conditions vary widely. Although
the editors have made every effort to ensure accuracy,
the reader remains responsible for the selection and use
of tools, materials and methods. Always obey local codes
and laws, follow manufacturer's operating instructions
and observe safety precautions.

Photo and Illustration Credits
13: Don Mannes; 119: Macida/Getty Images; 121 (3),
122 (top left), 123 (2): Alex Santantonio; 122 (scarifier):
Ox Tools; 122 (bottom right): FollowTheFlow/Getty
Images; 138: JP Wallet/Shutterstock; 164 (center),
165 (top left, top right, bottom left), 166 (two top left,
two bottom left): Structure Tech; 180 (bottom): American
Standard; 188 (left): Sterling; 188 (right): Swanstone;
205: kzww/Shutterstock; 207 (top left): Rust-Oleum;
209 (top left): HandyDeck; 209 (bottom right): DeckRite;
213 (bottom two): Decks Unlimited; 214 (fence): Benjamin
Rondel/Getty Images; 222 (layout design), 225 (top
right): Rain Bird; 236 (bottom): Sakrete; 250 (top):
Charles Knowles/Shutterstock; 250 (bottom), 251:
brizmaker/Shutterstock; 258, 259 (tech art): Mario
Ferro; 260: nexus 7/Shutterstock; 262: fcafotodigital/
Getty Images; 268: JGI/Jamie Grill/Getty Images

SAFETY FIRST—*ALWAYS!*

Tackling home improvement projects and repairs can be endlessly rewarding. But as most of us know, with the rewards come risks. DIYers use chain saws, climb ladders, and tear into walls that can contain big and hazardous surprises.

The good news: Armed with the right knowledge, tools and procedures, homeowners can minimize risk. As you go about your projects and repairs, stay alert for these hazards:

ALUMINUM WIRING

Aluminum wiring, installed in about 7 million homes between 1965 and 1973, requires special techniques and materials to make safe connections. This wiring is dull gray—not the dull orange characteristic of copper. Hire a licensed electrician certified to work with it. For more information, go to *cpsc.gov* and search for "aluminum wiring."

SPONTANEOUS COMBUSTION

Rags saturated with oil finishes, like Danish oil and linseed oil, and with oil-based paints and stains can spontaneously combust if left bunched up. Always dry them outdoors, spread out loosely. When the oil has thoroughly dried, you can safely throw them in the trash.

VISION AND HEARING RISKS

Safety glasses or goggles should be worn whenever you're working on DIY projects that involve chemicals, dust, and anything that could shatter or chip off and hit your eye. Sounds louder than 80 decibels (dB) are considered potentially dangerous. Sound levels from a lawn mower can be 90 dB, and shop tools and chain saws can be 90 to 100 dB.

LEAD PAINT

If your home was built before 1979, it may contain lead paint, which is a serious health hazard, especially for children 6 and under. Take precautions when you scrape or remove it. Contact your public health department for detailed safety information or call 800-424-LEAD (5323) to receive an information pamphlet. Or visit *epa.gov/lead*.

BURIED UTILITIES

A few days before you dig in your yard, have your underground water, gas and electrical lines marked. Just call 811 or go to *call811.com*.

SMOKE AND CARBON MONOXIDE (CO)

The risk of dying in reported home structure fires is cut in half in homes with working smoke alarms. Test your smoke alarms every month, replace batteries as necessary and replace units that are more than 10 years old. As you make your home more energy efficient and airtight, existing ducts and chimneys can't always successfully vent combustion gases, including potentially deadly carbon monoxide (CO). Install a UL-listed CO detector, and test your CO and smoke alarms at the same time.

FIVE-GALLON BUCKETS AND WINDOW COVERING CORDS

Anywhere from 10 to 40 children a year drown in 5-gallon buckets, according to the U.S. Consumer Products Safety Commission. Always store them upside-down and store ones containing liquid with the covers securely snapped.

According to Parents for Window Blind Safety, hundreds of children in the United States are injured every year after becoming entangled in looped window treatment cords. For more information, visit *pfwbs.org*.

WORKING UP HIGH

If you have to get up on your roof to do a repair or installation, always install roof brackets and wear a roof harness.

ASBESTOS

Texture sprayed on ceilings before 1978, adhesives and tiles for vinyl and asphalt floors before 1980, and vermiculite insulation (with gray granules) all may contain asbestos. Other building materials made between 1940 and 1980 could also contain asbestos. If you suspect that materials you're removing or working around contain asbestos, contact your health department or visit *epa.gov/asbestos* for information.

CONTENTS

CHAPTER 1
PAINTING & FINISHES

Prep Before You Paint.................................... 10
Master Interior Painting.............................. 16
Revive Kitchen Cabinets............................. 20
Spray-Paint an Exterior 26

Renew Your Wood Fence 32
Water-Based Basics 36
Wipe-On Poly... 40

CHAPTER 2
WOODWORKING & CABINETRY

Wood 101 48
Floating Shelves.. 54
12 Ideal Router Tips 61
Foolproof Dadoes & Rabbets 70

Tricks for Tighter Miters 74
Success with Melamine 79
All About Euro Hinges 84
Installing Cabinet Hardware...................... 90

CHAPTER 3
FLOORS, CEILINGS & WALLS

Install a New Floor in One Day.................. 96
Tiling Tricks 102
Choose Self-Leveling Underlayment 106
Spray-Texture a Ceiling.............................. 111

Taping Drywall... 114
Living with Plaster Walls 119
Plaster & Lath Tear-Off 124
Rock-Solid Handrails................................... 128

CHAPTER 4
DOORS, WINDOWS & TRIM

Install an Interior Door.............................. 134
How Much Does Window Replacement Cost?......... 138
Restore Your Old Windows 140

Working with Trim 147
Finishing Trim... 154
Essential Caulking Tips 158

CHAPTER 5

REMODELING, ENERGY SAVING & ELECTRICITY

Do's & Don'ts from Home Inspectors........................... 164
Avoid Framing Mistakes... 167
Leveling 101 172
Replacing a Refrigerator 176
Toilet Shopping Tips 180

A New Tub & Surround... 182
9 Things Electricians Do in Their Own Homes........ 189
Fire-Blocking Basics 192
Prevent Fires & Cut Your Energy Bill! 196

CHAPTER 6

EXTERIOR, LAWN & PAVING

Better Than Wood!.. 200
5 Solutions for a Shabby Deck.................................. 205
Build a Low-Upkeep Deck 210
Setting Fence Posts with Expanding Foam 214
Roof Tear-Off 216

Install an Irrigation System..................................... 221
Repair a Buried Cable 226
Cures for Top 5 Lawn Problems 228
Working with Bagged Concrete 234
Pour a Perfect Slab... 238

CHAPTER 7

GARAGE & AUTOMOTIVE

Garage Door Makeover.. 246
8 Garage Door Maintenance Tips 250
Space-Saving Garage Storage................................. 252
10 Tips to Save Gas.. 260

What to Do If 262
Change Your Engine Coolant 266
How to Buy a Reliable Used Car............................... 268

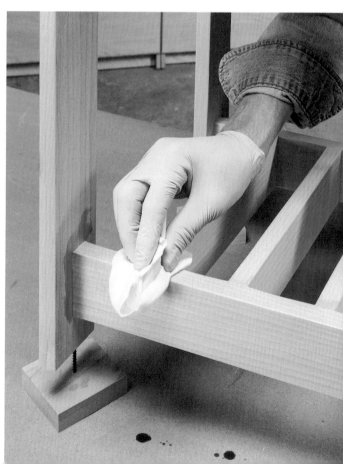

CHAPTER 1

PAINTING & FINISHES

Prep Before You Paint..10
Master Interior Painting..16
Revive Kitchen Cabinets...20
Spray-Paint an Exterior...26
Renew Your Wood Fence..32
Water-Based Basics...36
Wipe-On Poly..40

CAUTION:
If your home was built before 1978, check the paint for lead before you sand. For more info, go to *hud.gov/program _offices/healthy_homes.*

PREP BEFORE YOU PAINT

WHEN YOU NEED YOUR HOME TO LOOK ITS BEST, PEELING PAINT HAS GOT TO GO

Paying close attention to the prep work can make your paint job look as if you hired a pro. Here are tips and techniques for cleaning, scraping, filling and priming so your paint will stay put. We'll also help you identify and solve some specific problems that may have caused your paint to fail prematurely.

Applying the paint is easy. But creating a sound, dry surface for the new coat of paint is tough and time consuming. However, it's the key to any successful paint job.

CLEAN DEEP AND FAST WITH A PRESSURE WASHER

Paint just won't stick to a dirty or dusty surface (see **Figure A**, p. 13) You'll need to clean it even if there's very little scraping to do, and the fastest way is with a pressure washer. You can rent a pressure washer **(Photo 1)** and get a lot of loose paint and grime off your old painted surfaces fast.

These washers kick out a hard stream of water, so try it out on an inconspicuous spot on the house to get the hang of handling the wand. Be careful not to hit windows (they can break), and don't work the spray upward under the laps of siding. Remember, this is for cleaning, not blasting all the old paint off. Of course, some of the old loose paint will fall off, but too much pressure will gouge the wood **(Photo 2)**.

Don't try to pressure-wash while standing on a ladder. The recoil can knock you off balance. And finally, keep in mind that you won't be able to do any scraping and sanding for a couple of days until the surface dries thoroughly.

If the prospect of using a pressure washer is just too intimidating, you can get a stiff brush on a pole and a bucket with mild detergent to scrub the surfaces. Follow the scrub immediately with a rinse from your garden hose.

1 Pressure-washing removes loose paint and built-up grime and improves paint adhesion. Use the high pressure carefully, especially around windows. High-pressure water can break the glass. Avoid directing water up under the laps, and keep the nozzle at least 16 in. away from the wood.

2 Some loose paint will flake off while you wash the surface. But don't try to strip the paint—you'll gouge the wood.

KEEP YOUR SCRAPER SHARP

Old, flaking paint must be scraped from your wood surface or your new paint will eventually let go. Make sure the surfaces are dry first. Then scrape in the direction of the grain to avoid tearing the wood fibers and creating an unstable surface for your primer. Obviously, a sharp scraper is the best. You can buy hardened steel scrapers (**Photo 1**) or, for about twice the price, you can buy carbide scrapers (**Photo 2**). Good-quality scrapers all have replaceable blades. You can easily sharpen a steel scraper blade using a fine metal file. The carbide blades last up to 10 times longer but must be sharpened with special tools. Buy replacement blades to have on hand.

1 Follow the grain of the wood with long strokes. If nails are sticking up, pound them in. If the nail won't stay put, pull it out and drive in a new galvanized nail ½ in. away.

2 Pull down firmly with a sharp scraper to remove loose paint. Remember, you don't need to remove all the paint, just the stuff that flakes away with the scraper. Keep your scrapers sharp with a fine file. Tip: Don't scrape wet wood. You'll tear away the fibers and dig deep gouges into the wood.

3 Get into tight areas with a small 1-in. scraper. Heavy buildup of paint in corners will crack and let moisture in. Scrape and cut all excess paint out of the corners with a sharp putty knife.

4 While you're scraping, dig out any loose caulk around doors, windows and trim. Old, dried-out caulk loses its elasticity and will usually crack later. If your caulk is sound and adhering well, leave it in place.

DIAGNOSE COMMON PAINT PROBLEMS

Take a good look at your house before you start painting. You may have to correct some of the wrongs that the previous painter overlooked in desiring to get the job done fast. You may have peeling paint as shown in **Figures A, B and C.**

POORLY PREPARED SURFACE

You may notice the finished coat of paint peeling away from another coat underneath **(Figure A)**. This is the result of painting over a poorly prepped surface. Usually the surface wasn't cleaned before painting or the primer coat was left too long before the finish coat of paint was applied. You can remedy this situation by firmly scraping away the paint to get at the surface below. Scrape until you get down to a solid surface that may be part bare wood or a sound, previously painted surface. Sand and clean the surface thoroughly, let it dry, and prime all bare wood and spot-prime any small bare spots.

EXCESS MOISTURE

Sometimes you find paint and primer falling away from the bare wood surface **(Figure B)**. This is most likely caused by water getting behind the wood or even moisture from the home's interior. You can't repaint here unless you stop the source of the moisture migrating through the walls, especially from bathrooms and kitchens. Adding ventilation such as an exhaust fan in the room often helps. Many older homes have no vapor barrier, but applying a vapor barrier paint on the inside can sometimes do the trick. If you are stymied, consult a building contractor to help you solve the problem. Then scrape and sand to remove the loose paint.

ALLIGATORING

Another common problem is cross-grain cracking which is sometimes referred to as "alligatoring" **(Figure C)**. The source of this problem is usually paint buildup from several layers of oil-based paints. Unfortunately, there's no magic fix. You'll have to scrape off all the old paint down to bare wood and then sand the surface. Take precautions and gather this paint onto drop cloths or plastic for disposal because it may contain lead. Don't keep applying layers of paint to areas that don't need it, such as porch ceilings and eaves where the surfaces are protected. Often a good cleaning is all they need.

FIGURE A
Peeling after painting a poorly prepared surface

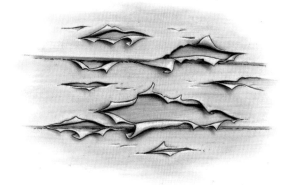

FIGURE B
Excess moisture getting behind the siding

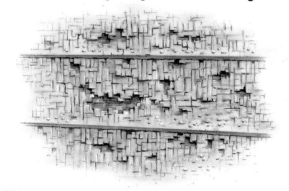

FIGURE C
Alligatoring from too many layers of oil-based paint

OTHER PROBLEMS

You may find mildew spots on the finished coat along shady areas. Buy a cleaner at paint supply stores to scrub the surface. You can usually stop mildew by increasing exterior airflow in that area, trimming plants close to the house and channeling water away. If the area is tough to air out, you can get mildewcide additives for your finish coat of paint.

FILL LARGE GOUGES BEFORE PRIMING

Fill large holes and gouges with a two-part resin filler such as Minwax High Performance Wood Filler. You have to mix these setting types of fillers, but they stick better to wood than other fillers. Remove any paint around the area before filling. Overfill each repair and then shape it once it has set with a file, sharp chisel and sandpaper. Blemishes deeper than ½ in. will need additional applications. Once the patch is dry, shaped and sanded, prime it to protect it from moisture.

You can fill nail holes with fillers too. For small, shallow blemishes, use an exterior spackling compound. Cracks can be filled with exterior caulk after priming.

SAND THE RIDGES

Feather the edge of a scraped area with a power sander to get rid of sharp edges. Ridges can later break the finished paint surface and allow moisture to get behind the paint.

Power sanders cut fast. Use a 60-grit paper for heavy ridges followed by 100-grit for a smooth look. Also sand shiny, old paint surfaces to give the topcoat better bite. After sanding, use a dry brush to whisk away any surface dust, especially on horizontal surfaces like windowsills.

USE A STAIN-BLOCKING PRIMER

You can choose either an oil or a latex primer and get great results. Oil primers, however, are generally more effective on new wood, metal and previously chalked surfaces. If you're priming over bare woods that have a high tannin content, such as cedar and redwood, ask your paint supplier for a special stain-blocking exterior primer. Stain-blocking primers will prevent a "bleed-through" of tannin through the primer and the topcoat and will stop old, rusty nail-heads from bleeding through as well **(Photo 1)**.

PRO TIP

The paint supplier can add pigment to your primer to get it close to the topcoat color. This is especially helpful when your topcoat is a darker color. You may even be able to cover the primed area and old paint surface with one coat of paint.

1 Spot-prime nailheads and knots with a special stain-blocking primer to prevent unsightly bleed-through from rust or wood resin. A pigmented shellac (BIN, for example) is a good product for this use.

PRO TIP

Always try to avoid priming or painting in direct sun. The extra heat can dry the primer and paint too quickly, preventing adequate penetration. It can also cause oil paints to develop blisters that will ruin the skin of the finish coat of paint.

2 Work the primer into cracks, especially where trim pieces meet siding. Even out the primer with long brush strokes and check for drips. Remember to work the primer under the siding laps and into tight spaces and hard-to-see spots. Surfaces with old paint that's still adhering well don't need a primer.

CAULK CORRECTLY

With all the caulks available, it can be hard to know what kind of caulk to buy to seal gaps. Most pros agree that acrylic caulk and siliconized acrylic caulk are the best for caulking around windows and doors and against corner boards. These caulks are paintable, long lasting and easy to clean.

Caulk sticks best to a primed surface. Squeeze enough caulk into the gaps to get a smooth bead that fills the void. Excess caulk will only increase the possibility of working loose over time.

1 Once you've primed the surface, caulk all the seams and cracks to keep out moisture and hide unsightly dark lines. Wipe excess acrylic caulk and shape it with a moist rag as you apply it. Let the caulk set (usually a couple of hours) before painting over it.

MASTER INTERIOR PAINTING

EIGHT TERRIFIC POINTERS FROM EXPERTS, AND FELLOW DIYERS, ON THE NO. 1 HOME IMPROVEMENT ACTIVITY

SPRING CLAMP

FERRULE

FINISH SETTLES IN THE BOTTOM OF THE JAR

1 LET PAINTBRUSHES SELF-CLEAN

Just hang your brush in a jar of solvent: water for latex paint, and mineral spirits or paint thinner for oil-based. Using a clamp, suspend the brush in the jar with the bristles fully submerged almost to the ferrule but not touching the bottom of the jar. Finish will slide off the bristles and settle on the bottom of the jar. If you're using paint thinner or mineral spirits, set the jar outside to keep fumes out of your house. Be sure it's away from children and pets. After a day or two, remove the brush and give it a thorough rinse in clean solvent.

JOINT COMPOUND

2 PATCH, PRIME, PATCH, PRIME

You've done a great job of patching and smoothing over all those pesky cracks, holes and dimples in your walls and ceiling, and you've rolled on the primer. So does that mean you're ready for the topcoat? Not so fast. Take a closer look at the surfaces with a portable work light. Chances are, you still have small imperfections you'll want to touch up with spackling or joint compound. Better to take care of these now because they'll really stand out after the final coat of paint goes on.

STIR STICKS

3 MAKE YOUR OWN STIR STICKS

Forget to grab stir sticks at the store when you picked up the paint? If you have a band saw and a hunk of 2x4, you can make your own! Take a 2-ft.-long 2x4 and draw a perpendicular line in the middle. Next, "rip" several ³/₁₆-in.-thick strips on the band saw up to the pencil line. Then, to release the stir sticks, chop the 2x4 at the pencil line. This method keeps your fingers a safe distance from the saw blade.

4 USE BABY WIPES FOR SMALL MESSES

Always have a package of baby wipes handy whenever you paint a room. They're great for wiping up small drips before you accidentally walk through them and track paint all over the house. And it beats keeping a bucket of water and rags around any day!

MARBLES

5 SHAKE AND TOUCH-UP PAINT

If there's only a little bit of latex paint left in the can and you want to save it for any touch-ups, put a half-dozen marbles in an empty water bottle and pour in the leftover paint. When pouring the paint into the bottle, hold the bottle steady in a roll of tape covered with a rag. Be sure to use a funnel or you'll have a mess on your hands. Next time you're ready to do a touch-up, shake the bottle, and the marbles will mix the paint.

DIY DEBATE
Paint walls or trim first?

We asked our Facebook followers whether they preferred to paint the trim or the walls and ceilings first and, boy, are people divided on this! We got more than 300 comments from DIYers and pros, but no clear consensus. However, we did learn some new tricks:

Paul G. paints in this order: "Hands, jeans, cat, kid, then finally the walls and trim."

And our keep-it-simple award goes to Brian G.: "I paint everything the same color, so it doesn't much matter."

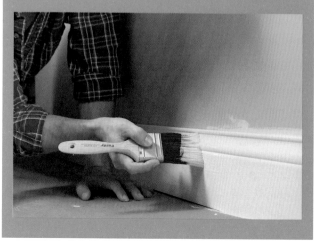

6 SHELTER BASEBOARDS FROM SPLATTER

When you're rolling paint onto walls or ceilings, a fine mist of paint settles on unprotected trim. For baseboards, forget about covering them completely. Just cover the top of each one with a "shelter" made from painter's tape. A single overhanging strip of 1½-in. or 2-in. tape catches roller splatters just as the roof overhang on a house keeps rain off the siding. Tape doesn't stick to dusty surfaces very well, so be sure to vacuum or wipe down your baseboards before masking. Also, press the tape down hard with a putty knife to prevent paint from bleeding underneath. For the best results, use self-sealing tape.

7 TAKE PHOTOS OF PAINT CAN LIDS

Have you ever thrown away a paint can and later wished you hadn't because you couldn't remember the name of the color you painted the bedroom? Paint can lids usually have labels with color information printed on them. Take photos of your paint can lids, print the images and tuck them away for future reference.

SELF-SEALING TAPE

DIY DEBATE
Angled or straight bristles?

We asked our Facebook followers whether they preferred paintbrushes with straight or angled bristles for tasks like cutting in around windows or painting trim. Most said they preferred angled, but we did hear from a few straight-bristle brush fans. And lots of people use both. As Lea D. told us, "Angled for corners and cutting in, and flat for all-over coverage."

8 SPLURGE ON SELF-SEALING TAPE

With regular painter's tape, you run the risk of "paint bleed"—paint creeping underneath the tape, leaving a ragged line where a wall meets trim or meets another wall or ceiling. We like self-sealing tapes like FrogTape and ScotchBlue Edge-Lock tape because they're specially designed to prevent paint bleed, giving you crisp, straight lines. They cost a lot more than regular masking or painter's tape, but they're worth it.

REVIVE KITCHEN CABINETS

A SIMPLE AND INEXPENSIVE DIY MAKEOVER

EASIER THAN YOU THINK

You don't need to spend thousands of dollars on new cabinets to give your kitchen a stunning new look. If your cabinets are in good shape, you can give them a fresh face with paint. Even including the sprayer, the project is pretty inexpensive.

Professional painters typically spray-paint doors to produce an ultra smooth finish. We'll show you how to spray-paint your doors and drawers, with just a short learning curve to use the sprayer effectively (for more sprayer tips, see p. 26). You could also spray the cabinet frames, sides and trim, but masking off the cabinet openings (and the rest of the kitchen) takes a lot of time, so just use a brush for those areas.

Remember, a painted finish won't be as tough as a factory finish, and even if you're careful, you can still end up with paint runs and have brush marks on your cabinet sides. But if you like the style of your cabinets and they're structurally sound—and you're willing to invest the time to paint them—this project is for you.

All the materials you need are available at home centers and paint stores. Plan to spend four or five days to complete the job—you'll have to let the paint dry overnight between coats and you can paint only one side of the doors per day.

NEW-LOOKING CABINETS IN 3 STEPS

PREP

PRIME

PAINT

1

2

3

WASH, RINSE, TAPE, REPEAT

As with any successful painting project, preparation is the key—and the most time-consuming step. Start by removing the cabinet doors and drawers as well as all the hardware. Label the doors as you remove them so you'll know where to reinstall them. Writing a number in the hinge hole (for Euro hinges) or where the hinge attaches works great—it's the only part not painted.

Take the doors and drawers to the garage or another work area and spread them out on a work surface. It's surprising how much space doors and drawers eat up—even if you have a small kitchen. An extension ladder placed over sawhorses gives you a surface where you can set the doors. Wash the fronts and the backs of the doors and the drawer fronts to remove grease (**Photo 1**). Then stick tape in the hinge holes or where the hinges attach to keep paint out.

Wash the grease off the cabinet frames in the kitchen too. Then tape off everything that abuts the cabinet frames (**Photo 2**). Use plastic sheeting or brown masking paper to cover appliances. Use rosin paper for countertops—it's thick enough to resist tears and won't let small paint spills seep through.

PRIME FOR A FRESH START

Some cabinets have a catalyzed lacquer finish that is very hard. Primer won't form a good bond to this surface unless you scuff it up first. Sand any damaged areas on the doors or cabinet frames with 320-grit sandpaper to remove any burrs or ridges, then fill the areas with spackling compound (**Photo 3**).

Lightly sand the doors and cabinet frames, trim and sides with 320-grit sandpaper. Sand just enough to take off the shine—you don't need to sand off the finish. Vacuum the dust off the wood using a bristle attachment. Before you're ready to apply the primer, wipe down the doors and frames with a tack cloth. Running the cloth over the surface is enough—you don't need to scrub to remove the fine dust particles.

Apply a stain-killing primer (Bulls Eye 1-2-3 and BIN are two brands) with a paintbrush (**Photo 4**). You can use a cheap brush—even a disposable one—for this. Don't worry about getting a uniform finish or brushstrokes in the primer (you'll remove them later with sandpaper). The doors and frames don't have to look pretty at this stage. But don't use a roller. It leaves a texture that will affect the finish. Besides, brushing is almost as fast as rolling, and you can use the bristles to work the primer into crevices.

Once the primer is dry (just one or two hours), lightly sand the doors and cabinets with 320-grit sandpaper to remove any brushstrokes (**Photo 5**). Sandpaper

1 WASH OFF YEARS OF KITCHEN GREASE
Clean away all the grease with warm water and dish detergent or the primer and paint won't adhere. Rinse clean with water.

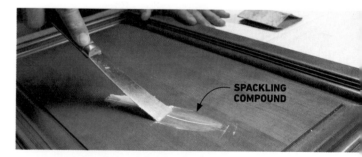

2 TAPE OFF AND COVER EVERYTHING
Tape off the walls, ceiling and flooring, and cover the countertops with rosin paper. Wrap appliances and the vent hood with plastic sheeting or masking paper.

3 FIX SCRATCHES, HOLES AND DINGS
Work spackling compound into damaged areas with a putty knife. Fill in holes from handles and hardware if you are replacing those features and will need holes in different places.

4 PRIME DOORS AND CABINET FRAMES WITH STAIN-BLOCKING PRIMER

The primer covers any stains and seals in cooking odors. Prime one side of all the doors, let them dry while you prime the cabinet face frames and sides, then prime the other sides of the doors.

5 SAND DOORS AND CABINETS WITH FINE-GRIT SANDPAPER

Sand with the grain. Be careful not to round over corners. After sanding, wipe the surface clean with a tack cloth.

STILE

RAIL

6 START IN A CORNER TO PAINT CABINET FRAMES

Use a high-quality paintbrush to paint an entire rail or stile, including the inside edge, before moving to an adjacent rail or stile.

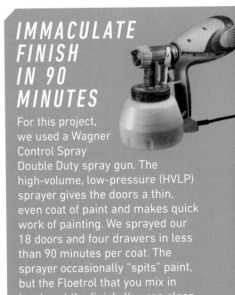

IMMACULATE FINISH IN 90 MINUTES

For this project, we used a Wagner Control Spray Double Duty spray gun. The high-volume, low-pressure (HVLP) sprayer gives the doors a thin, even coat of paint and makes quick work of painting. We sprayed our 18 doors and four drawers in less than 90 minutes per coat. The sprayer occasionally "spits" paint, but the Floetrol that you mix in levels out the finish. You can clean the sprayer in about 10 minutes.

The paint experts we talked to say you can get a nice-looking finish with non-HVLP sprayers too.

The advantages of an HVLP sprayer are that the spray is easy to control and the low pressure produces little overspray, so most of your paint ends up where you want it—on the doors.

works better than a sanding sponge—you can feel the rough spots through the paper, and paper doesn't round over corners as sponges do.

If you have doors with coarse wood grain (like oak) and want a smooth finish, fill in the grain with spackling compound (MH Ready Patch is one brand). Use a putty knife to skim-coat the door with compound, working it into the wood grain. Wait for it to dry, sand it with medium-grit sandpaper, then prime it again.

COMPLETE THE TRANSFORMATION

Use a gloss or semigloss latex enamel paint for a finish that resists stains and fingerprints. To get started, pour a gallon of the paint into a bucket and thin it with half a cup of water and half a quart of Floetrol paint additive. The water and the Floetrol level out the paint when it's applied and slow the drying process, helping eliminate brush and lap marks. The thinner paint also provides a more even coat when you're spraying.

Paint the cabinets with a brush **(Photo 6)**. Paint an entire rail, stile or trim piece before the paint dries, then move on to the next part of the cabinet. Paint any exposed sides of cabinets with a brush. Most light brush marks will disappear as the paint dries.

Before spray-painting the doors and drawer fronts, construct a makeshift booth to contain the airborne spray. Assemble a work surface (putting boards over sawhorses works great), then hang plastic sheeting around the work area. Ventilate the room—even if it's just a fan blowing out an open window.

Fill the spray container with the paint mixed with Floetrol and water. Wear a mask respirator. Test the spray pattern on cardboard, keeping the nozzle 10 to 12 in. from the surface **(Photo 7)**. Sweep your entire arm back and forth across the cardboard; don't just use your wrist. When you're ready to paint, set a block of wood or a cardboard box on the work surface to elevate the doors. Place a lazy Susan turntable over the box, then set the door on top **(Photo 8)**.

Spray the back of the doors first. This lets you get used to spraying before you paint the front. Start by spraying the edges. Rotate the door on the turntable to paint each edge so you won't have to change your body position. Move your arm across the entire edge of the door, starting the spray before the paint lands on the door and spraying past the end. Keep the nozzle 10 to 12 in. from the door. After painting all four edges, start at the top of the door and spray in a sweeping motion back and forth, moving down just enough each time to overlap the previous pass by 50% until you reach the door bottom.

7 PRACTICE SPRAY PAINTING ON CARDBOARD
Adjust the nozzle to get a vertical fan pattern and fix the flow rate so the paint covers without running.

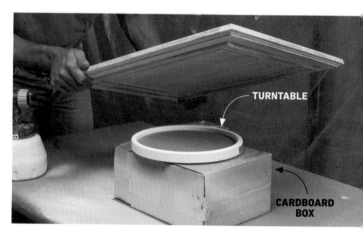

TURNTABLE

CARDBOARD BOX

8 SET DOORS ON A TURNTABLE WHEN SPRAY PAINTING
Stand in one spot and rotate the door on the turntable to paint each side. Keep the nozzle 10 to 12 in. from the door and maintain a consistent angle while spraying the paint.

FIRST COAT OF PAINT

9 PAINT THE EDGE AND DETAIL WORK
Paint one side, then turn the door to paint the adjacent edges and details. Start the spray before paint lands on the door, and keep spraying past the edge. Don't worry if you missed a spot. You can catch it on the second coat.

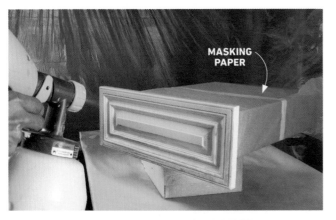

MASKING PAPER

PAINT RUN

10 PAINT DRAWERS WITH THE SPRAYER

Wrap the insides of the drawers with plastic or paper. Paint the backs first, then the edges and then the faces, starting at the top and working down. Start and stop the spray past the sides of the drawer.

Let the paint dry overnight. Then give the cabinet frames, sides and trim a second coat. Spray a first coat on the door fronts **(Photo 9)**.

Cover the drawers so only the paintable surface is visible. Set the drawer face down on the turntable and spray the back. Then place the drawer on its bottom and spray the front **(Photo 10)**. Be careful not to overspray. It's easy to get runs in the paint on drawer fronts. If you catch paint runs while they're still wet, gently brush them out with a paintbrush **(Photo 11)**.

Let the doors and drawers dry overnight, then give them a second coat. The backs of the doors really need only one coat.

When the doors are dry, install the hardware and hang the doors **(Photo 12)**. If any paint seeped into the hinge holes, scrape it out so the hinges will fit snugly.

11 FIX PAINT RUNS

Catch paint runs with a paintbrush while the paint is still wet. If the paint is dry or tacky, wait until the next day, then sand out the run or imperfection and repaint.

12 REINSTALL DOORS AND DRAWERS

Attach the hinges to the doors first, then simply screw them to the cabinet frames to finish your kitchen.

Figure A Painting Doors

Spray the door edges first. Then spray any detail work. Then spray the entire door, starting at the top and sweeping your arm back and forth until you reach the bottom. Keep the angle of the spray gun consistent as you spray.

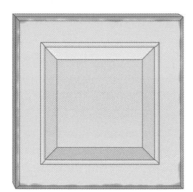  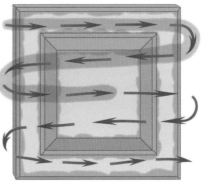

SPRAY-PAINT AN EXTERIOR

DON'T LET A HANDY PIECE OF EQUIPMENT INTIMIDATE YOU

MEET THE PRO

Daryl Becker, a professional painter, has overseen projects ranging from minor residential touch-ups to painting the entire exteriors of Lowe's and Target stores.

Every professional painter owns an airless paint sprayer. There's just no more efficient way to deliver paint onto a surface, and for most pros, every minute saved is money in the bank. The smooth, even finish that sprayers deliver just can't be matched with a brush or roller.

Working with a paint sprayer may seem somewhat intimidating, but it takes only a few minutes to get the hang of the proper technique. We visited the training/testing facility at Schoenfelder Renovations in Hopkins, Minnesota, where Daryl Becker showed us the basics. He also shared some extra gems you won't read about in the operator's manual for your paint sprayer. Here we'll focus on exterior painting, but most of these tips apply to any painting job that involves a sprayer.

MOTOR

OFF/ON

MAGNUM X7

PRESSURE
CONTROL
KNOB

PRIME
TUBE

SUCTION
TUBE

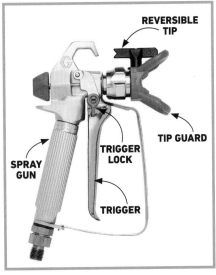

REVERSIBLE
TIP

SPRAY
GUN

TRIGGER
LOCK

TIP GUARD

TRIGGER

WHAT'S AN AIRLESS SPRAYER?

Airless sprayers work by pumping paint at very high pressures (up to 3,000 psi). They can suck paint from a large bucket (fewer refills), and the gun is lighter because it's not attached to the paint reservoir, as is the case with many air sprayers. Airless sprayers can spray both paint and finishes. There are different tips for different materials.

An entry-level model will cost about $250. The Graco X7 model shown retails for about $450 at home centers. Pros use models that range from $500 up to several thousand dollars. The basic operations of the machines are the same; what you get for your extra dollars is mostly durability. You can also rent an airless sprayer for a lot less.

ADJUST THE SPRAYER, STARTING WITH LOW PRESSURE

The thickness of the paint will determine the proper pressure setting on the sprayer. Start with the pressure on low and make a pass on a scrap piece of cardboard or rosin paper. If the pressure is too low, the spray pattern will be uneven and there will be "fingers" on the edges. Keep upping the pressure until you get a nice, even spray pattern with a consistent edge. If the pressure is all the way up and the pattern is still weak, you may have to go up one tip size.

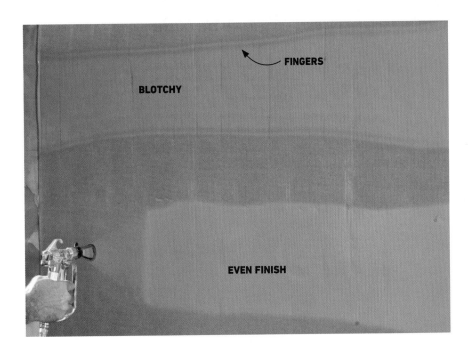

FINGERS

BLOTCHY

EVEN FINISH

ALWAYS KEEP THE GUN PERPENDICULAR TO THE WALL

To achieve a consistent layer of paint, the tip of the sprayer should be held about 12 in. from the surface, and the gun should always remain perpendicular to the wall. This technique is the foundation for a professional finish. It seems tricky at first, but after only a few passes you'll be painting like a pro. Practice on a low-visibility wall until you get the hang of it.

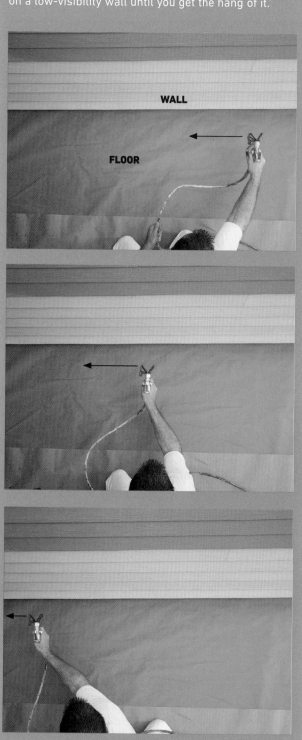

WALL

FLOOR

KEEP A LID ON IT

Always keep the lid on the bucket. Just remove the small cap and stick the intake tube into the smaller hole. This will keep debris out of the paint and prevent clogs. Plus, an open bucket dries out faster, and dried clumps of paint can also clog the works. Always use a 5-gallon bucket. If your project only requires 3 gallons, pour that amount into an empty 5-gallon bucket and draw your paint from that.

TAPE OFF WINDOWS AND DOORS

Before you crack open that first bucket of paint, tape off your windows and doors. Try dispensers that roll out the tape and plastic at the same time. You can buy a high-end dispenser like the 3M M3000K (shown here) at paint stores. More basic models can be purchased at home centers. Only the face of the trim needs to be protected.

50% OVERLAP

GUN ANGLE

OVERLAP 50% AND KEEP THE GUN MOVING

Overlap the pattern about 50%. Release the trigger at the end of each pass. Start the gun in motion before pulling the trigger. If you start spraying with a stationary gun, you'll get a glob of paint. When spraying under lap siding or the side of trim boards, angle the tip upward so you get enough paint on the bottom portion of the board. Always start at the top of the wall and work your way down.

BACK-BRUSH THE NOOKS AND CRANNIES

If you thought you could just blast the wall with a sprayer and call it a day, bad news. The paint sprayer is only a paint delivery system. In order to achieve a coating that will last for years, you need to push the paint into every crack and crevice and underneath every lap with a brush. It seems like a tedious extra step, but it's absolutely necessary.

PAY ATTENTION TO THE WEATHER

Our expert said one of the most common mistakes newbies make is ignoring the weather. Painting a wall in direct sunlight on a really hot day is next to impossible—the paint dries before there's time to back-brush and back-roll. If you can, pay attention to where the sun shines on the house at different times of the day. Plan your painting day so you can stay on the shady side. And make sure you don't get rained on. Most paint containers specify the length of time the paint must be dry before being exposed to water.

BACK-ROLL, THEN RECOAT

After you back-brush, it's time to back-roll. Don't spray an area so large that the paint dries before you can roll it out (drying times can vary greatly depending on the weather). A roller with a thicker nap is better at reaching the uneven surfaces. Many pros use a roller with a ¾-in. nap because it gets up into more of the recessed areas. While it may be tempting to roll lap siding horizontally, always roll in an up-and-down motion. It's hard to stop paint from dripping off the bottom of laps if you roll horizontally.

One coat may be enough if you're just freshening up the paint with a new coat of the same color. But if you're working with new siding or changing colors, a second coat will be needed. But no back-brushing or back-rolling is necessary on the final coat, so it goes fast, and the final coat hides many of the smaller brush and roller marks.

USE A SHIELD TO GET CLOSER

If you plan to spray your soffits, do that first. When it comes time to paint the walls, use a shield to protect the soffits from overspray. The pros use shields like this one, but you could get by with a sturdy piece of cardboard. The same trick works with the foundation, electric meters or whatever else you don't want to mess up with overspray. And the shield doesn't have to be precisely positioned; you can come back and clean up the line with your brush.

SHIELD

SPRAY THE EDGE OF THE TRIM THE SAME COLOR AS THE WALL

Only tape off the face of the windows and doors, then spray the edges of the trim at the same time as the walls. After the walls are done, come back and roll on the trim color. Eliminating the laborious task of cutting in the edge of the trim around each and every lap in the siding may seem like cheating, but it's not. First, no one will ever notice. Second, the caulking between the trim and the siding is rarely perfect, and trying to cut in paint over blobs of caulking rarely results in a nice clean line.

AVOID OVERSPRAY MESSES

Even a finely tuned spray pattern will create some overspray. Wind and high humidity will cause the overspray to travel farther. Make sure you cover plants, decks and walkways, and be sure to move cars and any other items you don't want paint on.

EDGE OF TRIM SAME AS SIDING

CAUTION:
Houses built before 1978 may contain lead paint. Before disturbing any surface, get a lab analysis of paint chips from it. Contact your public health department for information on how to collect paint samples and where to send them.

REVERSE THE TIP TO PURGE CLOGS

Most spray tips have an arrow on them because they're reversible. A forward-pointing arrow means you're ready to paint. If you start to get an uneven spray pattern, you probably have a clog in the tip. To purge the debris, turn the tip 180 degrees and spray some paint onto a piece of cardboard or rosin paper for a couple of seconds. Then turn the tip back around and continue painting. If you still aren't getting good results, you may need to clean the tip or one or more of the inline filters (located in various places depending on the sprayer).

RENEW YOUR WOOD FENCE

SHABBY TO HANDSOME IN THREE EASY STEPS

Has your cedar fence lost its rich, warm glow? Who invited that shabby-looking impostor to the backyard party? Don't worry—underneath that thin gray skin, the glow still remains. All you have to do is remove the surface layer of aged wood cells to expose a fresh layer of wood. The process is a breeze. In fact, with a power washer, it's as simple as washing your car. Then apply an exterior wood oil stain to preserve this new layer of wood. It'll prolong the life of your fence to boot.

WASH *REPAIR* *STAIN*

POWER-WASHING MAKES THE CLEANING TASK EASY

Power washers are aggressive. They'll strip the wood as well as clean off the dirt and grime, but you can also erode the wood too deeply and ruin it. The key is to use the right sprayer tip and technique. In any case, the power washer's spray will slightly raise and roughen the grain on smooth wood. That's actually good—it allows more sealer to soak in and improves the finish.

Power washers are inexpensive to rent. Rent one that operates at 1,500 or 2,000 psi, and avoid more powerful 3,000 or 3,500 psi units. Be sure to get both 15- and 25-degree spray tips. Have the rental people demonstrate the washer's use. It's an easy machine to run.

To avoid damaging the pump, don't run the power washer without first filling the pump and hoses with water. To do this, attach both hoses (Photo 1), snap in a 25-degree tip, turn on the garden hose spigot and hold down the trigger on the wand until water squirts out. Release the wand trigger and start the engine. If it's hard to pull the start cord, pull the wand trigger to release the water pressure.

Clear the area along the fence by tying back plants that are growing alongside it. Wear water-repellent clothing—you will get wet from the spray.

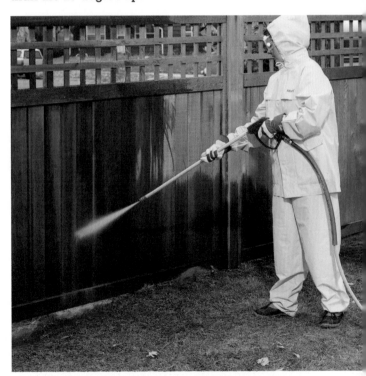

SPRAYER TIP

Start spraying with the wand tip 18 in. from the wood surface. Move in closer as you swing the tip slowly along the length of the board (Photo 2). Keep the width of the fan spray aligned across the boards. The wood's color will brighten as the surface is stripped away. Watch closely and stop stripping when no more color change occurs. You don't have to remove too much surface to expose fresh wood, and continuing to spray won't improve the color.

Be patient with yourself and the job. It takes a bit of practice to arrive at the proper tip distance and speed of movement, but you'll catch on fast. It's better to make two or three passes than to risk gouging the surface trying to accomplish this job in one pass. As you gain experience, you can switch to a 15-degree tip. This tip cuts more aggressively and works faster than the 25-degree tip.

SPRAY WAND

WAND TIP

GARDEN HOSE

HIGH-PRESSURE HOSE

1 Connect a garden hose and the power washer hose to the machine. Snap a 25-degree tip onto the end of the wand. Turn on the water to the garden hose and pull the trigger on the spray wand until water squirts out. Now start up the power washer's engine.

2 Hold the tip of the wand about 18 in. from the fence and move the spray the length of the boards. Pull the trigger and keep the sprayer tip moving to avoid gouging the wood. Use a variety of attack angles to strip inside corners.

SIMPLE REPAIRS ADD YEARS

With the fence clean, it's time to fix or replace damaged boards, refasten loose boards and countersink any protruding nails. Use waterproof glue **(Photo 3)** to repair any split and broken boards. Drive corrosion-resistant screws **(Photo 4)** instead of nails to pull loose pieces tightly together. If a gate is sagging, straighten it with a turnbuckle support **(Photo 5)**. Also coat the posts **(Photo 6)** where they emerge from the ground or concrete with a wood preservative. This is the area that rots first.

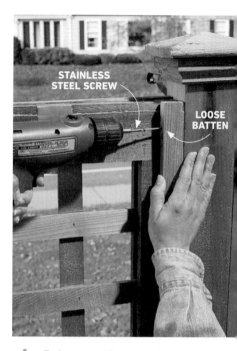

STAINLESS STEEL SCREW

LOOSE BATTEN

WATERPROOF GLUE

TAPE CLAMP (STRAPPING)

GLUE LINE

4 Drive weather-resistant or stainless steel screws to tighten loose boards. Recess the head ¼ in. and fill with a light-colored caulk.

3 Glue split and broken pieces when the wood has dried for at least 24 hours. Apply waterproof glue, and clamp or tape the pieces firmly together.

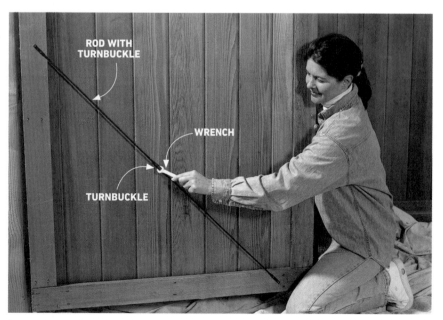

ROD WITH TURNBUCKLE

WRENCH

TURNBUCKLE

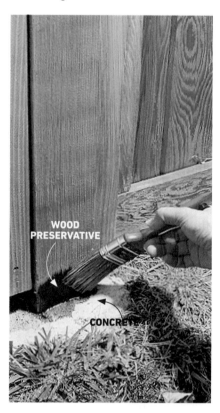

WOOD PRESERVATIVE

CONCRETE

5 Realign any sagging gates with a turnbuckle. We spray-painted the shiny turnbuckle black to make it less conspicuous.

6 Brush a wood preservative into the posts around the base to help prevent rot at this vulnerable area.

STAIN MAKES THE FENCE LOOK BRAND NEW

To preserve the natural color of the wood, use an exterior semitransparent oil stain. It seals the wood while allowing the grain and color variations to show through. And its pigments add an overall color tone. Make sure the stain contains ultraviolet inhibitors, which will slow down bleaching by sunlight, and a mildewcide to slow fungal growth. Look for samples on cedar at the paint store, or bring in your own piece of wood to test. A test sample is the best way to ensure a satisfactory result.

Before applying the stain, be sure the fence is dry. Allow at least 24 hours. If it's cool and humid, allow another 24 hours.

Use a paint roller with a "medium nap" cover **(Photo 7)** to apply a soaking coat to the wood. Let the wood absorb as much stain as it can. Roll about a 3-ft. section of fence and then brush **(Photo 8)** the stain into the wood. If the wood still appears dry, roll on additional stain. Work the stain into all recesses and corners. The roller applies the stain, but you need the brush to work it well into the wood's surface. Coat detailed areas with a trim roller and smaller brush **(Photo 9)**. Keep wet edges to prevent lap marks.

Most semitransparent oil stains are guaranteed to last two to five years. (Solid-color stains last longer but are more difficult to renew.) Fences usually face severe weathering, so expect the finish to last no more than three years. Plan on recoating the fence

7 Roll into the dry wood a soaking coat of semitransparent stain. Coat about 3 ft. of fence, then proceed to the step shown in Photo 8.

within this time frame to keep your fence looking fresh. Before recoating, wash the fence with a garden hose sprayer, and use a bristle brush on stubborn dirt deposits and stains. Let the fence dry and stain it using the same method.

8 Brush the stain into the wood grain and all corners and gaps. Brush out any runs or drips.

9 Work the stain into small and tight areas with a trim roller and a 2-in. brush. One generous coat should be enough.

WATER-BASED BASICS

YOU MIGHT HAVE DITCHED THESE FINISHES YEARS AGO, BUT TODAY'S PROS ARE GIVING THEM A SECOND CHANCE

If you used water-based wood finishes years ago and gave up in frustration, give them another try. Newer versions have many advantages over solvent-based finishes: They dry much faster, so less dust can settle into the wet coat and there's less waiting between coats. Cleanup takes soap and water, not chemicals. They are low odor, pose no fire hazard and are better for the environment.

But water-based finishes aren't perfect. They raise the grain and are very sensitive to temperature and humidity. They're nonyellowing, which is good, but they can also produce a bland appearance on darker woods.

To help you achieve a great finish every time and avoid the pitfalls, here are our pro's top 10 tips for using water-based finishes.

1 RAISE THE GRAIN FIRST

Always raise the grain on raw wood before applying a water-based finish. Simply brush, sponge or spray on some distilled water, and let it dry thoroughly (overnight is best). Then resand with your final grit paper to break off the whiskers. Now when you apply the finish, the grain will stay down.

MEET THE PRO

David Munkittrick has more than 30 years' experience in woodworking. He is an active freelance journalist, furniture designer and builder. He lives and works on an old farmstead in western Wisconsin where the pig barn has been repurposed as his wood shop.

BEFORE ADDING WATER	AFTER WATER DRIES

1

2 SEAL OIL-BASED STAIN

Oil and water don't mix. Water-based poly can have adhesion problems when applied over an oil-based stain that's not thoroughly cured. That's why you should always apply a barrier coat of dewaxed shellac to seal oil-based stain. After the shellac dries, a light scuff-sand will leave an excellent surface for the poly to grip.

The instructions on the can will indicate that you can apply a water-based clear coat right over an oil-based stain if the stain has thoroughly cured. However, the curing time can be several days, especially with an open-grain wood such as oak where the stain can sit uncured deep in the pores. Play it safe and seal the stain with shellac. Zinsser SealCoat is a dewaxed shellac available at most home centers and hardware stores.

WET FINISH · DRY FINISH

3 LAY IT DOWN AND LEAVE IT

Water-based poly should be laid down with a few quick strokes. Don't worry too much about the appearance of the wet finish. It will look awful at first, but water-based poly has an amazing ability to pull tight as it cures, like shrink-wrap. The brush marks will disappear—we promise. If you go back and try to rework the film, you're likely to cause a big mess. Resist the urge. If you see a dust speck, just leave it alone and fix the problem later with sandpaper and another coat.

4 CHOOSE THE RIGHT APPLICATOR

Buy a top-quality, fine-bristle nylon brush for spindle work, inside corners and narrow edges. The nylon bristles won't absorb the water from the finish and become mushy as natural bristles will. Our pro uses a Golden Taklon brush, but there are other ones available. Each fiber is extruded to a point to resemble a natural bristle. The brush is soft, and the variable fiber diameters create more space for holding material, meaning fewer dips in the can. For large, flat surfaces like tabletops, turn to a paint pad. It will allow you to lay down an even coat in seconds and maintain a wet edge, even over a big area.

GOLDEN TAKLON BRUSH

PAINT PAD

5 USE SYNTHETIC ABRASIVES, NOT STEEL WOOL

Synthetic wool is a must-have product with water-based finishes. Traditional steel wool will leave behind bits of steel, which will react with the water and leave rust stains in the clear coat. Synthetic wool comes in various grades and is available where water-based finishes are sold, including at home centers, hardware stores and woodworking stores. Use coarse to medium synthetic wool between coats. To rub out the last coat, turn to fine and extra fine.

6 REFINISH KITCHEN CABINETS WITH WATER-BASED POLY

The low odor of water-based poly makes it ideal for refinishing existing kitchen cabinets in place. It doesn't matter what the old finish was, as long as you prep the surface properly before applying the water-based product. First use a degreaser cleaner like Formula 409 or Fantastik to clean away any buildup of grease or cooking oil. Scuff-sand the old finish with fine synthetic wool, then seal with Zinsser SealCoat. Sand the seal coat with fine synthetic wool, then brush on two to three coats of water-based poly to complete the job.

7 STRAIN YOUR POLY FIRST

Unless you're using a brand-new can of poly, always strain it with a medium-mesh strainer before applying it. Once the finish is used, it will be polluted with little bits of dried or semi-dried varnish, which will wreck your new finish. Basic stands and replacement meshes like those shown are available at woodworking stores and online.

8 USE AN EXTENDER IN HOT, DRY CONDITIONS

Water-based finishes are more sensitive to temperature and humidity than their oil cousins. It's best to apply your water-based poly when the air temperature is between 70 and 80 degrees F and the humidity is below 70%. If the air is both hot and dry, the poly may set so fast that it will be difficult to maintain a wet edge as you brush, or the film may not level properly before it sets.

The solution is to add an extender to slow the drying time. This is especially useful when you're coating a large piece like a dining table. One choice is General Finishes Dry-Time Extender, No. 21217. Floetrol is another great additive for slowing things down. It's designed for latex paints but works great with satin or semigloss water-based poly and is readily available at paint stores.

9 ADD COLOR FOR THE LOOK OF OIL-BASED POLY

Water-based poly dries water-clear and can leave wood with a cold look, especially on dark woods like walnut. To get the warm glow of oil-based poly, add a few drops of dye. TransTint Honey Amber is a great product (No. 21979). Make a weak solution of dye and water, then stain the wood before you apply the poly. Believe it or not, you can also add dye directly to the poly before you brush it on.

A third coloring option is to seal the raw wood with wax-free shellac, then topcoat with water-based poly. Whichever method you choose, experiment on scrap wood to make sure you'll get the look you want.

10 MIST YOUR WOOD BEFORE STAINING

Dry wood can aggressively suck up dye or stain, making it hard to control the color penetration. The result can be a dark, blotchy mess. For added control, try wetting the wood with distilled water right before you apply the dye or stain. (Be sure you've raised the grain first; see Tip 1.) The increased open time makes the color easier to control. A household pump sprayer or sponge works well.

MEET THE EXPERT

Tom Caspar has been a professional woodworker and custom furniture builder for more than 40 years.

WIPE-ON POLY

THE FAST, EASY, GOOF-PROOF FINISH

The best choice for a clear coating is often a specialized finish like pre-catalyzed lacquer—but that assumes you have a spray booth outfitted with high-end equipment. For most of us, polyurethane provides a combination of cost and durability that's very hard to beat. With wipe-on poly, you also get goof-proof simplicity, speed and convenience.

STANDOFF · SCREW

SET THE STAGE

Use resin paper, a drop cloth or newspaper to protect your worktable from drips. If your project has legs, make standoffs for them to perch on. Standoffs allow you to wipe finish all the way down to the ends of the legs. They poke holes in the wood, so if you have parts that must be finished on both sides, such as a shelf, set them on blocks covered with cloth instead.

CUT UP AN OLD T-SHIRT

Cut a T-shirt into 6-in. squares. Fold each square in half, twice, to make applicators. White fabric is best because any lint left in the finish is less likely to show.

WIPE-ON POLY PROS & CONS

+**FAST.** Coat a project in less than half the time it takes to brush on a finish.

+**EASY.** No skill or expensive brush needed.

+**DUST TOLERANT.** The coating is thin and dries fast, so "nubs" caused by airborne dust are less likely.

+**NO CLEANUP.** Just dispose of the cloth, container and gloves. No brush to clean!

-**EXPENSIVE.** On average, wipe-on poly costs twice as much as brush-on poly.

-**SLOW BUILD.** Three coats of wipe-on will match the buildup from one coat of brush-on. But the speed of wipe-on application can make up for those extra coats.

MEET THE TEAM

We tried four versions of wipe-on poly. In terms of results, we found only small differences and were happy with each. Most home centers carry various sheens, but only one brand. All these options, and more, are available online. Prices start at about $15 per quart.

Minwax is the most common brand of oil-based wipe-on poly. Like other oil-based coatings, it adds a slight amber color to the finish. That can be good or bad, depending on the project.

Minwax water-based wipe-on poly dries faster than oil-based products, so you have to move fast. Unlike the others, it has no amber hue.

General Finishes Arm-R-Seal is formulated for brushing or wiping. It's slightly less amber than the other oil-based finishes.

Watco wipe-on poly is most like the Minwax oil-based product. Be careful when shopping; Watco's beloved Danish oil finishes come in a similar container and it's easy to grab the wrong product.

MISSED A SPOT!

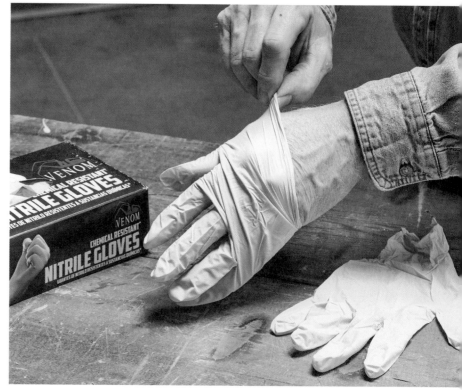

BRIGHT LIGHTING IS CRITICAL

Good lighting can help you avoid leaving drips, sags and pesky "holidays" (spots skipped by accident). When you have just applied finish to an area, check to see that all of it looks shiny and wet. Use a portable light if you're working in a dim room.

WEAR GLOVES

Always protect your hands with disposable vinyl or nitrile gloves. You can usually reuse them two or three times before they get too gummed up.

POUR IT INTO A PLASTIC TUB

A margarine or cottage cheese tub is just right for wipe-on. Dip your rag into the finish, squeeze out the excess and wipe on. With the lid in place, the container will keep the poly fresh for a couple of days. After a few days, the solvent will begin to degrade the plastic, so don't use plastic for long-term storage.

BRUSH FIRST, THEN WIPE

When you need a thick, protective buildup of poly on a door or tabletop, you have three choices: Go with brush-on poly, apply several coats of wipe-on or do a combination of both. You can, for example, brush on two coats for a heavy build, then apply wipe-on for a flawless surface. Sand the brushed-on finish absolutely smooth and apply at least two wipe-on coats for a consistent sheen. To make sure the two finishes bond to each other, they should both be oil-based or water-based. Using products from the same company is a good idea too.

PAINT PAD

COVER LARGE AREAS FAST

A paint pad holds more finish than a rag and wipes it on faster. You can reuse a paint pad too. After each coat, just store it in a sealed plastic tub or plastic bag. Get a paint pad at any home center for about $5.

KEEP THE COATS LIGHT

Three thin coats of wipe-on finish will look smoother than one or two thicker coats. For the best results, don't sand after the first coat. (You might sand through it!) Apply a second thin coat, then lightly sand with 220-grit sandpaper. Then apply a final thin coat.

WIPE OFF INTRICATE PROJECTS

On most surfaces, you wipe on the finish and just let it dry. If your project has lots of hard-to-access surfaces, try a different approach. Apply the finish to a limited area, then use dry rags to wipe it off after a few minutes. This way, you don't have to worry about accidentally smearing finish on an area you've already covered. Just wipe it off.

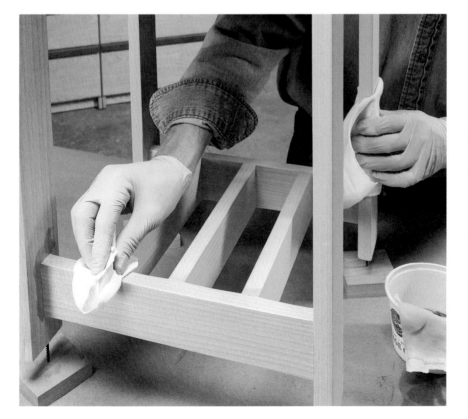

PERFECT FOR TRICKY SURFACES

Wipe-on is a slick solution for hard-to-brush items. Sometimes it even beats spraying. You can work the finish into tight spots where spray would "bounce" out.

FRESHEN UP AN OLD FINISH

If your old furniture or woodwork looks dull and lifeless, try renewing it with a few coats of wipe-on finish. Wash it first with dish soap and water, then lightly sand the old finish with 220-grit sandpaper. Vacuum off the dust, then apply the finish as usual. Apply at least two coats to achieve an even sheen.

LET STAIN DRY OVERNIGHT

Applying poly too soon after staining is always risky. And it's even riskier with wipe-on poly. If the stain isn't completely dry, wiping it with a rag soaked with finish will cause it to smear.

SAND BY HAND

Don't use an electric sander between coats. It will remove too much finish. Sand by hand instead. Fold the paper in thirds so it doesn't wrinkle, then hold it flat with two or three fingers. Be careful near sharp or slightly rounded edges, though. Sanding too hard might cut through the finish and leave bare wood. It's best to not sand those edges at all.

WET RAGS ARE A FIRE HAZARD

Take no chances. If rags wet with finish are wadded up, they can heat up, smolder and catch on fire as they dry. However, wet rags are safe if you dispose of them properly. Take them outside and separate them. Place them on concrete or asphalt, or hang them with clothespins to dry overnight. Be sure to keep them away from kids and pets. Once the rags are stiff, they're no longer a fire hazard. You can put them in the trash.

WANT ULTRA SMOOTH? TRY STEEL WOOL

If you're using an oil-based finish and you want to make a surface smooth as glass, apply the last coat with "00" steel wool. Rub hard. The steel wool will cut through any nibs or dust on the surface. To capture the grit and to maintain an even sheen, use a bunch of dry rags to wipe off the finish before it dries. This will leave only an ultra thin film of finish on the surface.

CHECK FOR DRIPS

There isn't much that can go wrong with wipe-on. But you can end up with a few drips or sags. Immediately after you wipe on the finish, give the whole project a quick inspection and wipe away any mistakes.

CORRECT BAD BRUSHWORK

When brush-on poly goes wrong—dust nubs, sags, brush marks—you can correct it. After the finish has fully dried, wet-sand with soapy water or mineral spirits and 400-grit wet/dry paper. After you've sanded the finish flat and smooth, a couple of light coats of wipe-on poly will give you a perfect surface.

WET/DRY SANDPAPER

CHAPTER 2

WOODWORKING & CABINETRY

Wood 101 48
Floating Shelves 54
12 Ideal Router Tips...................................61
Foolproof Dadoes & Rabbets 70
Tricks for Tighter Miters 74
Success with Melamine 79
All About Euro Hinges 84
Installing Cabinet Hardware 90

WOOD 101

WOOD MOVEMENT CAUSES HEARTBREAK WHEN PROJECTS CRACK AND WARP. SAVE SOME NIGHTMARES BY MASTERING THESE SIMPLE TECHNIQUES.

When humidity is high, wood absorbs moisture and swells. When humidity drops, wood shrinks. Each of these "movements" is gradual, so you probably won't notice weekly changes. But seasonal changes cause problems you can't miss, such as sticking doors, ugly gaps in woodwork or a crack in a tabletop.

Movement occurs whether wood is fresh from the mill or centuries old, whether it was kiln dried or air dried. And it exerts tremendous force that's almost unstoppable. But with a little knowledge, you can minimize the consequences. Jeff Gorton will explain the basics of wood movement and show you real-world solutions.

WOOD MOVEMENT 101: ABC (AND D!)

1. NOT MUCH MOVEMENT LENGTHWISE

MOST MOVEMENT ACROSS WIDTH

1. WIDTH MOVEMENT IS THE MAIN ISSUE

Wood moves as its moisture content changes. Wood doesn't move much lengthwise, so you don't have to worry much about boards getting shorter. But a board can move quite a bit across its width. A board that's 6 in. wide during a humid summer might shrink by 1/32 in. in winter. That's not much, but it's enough to cause a crack in a tabletop or gaps between floorboards.

2. MOVEMENT IS CAUSED BY MOISTURE CONTENT

When wet wood dries, it shrinks. The amount of movement is determined by the type of wood and the degree of change in its moisture content. Applying a sealer or paint can moderate wood movement. But it's nearly impossible to seal wood so completely that its moisture content stays constant.

2. DRY WOOD SHRINKS

WET WOOD SWELLS

3. WOOD CAN ALSO CHANGE SHAPE

Movement within a board isn't uniform; one section might move more than another. That leads to warping, twisting and cupping. Most of these changes happen in the initial drying phase, but wood can change shape later too.

3. MOVEMENT ISN'T UNIFORM

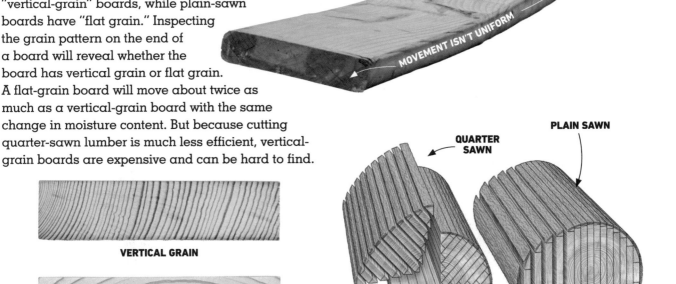

4. VERTICAL GRAIN IS MORE STABLE

How a board is cut from the log also affects how much it moves. Quarter-sawing yields "vertical-grain" boards, while plain-sawn boards have "flat grain." Inspecting the grain pattern on the end of a board will reveal whether the board has vertical grain or flat grain. A flat-grain board will move about twice as much as a vertical-grain board with the same change in moisture content. But because cutting quarter-sawn lumber is much less efficient, vertical-grain boards are expensive and can be hard to find.

QUARTER SAWN

PLAIN SAWN

4.

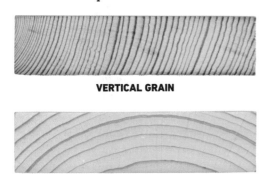

VERTICAL GRAIN

FLAT GRAIN

BUTT JOINT

BUTT JOINT

1

10 TECHNIQUES: HOW TO TAME WOOD MOVEMENT

1 AVOID MITERS OUTDOORS

Miter joints hide end grain and look more refined. But the effect is ruined when the miters don't meet tightly. Huge changes in humidity, and wetting and drying from rain and sun, cause wood to move more outdoors than it would indoors. So whereas a miter joint will look good for decades indoors, it may start to look really bad after only one season outdoors. That's why it's usually better to avoid miters outdoors whenever possible. Use a butt joint instead.

2 PLAN FOR DECK BOARD MOVEMENT

Deck boards can shrink or expand after they're installed, depending on how much moisture they contained when you fastened them down. To allow for this, space wet treated boards with a 16d nail (⅛ in.) and dry boards such as cedar decking with a carpenter's pencil (5⁄16 in.).

3 ALLOW EXPANSION SPACE FOR WOOD FLOORS

If you are installing an engineered wood floor, be sure to follow the instructions carefully because they include all the information you need about spacing. In general, floating wood floors that aren't nailed or glued down require about a ½-in. space around the perimeter and enough clearance at thresholds, doorjambs and other obstructions to allow movement. Solid wood floors also require at least a ½-in.-wide expansion space around the perimeter.

2

3

EXPANSION SPACE

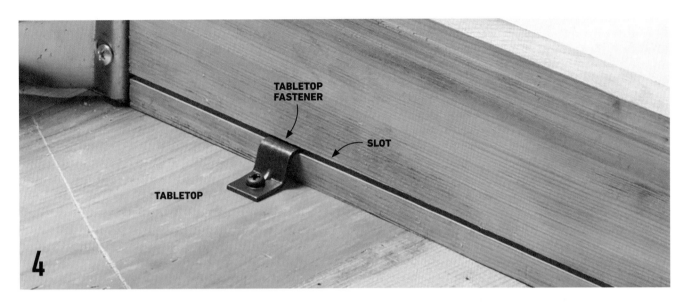

TABLETOP FASTENER

SLOT

TABLETOP

4

5

6

FLOAT TABLETOPS

4 One of the most common errors that beginning woodworkers make is to securely fasten wood tabletops to the underlying frame. Tabletops tend to be wide, and wood moves a lot across its width. Restricting the movement with screws or nails can cause the top to crack as it shrinks. To avoid this, use special tabletop fasteners or some other method that holds the top down but still allows the top to expand and contract.

LET WOOD ACCLIMATE

5 Since the relative humidity of your indoor space may be quite different from the humidity where your trim or flooring was stored, you should always allow time for the material to acclimate. The wider and thicker the trim or flooring boards are, the longer you should leave them in the space before installation. Thin, narrow trim may take only a day or two to reach equilibrium with the room's relative humidity. Wide or thick boards should be left in the room for at least four days before you install them. Of course the trim or flooring will still move a little after it's installed, but at least most of the change will have occurred beforehand.

AVOID WIDE BOARDS

6 Of course there are times when you have to use a wide board or you want to use one because it looks better. But always be aware that movement in wide boards, whether it's cupping, twisting or something else, will be more pronounced than in two or more narrower boards. Gluing several narrow boards together will result in a more stable tabletop than gluing two wide boards together.

7 USE MANUFACTURED WOOD TO HOLD PAINT BETTER

If you're planning to paint an exterior project, consider building it from a manufactured product rather than solid wood. Wood movement requires the paint to flex constantly, and eventually the paint cracks and peels. Manufactured wood substitutes from companies like Louisiana-Pacific, Azek or James Hardie are more stable than solid wood. And because these products move less, they provide a better surface for paint.

8 PREFINISH TONGUE-AND-GROOVE

As tongue-and-groove boards expand and contract, the spaces between them change a little. If you don't prefinish the boards, you'll see exposed raw wood on the tongue when the boards shrink. But finishing the boards before you install them will solve this problem. Just be careful to avoid a buildup of finish in the groove; it could make the boards difficult to fit together.

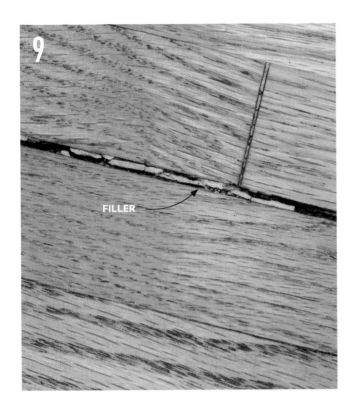

9

FILLER

10

CABINET
DOOR PARTS

SUBSTITUTE SHEETS FOR BOARDS

As you're planning your next woodworking project, don't assume it has to be built entirely from boards. Veneered sheets of plywood and MDF are more stable and are a good alternative to solid lumber. These veneered sheets are less likely to bow or cup, and won't crack like lumber. Choices at home centers are usually limited to oak, birch or maple veneers. If you're looking for something else, such as cherry or walnut, check with a local hardwood lumber supplier or a full-service lumberyard.

STICKING DOORS

Sticking and rubbing doors are a common problem caused by wood movement. High humidity is usually the culprit, so some problems can be avoided or solved by keeping the humidity levels in your house low. But when this isn't practical, you'll have to resort to solutions like tightening door hinge screws or planing or sanding the door edge.

9 DON'T FILL CRACKS ON WOOD FLOORS

If you have wood floors, especially old ones, you probably have some cracks between the boards. It's tempting to try to hide the cracks with wood filler, but it's not a good idea. As the floorboards expand and contract, the filler will crack and fall out, leaving you with an unsightly mess that's hard to fix.

10 LET PARTS WARP BEFORE ASSEMBLY

When you go to all the trouble to build cabinet doors, you want to make sure they aren't going to warp or twist after assembly. One way to prevent this is to cut your parts, then stack them with spacer boards (stickers). Let them acclimate for about 24 hours before building the doors. Be sure to cut extra parts so you can replace any boards that warp.

MEET THE EXPERT

Jason White has more than 20 years of woodworking experience.

FLOATING SHELVES

CUSTOM ACCENTS TO SUIT YOUR ROOM

You can buy floating shelves in stores or online for about $20 to $80 each. But before you do that, consider building your own.

For about the same cost, you can get the exact size, thickness and look you want. You can even finish them to match your trim or furniture. And your homemade shelves will be sturdier than most store-bought shelves—ours can support about 50 lbs. each. Plus, you'll earn serious bragging rights when you're done.

MONEY, TIME AND TOOLS

A pair of shelves cost us about $150 to build. We were able to make two shelves from a single 4 x 8-ft. sheet of ½-in.-thick red oak plywood. It can be tough to find locally, so call around before you shop, or choose different plywood.

Our shelves are 2½ in. thick and 72 in. long, so finding veneer long enough on store shelves is also a challenge. You can special-order it at some home centers, however. We bought ours online from Rockler Woodworking and Hardware (*rockler.com*), where a 24-in. x 96-in. roll costs about $100 shipped. You can find less expensive veneer, but we love this stuff because you don't have to heat it or apply any glue—it's just peel and stick! Expect to spend about an additional $10 to $20 on stain and other assorted materials.

It took us a couple of hours to build each shelf, including sanding, staining and mounting on the wall. We made ours using a circular saw and cutting guide, but you can make them much faster with a table saw. And you can certainly hand-drive small nails, but it's much faster and easier to use a pneumatic brad nailer (you can buy one at Harbor Freight Tools for about $30). You'll need a small compressor to power it. It also helps to have a random orbit sander, especially for sanding the sides flush before applying the veneer (see p. 56). Bonus points if you own a belt sander for scribing!

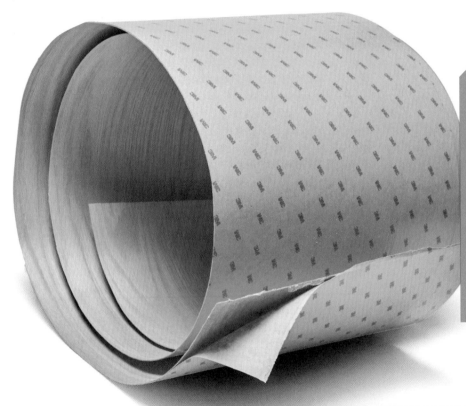

SELF-STICK VENEER FOR THE LOOK OF SOLID WOOD

A shelf made from a single plank looks great, but long, thick planks can be hard to find, expensive or both. So we cheated and used adhesive-backed veneer made from real wood, which is easy to cut and apply and creates the seamless look of solid timbers. To see how to apply it, check out Photos 4-6.

BUILD CUTTING GUIDES FOR PERFECT CUTS

It's hard to get nice, straight cuts without something to help guide your circular saw. That's where a cutting guide comes in. We used a self-squaring crosscut guide for short cuts and a longer guide for "rip" cuts. The guide shown here is just a narrow piece of ¾-in. plywood attached to a wider piece of ¼-in. plywood, with a squaring fence on the bottom. The base of the saw rides against the guide's "fence." To see how to make one, go to *familyhandyman.com* and search for "circular-saw cutting guide."

CUTTING GUIDE

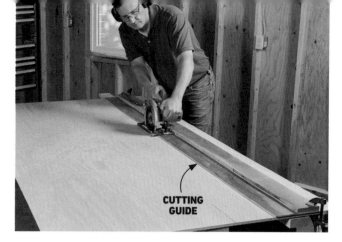

1 CUT THE PARTS

Using a 60-tooth blade in your circular saw and a cutting guide, cut all the parts to size. A 4 x 8-ft. sheet of plywood will yield enough parts for two shelves.

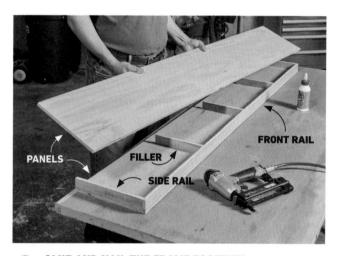

2 GLUE AND NAIL THE FRAME TOGETHER

Apply carpenter's glue to the edges of the rails and fillers and nail on the first panel with 1-in. brads. Then flip the shelf over and nail on the other panel.

3 SAND THE FRONT AND SIDES FLUSH

Using a random orbit sander and 100-grit sandpaper, sand the front and sides of the shelf so that the rails and panels are flush with each other. This will give you a flat, smooth surface on which to apply the veneer.

CUT AND ASSEMBLE THE PARTS

Set a full sheet of ½-in. plywood on three or four 2x4s laid across sawhorses **(Photo 1)**. Measure and mark the plywood for each of the shelf parts and use a circular saw and cutting guide to make your cuts. The cutting guide will help keep your cuts perfectly straight and minimize chip-out.

Next, glue and nail all the parts together **(Photo 2)**. It helps to draw pencil lines on the top and bottom panels first so you'll know where to drive the nails for the fillers after you cover them with the top and bottom panels. With all eight parts cut to size, it's fairly easy to assemble the shelf with glue and nails. (See **Figure A**, p. 60.) Start by laying the front rail (C) on end on top of your worktable (an old hollow-core door or plywood scrap on sawhorses works great), plus a couple of short support blocks cut from a 2x4. These blocks will support the top panel (A) while you glue and nail it onto the front rail. Carefully align the top and front pieces and use an 18-gauge pneumatic brad nailer to drive 1-in. brads.

Now stand the side rails (D) on end and glue and nail them to the top panel. Flip the whole thing over and install the fillers (E) with glue and brads. The fillers should be evenly spaced, but don't be too fussy because they'll be hidden once you install the bottom panel (B). Nail through the front rail into each of the fillers.

Then flip the whole thing over again and nail through the top panel into each of the fillers. Now flip the whole works over one more time and nail through the bottom panel into the fillers.

APPLY THE WOOD VENEER

The top and bottom panels have exposed plywood edges that get covered with veneer. If those edges aren't perfectly smooth and flush with the faces of the front and side rails, the veneer won't stick properly. Sand everything flush with a random orbit sander and 100-grit sandpaper **(Photo 3)**. Lay out the roll, veneer side down, and draw a straight line using a marker and straightedge at 3 in. wide along the entire length of the roll. This will give you ¼ in. of overhang when you apply the veneer to the front and sides of the shelf.

Cut along the line with a pair of scissors and then cut the strip of veneer into three pieces for the front and two sides, leaving them long enough so there's ¼ in. of overhang on each end **(Photo 4)**. Apply the veneer to the sides first, being careful to keep the veneer aligned with the shelf **(Photo 5)**. Don't peel and stick more than a few inches at a time, and rub a block of wood over the veneer to press it on. Cutting the pieces slightly oversize helps in case you don't get it on perfectly straight.

Pull an edge-banding trimmer apart and use one of the two sides to trim the veneer flush with the shelf **(Photo 6)**. This method works well going with the grain of the veneer, but not when trimming across it. For the short cuts across the grain, back the veneer up with a block of wood and trim the veneer flush (on the sticky side) with a sharp utility knife. A handheld router with a flush-trimming bit also works well. Install the front veneer piece after the sides. Then drill several countersink holes in the back of the shelf for some No. 8 wood screws **(Photo 7)**. Space the holes about 12 in. apart and ¾ in. from the back edge.

MAKE A WALL CLEAT

Cut a wall cleat (H) out of a straight 2x4 and make it 1¼ in. x 1⅜ in. x 70¾ in. **(Photo 8)**. Use your circular saw and the same cutting guide you used to cut the plywood pieces to width (set another 2x4 under the guide to keep it from tipping). Rip the cleat to width and then crosscut it to length. The narrow part of the cleat should slip into the hollow opening in the shelf with just a bit of wiggle room.

Using an electronic stud finder and painter's tape, find and mark the stud locations on the wall. Transfer the stud locations to the wall cleat and predrill holes in the cleat slightly smaller than the diameter of the shanks of the lag screws. Hold the cleat to the wall and drill pilot holes in the wall using the cleat as a drilling guide.

Drive 4-in. lag screws through the cleat and into the wall **(Photo 9)**. Start by driving a lag screw on one end of the cleat, check for level, then screw down the other end before driving the middle screws.

FIT THE SHELF TO THE WALL

Slip the shelf onto the cleat and tight to the wall. If your wall isn't perfectly flat, you'll see some small gaps between the shelf and the wall. You can eliminate those gaps by "scribing" the shelf to fit the contours of the wall **(Photo 10)**. This step is optional—skip it if you don't mind the gaps. To scribe, drag a pencil against the wall and trace a line onto the top of the shelf. The line follows the contours of the wall.

Now use a belt sander to sand up to the pencil line **(Photo 11)**. Trying to sand freehand with the belt sander is tricky because if you don't hold the

4 CUT THE VENEER TO SIZE
Using scissors, cut three pieces of oak veneer big enough to cover the front and sides of the shelf. Make them 3 in. wide so you'll have ¼ in. of overhang on each side.

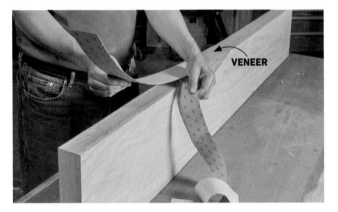

VENEER

5 STICK ON THE VENEER
Peel off the back and stick on the veneer, leaving a little bit of overhang on all four edges. Press the veneer on firmly with a block of wood.

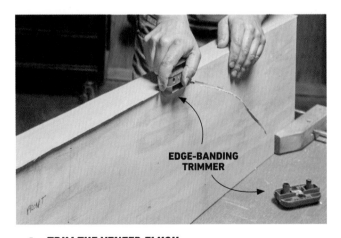

EDGE-BANDING TRIMMER

6 TRIM THE VENEER FLUSH
Using half of a handheld edge-banding trimmer, trim the veneer flush with the edges of the shelf. You can also use a router with a flush-trimming bit.

7 DRILL HOLES FOR SCREWS

Drill countersink pilot holes in the top of the shelf for some No. 8 wood screws. Drill them ¾ in. from the "wall" edge and space them about 12 in. apart.

COUNTERSINKING DRILL BIT

8 CUT THE CLEAT TO SIZE

Using a circular saw and a cutting guide, rip a wall cleat out of a 2x4. Make sure the 2x4 you're cutting from is dead straight.

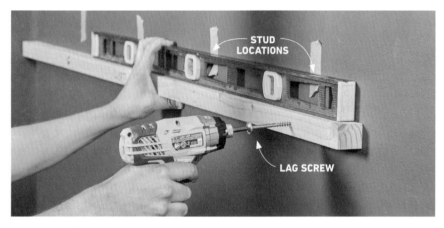

STUD LOCATIONS

LAG SCREW

9 SCREW THE CLEAT TO THE WALL

Drill pilot holes in the cleat and wall and secure the cleat with 4-in. lag screws. There's no need for fender washers if you use washer-head type screws like the ones shown.

BELT SANDER CLAMPED TO WORKTABLE

SCRIBE LINE

10 SCRIBE FOR A TIGHT FIT

Hold the shelf over the cleat, firmly against the wall, and drag a pencil along the wall to trace a scribe line onto the shelf. Scribing and sanding (next photo) allow shelves to fit perfectly against wall contours, but you can skip these steps if you don't mind a few gaps.

11 SAND TO THE SCRIBE LINE

Using a belt sander clamped to a sacrificial worktable, sand up to the scribe line on the shelf.

WOOD FILLER

12 FILL NAIL HOLES
Push "stainable" wood filler into the nail holes, leaving it slightly proud of the plywood in case of shrinkage.

13 SAND AND STAIN THE SHELF
Sand all the sides of the shelf using 100- and 150-grit sandpaper. Remove all dust after sanding with the 100-grit to prevent loose granules from scratching the plywood's surface.

sander perfectly perpendicular to the shelf, the scribe on the top and bottom panels won't match and the shelf won't fit tight to the wall. Instead, turn the belt sander on its side and clamp it on top of a temporary worktable like an old door or scrap of plywood. Turn it on and adjust the belt tracking so that the belt just barely disappears below the surface of the worktable (not all belt sanders let you do this). Run the shelf flat against your worktable and slowly sand up to the pencil line.

SAND, STAIN AND INSTALL

Using a fingertip or putty knife, push some "stainable" wood filler into each of the nail holes **(Photo 12).** The filler might shrink when it dries, so leave a bit extra in each hole—enough that it sits proud of the plywood. Once it dries, sand all sides of the shelf using a random orbit sander and 100- and then 150-grit sandpaper. After sanding with the 100-grit, vacuum or wipe off the sawdust so loose granules don't scratch up the shelf when you sand with the 150-grit. Vacuum up the dust or simply wipe it off with a tack cloth and apply stain following the directions on the can **(Photo 13).** If you want the shelf to look darker, wait a few hours and apply a second coat. Wait a day or two after staining

and then brush on three coats of polyurethane for protection.

Holding the shelf over the cleat and tight to the wall, drive 1⅝-in. wood screws through the pilot holes that you drilled earlier and into the wall cleat **(Photo 14).** Drive one of the middle screws first to help hold the shelf in place while you drive the others.

With the shelf secured, cover the exposed screw heads with a "non-hardening" type of wood filler colored to match your stain **(Photo 15).** This type of putty stays soft, allowing you to dig it out should you decide to remove the shelf someday.

MATERIALS LIST (2 Shelves)

ITEM	QTY.
4' x 8' sheet of ½" red oak plywood	1
24" x 96" roll of peel-and-stick veneer (enough for seven or eight shelves)	1
2x4	1
Non-hardening wood putty	
Tack cloths	
1⅝" (No. 8) wood screws	
4" lag screws	
Stainable wood filler	
Wood stain	
Cotton rags	
Disposable foam paintbrushes	
1" brad nails (18 gauge)	
Carpenter's glue	

WOOD
SCREW

NON-HARDENING
WOOD PUTTY

14 ATTACH THE SHELF TO THE CLEAT

Hold the shelf against the wall and drive 1⅝-in. wood screws through the shelf's pilot holes and into the wall cleat.

15 HIDE THE SCREW HEADS

Hide the screw heads with wood putty that matches the color of your stain. Use non-hardening putty so you can dig it out if you decide to remove the shelf someday.

Figure A **Exploded View**
OVERALL DIMENSIONS: 72" LONG x 11" DEEP (AFTER SCRIBING ⅛" OFF THE BACK) x 2½" THICK

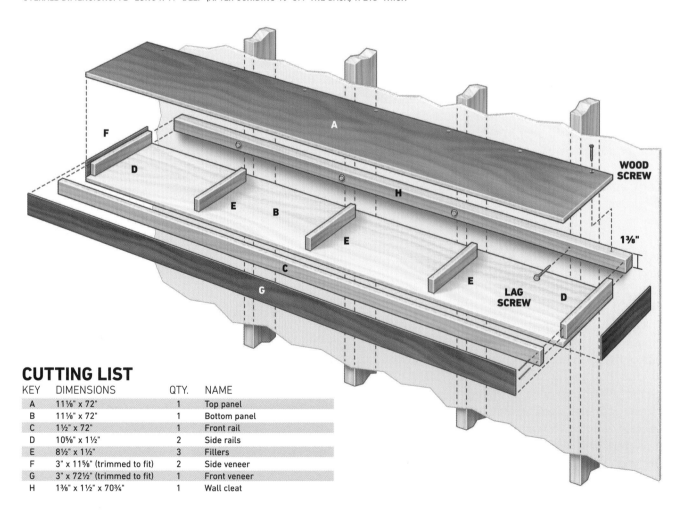

WOOD
SCREW

1⅜"

LAG
SCREW

CUTTING LIST

KEY	DIMENSIONS	QTY.	NAME
A	11⅛" x 72"	1	Top panel
B	11⅛" x 72"	1	Bottom panel
C	1½" x 72"	1	Front rail
D	10⅝" x 1½"	2	Side rails
E	8½" x 1½"	3	Fillers
F	3" x 11⅝" (trimmed to fit)	2	Side veneer
G	3" x 72½" (trimmed to fit)	1	Front veneer
H	1⅜" x 1½" x 70¾"	1	Wall cleat

12 IDEAL ROUTER TIPS

LEARN HOW THE PROS MAKE EASY WORK OF ROUTING

1 CLEAN UP A BAD CUT

An imperfect saw cut—one that's not quite straight or smooth, or one that's burned or splintered—is easy to clean up with a router and a pattern bit. Just clamp a straightedge to the board and let the bearing-guided bit create a flawless edge.

2 EASE SHARP EDGES

Whether it's furniture, trim or cabinetry, sharp edges are a potential problem. They're more likely to chip or dent with everyday use. Sharp edges also create a weak spot in paint and other coatings, leading to cracking and peeling, especially outdoors. To prevent trouble, ease sharp edges with a quick rub of sandpaper. Or better yet, round them with a 1/16-in.-radius round-over bit.

3 HOLD DOWN WITH HOT GLUE

Routing parts that are too small to hold down is dangerous for you and your project, since the router can send parts flying across the shop. But you can secure small parts without driving screws through them. All it takes is some hot glue. When you're done, just twist the routed part to break it free.

4 TAKE SMALL BITES FOR CLEANER CUTS

The best way to ensure a smoothly routed profile without chatter, chipping or burns is to cut in two or three passes, lowering the bit after each pass. On your final pass, take off just a smidgen of wood for the cleanest cut.

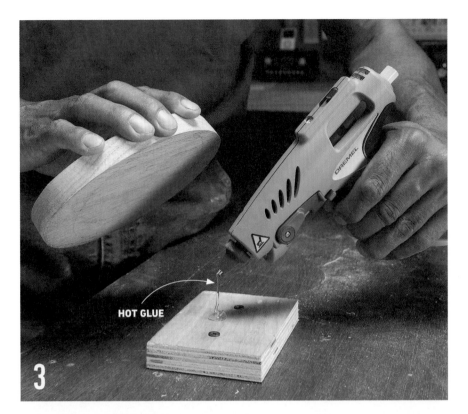

HOT GLUE

3

4

5   ROUTE SKINNY MOLDINGS? NO PROBLEM

If you've ever tried to rout a profile on a skinny strip of wood, you already know that it's dang near impossible. So instead, start with a wide board. Cut the profile, then rip it off using your table saw.

6

USE BISCUITS WITHOUT A BISCUIT JOINER

If you want to use biscuits but don't want to shell out $100 or more for a biscuit joiner, stick a ⁵⁄₃₂-in. slot cutter in your router and cut perfect slots for biscuits. You can cut short slots sized for biscuits or save time by cutting a continuous slot as shown here. You'll find slot cutters online; you'll even find router sets intended especially for biscuits. Just remember that there are situations where a router is no substitute for a biscuit joiner— for example, when cutting into beveled edges.

SLOT CUTTER

BISCUIT

7

SCREW THROUGH
BOARD INTO TABLE

UNIMPEDED
ROUTING

SPACER ON OTHER
SIDE OF "BRIDGE" IS
SAME THICKNESS

7 AVOID ROAD BLOCKS

Clamps can lock down a board while you rout, but they also get in the way, forcing you to stop and reposition them. A "bridge clamp," on the other hand, holds the work in place and leaves an unobstructed path for your router.

8 SAND FIRST, ROUT LATER (NOT SHOWN)

Always smooth the edge of a board before you rout a profile. Otherwise, the bearing follows any humps or dips along the edge and transfers those imperfections to your finished profile.

9

BREAKOUT BLOCK

9 ***STOP END-GRAIN BREAKOUT***
When a router bit exits end grain, splintering is almost inevitable. But you can prevent that by clamping on a scrap wood breakout block. That way, the block itself is at the end of the cut, and it's the block that suffers the damage.

10 STOP SLIPS

Rubbery router pads have an almost magical power to keep boards from sliding around as you rout (no clamps needed). But you do not have to run around searching for a router pad. Pads to keep rugs from slipping are available at discount stores and—as far as we can tell—are the same material as router pads.

11 ROOST ROUTER BITS

The best router bit storage is a custom-made holder specially designed to suit your personal collection and is hand-crafted from natural materials. In other words, it's a scrap of wood with ⅛-in. and ¼-in. holes drilled in it. You can even drill a couple of holes in the edge and hang it on pegboard if you like.

11

12 ADD EXTRA SUPPORT FOR NARROW STOCK

A router base tends to tip when riding across a narrow strip of wood. For extra stability, screw a wider board to your workbench alongside the narrow strip. Also screw on a stop board to keep the workpiece from skiing forward as you rout.

FOOLPROOF DADOES & RABBETS

///

THIS EASY CUTTING METHOD GUARANTEES THE STRONGEST JOINTS POSSIBLE

Dadoes, grooves and rabbets are the workhorses of cabinet and bookcase construction. They're used in woodworking projects to make stronger joints.

Dadoes and grooves are flat-bottomed recesses that strengthen supporting shelves and connecting panels. A dado runs perpendicular to the grain of the wood while a groove runs parallel to the grain. A rabbet is like a dado that's missing a side. It's essentially a notch cut into the edge of a board or piece of plywood.

You can cut dadoes, grooves and rabbets in many different ways. In this article, however, we're going to show you a simple, foolproof cutting method that requires only a router, a pattern bit and two straight guides.

RABBET

DADO

HOW A PATTERN BIT WORKS

The bit we're using is called a top-bearing pattern bit or top-bearing flush-trim bit. The bearing follows along the straight router guide as the cutters carve out the recess. Since the bearing and the cutters have the same diameter, you just line up the edge of the guide or pattern with the marks for the dado, groove or rabbet and run the router bit along the guide. Using two guides as we show here allows you to cut an exact size dado for any wood thickness that's greater than the bit diameter. The router bit can't go off track either, since it's trapped between the guides.

Most home centers and hardware stores don't stock top-bearing pattern bits, but they're readily available online and at woodworking stores. The bits come in different diameters and lengths. Make sure to buy a bit that's narrower than the thickness of the spacers **(Photo 4).** We're using a ½-in.-diameter bit with 1-in.-long cutters (Freud No. 50-102).

CUTTER

GUIDE BEARING

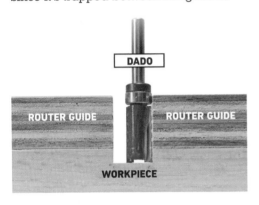

DADO

ROUTER GUIDE **ROUTER GUIDE**

WORKPIECE

RABBET

ROUTER GUIDE

WORKPIECE

ROUTER GUIDE

HOW TO CUT PERFECT DADOES

1 MAKE TWO STRAIGHTEDGE GUIDES

The dado cutting method we show here requires two perfectly straight guides. You can make your guides any length you want, and whatever thickness is required for your router bit. Since the bit we're using has relatively long cutters, we needed a 1-in.-thick guide to give the bearing something to ride against and the clearance necessary for the bit to reach the bottom of the dadoes.

To make guides like those shown here, cut four 6-in.-wide-by-4-ft.-long strips of ½-in.-thick plywood. Glue pairs together to make two 1-in.-thick strips. When the glue is dry, use a table saw or circular saw and straightedge to trim the guides and create one perfectly straight edge. Draw an arrow toward the straight edge of each strip to remind you which edge you should use for the guide **(Photo 3).**

When you're done trimming the edges, check the straightness of the guides by placing them next to each other on your workbench, with the arrows facing, and press them together. The guides should fit tight with no gaps. If there is a gap, recut one or both pieces until they fit tightly together.

2 MARK THE LOCATION OF THE DADO

You need to mark only one edge of the dado. Then draw an "X" to indicate which side of the mark the dado goes on. A good tip is to make three, not just two, marks across the workpiece. Then when you line up your straightedge with the marks, if one of the marks doesn't line up, you'll know you've made a layout mistake.

3 CLAMP THE FIRST GUIDE

The method we're using requires two guides, one for each side of the dado. This allows you to cut a perfect-width dado regardless of the thickness of the material. Line up the guide with the marks and clamp it securely. Be careful to position the clamps where they won't interfere with the router base as you're cutting the dado.

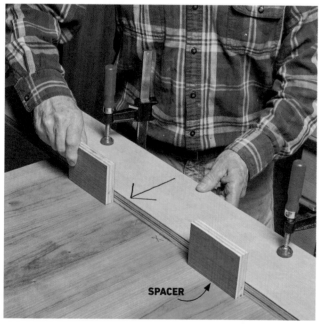

SPACER

4 ADD SPACERS

When you're cutting out the parts for your cabinet or bookcase, save a few scraps of the material. Then use those scraps as spacers. This ensures that the thickness of the material you're using will match the dado widths perfectly.

5 CLAMP THE SECOND GUIDE

Press the second guide against the spacer blocks and clamp it. Make sure the clamps won't interfere with the router base. Remove the spacers and you're ready to cut the dado.

6 ROUT THE FIRST SIDE OF THE DADO

Since the dado we're cutting is a little less than ¾ in. wide and we're using a ½-in. bit, it will take two passes, one along each router guide, to complete the dado. First adjust the router depth. This will be the thickness of the guides plus the desired depth of your dado. We set the router to cut a ¼-in.-deep dado. If you're positioned as shown in this photo, start at the left side and move the router left to right, keeping the guide bearing pressed against the guide farthest from you. The rule of thumb is to rout inside cuts like this in a clockwise direction.

7 FINISH UP WITH A SECOND PASS

Complete the dado by moving the router right to left, keeping the guide bearing in contact with the guide closest to you. Before you remove the clamps and guides, inspect the dado to make sure both edges are straight and smooth. If you find any imperfections, run the router over that area again. That's all it takes to cut a perfect dado.

HOW TO CUT PERFECT RABBETS

1 POSITION THE GUIDE

There's more than one way to cut a rabbet, including buying a special rabbeting bit. But since you already have the guide and a pattern bit, why not use them to cut rabbets too? Here we're cutting a ¼ x ¼-in. rabbet in the back of a cabinet side to accept the ¼-in. plywood back. Use a scrap of the same plywood to set the position of the guide, then clamp the guide into place.

2 ROUT THE RABBET

Starting at the left end, run the router left to right along the guide to cut the rabbet. You can use this same technique to cut wider rabbets like the one along the top edge of the cabinet, but you'll have to make one pass along the guide and then clean up the remaining wood using the router freehand. That just means holding the bearing a tad away from the straightedge to remove the rest of the wood. Be sure to keep the router base tight to the guide at all times.

TRICKS FOR TIGHTER MITERS

///
PICTURE-PERFECT MITERED JOINTS ARE EASIER THAN YOU THINK

When they are done well, mitered joints look good. They hide end grain and match face grains nicely. But they're also a pain in the neck, requiring precise cuts and fussy fastening. Are you in pursuit of the perfect miter joint? These tips for tighter miters cover common situations that you'll undoubtedly encounter in your workshop.

1

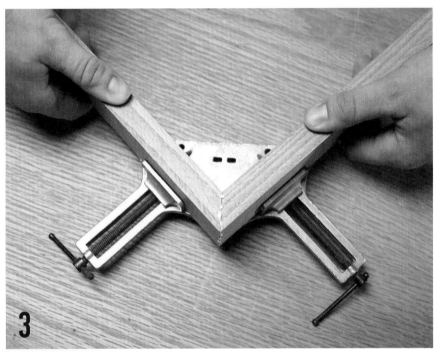

2

USE SCRAP WOOD GUIDES FOR A PERFECT FIT

1 It's dang near impossible to get the length and position of a mitered part right unless you can butt it up against the adjoining miters. To provide a guide, tape or clamp mitered scraps in place. Remove the scraps as soon as you glue the part in place—otherwise, stray glue might make those temporary guides permanent.

ALIGN WITH BISCUITS

2 It's not easy to align and clamp miters, especially when they're lubricated with a coat of slippery glue. That's why woodworkers often use biscuits on miter joints even where extra strength isn't needed. Cutting biscuit slots is a minor job that provides major help at glue-up time.

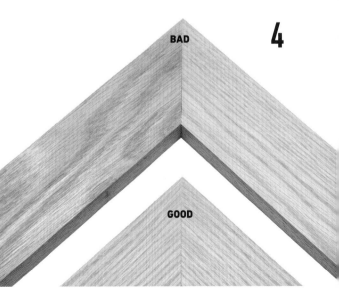

3

SQUARE UP WITH CORNER CLAMPS

3 With some miter-clamping methods, you need to grab a square and make sure the corner is exactly 90 degrees. Not so with corner clamps; they automatically hold parts perfectly square. They're available at home centers or online for $10 to $50 apiece.

MATCH WOOD GRAIN

4 Whether you're banding a tabletop or making a picture frame, make sure the wood color and the grain pattern match at the miters. Selecting matching wood at the lumberyard takes only a few extra seconds and gives you much better-looking miters.

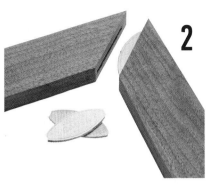

BAD

4

GOOD

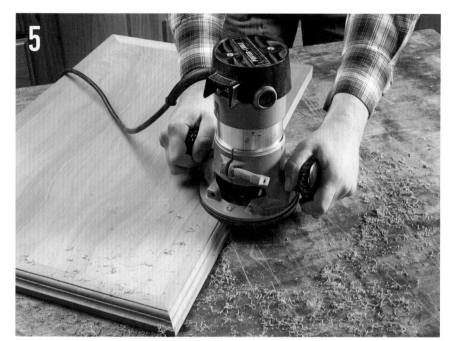

5

MITER, ASSEMBLE THEN ROUT

Shaped moldings can be tough to miter, align and clamp. So make life easier by starting with plain square stock. Then, after assembly, grab your router and shape the edges. The risk with this method is that you'll gouge or splinter parts that are already in place. The best way to avoid disaster is to make a series of shallow passes instead of one full-depth cut.

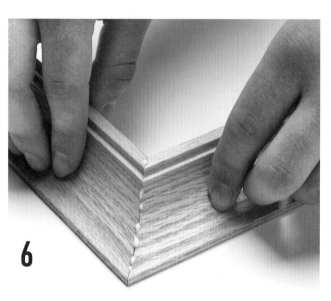

6

7

CLAMP WITH YOUR HANDS

When you're dealing with small or other hard-to-clamp parts, your hands make the best clamps. Simply rub the glued surfaces together and hold them tightly on a flat surface for about a minute. Let go and allow the joint to set for 30 minutes before handling it.

SLOW DOWN YOUR GLUE

It is hard enough to align and clamp miters without rushing to get it done before the glue begins to set (in 5 to 10 minutes, and even faster in warm, dry conditions). Slow-setting wood glues, give you an extra 10 minutes or so.

If you can't find a slow version at your favorite home center, make your own. If you add 1 part water to 20 parts wood glue, you'll gain about five minutes of working time. The water will also weaken the bond very slightly. So if strength is critical, order slow-setting glue online. Titebond Extend is one common brand.

8

8 MICRO-ADJUST WITH PAPER SHIMS

If you've ever tried to adjust the angle of your miter saw by one-tenth of a degree, you already know how hard micro-adjustments are. Here's an easier way: Slap a few sticky notes on the fence, make test cuts, and add or remove sheets until you get exactly the angle you want.

9 FEEL THE DIFFERENCE

When you are building a box or frame, the opposite sides have to be exactly the same length. To make sure they are, do the touch test: Set the parts side by side and run your finger over the mitered ends. You may not be able to see a slight length difference, but you'll feel it.

9

10 CLOSE UGLY GAPS

You can close a miter gap by rubbing it with a screwdriver shank or any hard, smooth tool. We used the end of a utility knife. That crushes the wood fibers inward to make the gap disappear. Even professional woodworkers sometimes resort to this crude trick.

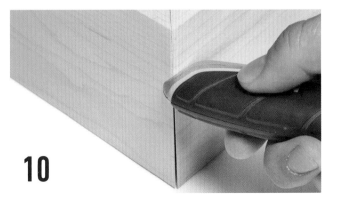

10

11 MAKE YOUR OWN CORNER CLAMPS

This is an old favorite among woodworkers: Clamp on notched blocks, then add a bar clamp or two to squeeze the joint. This allows you to put a lot of pressure on the joint without buying any special clamps. If you're assembling a four-sided project such as a picture frame, join two corners first. Then, after the glue has set, join the two halves of the frame.

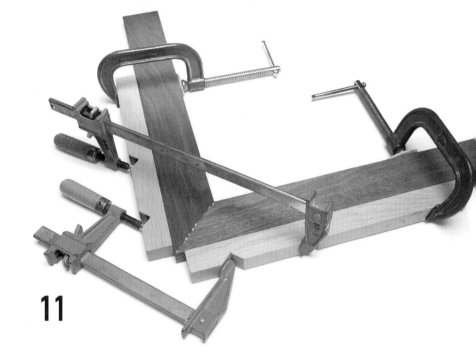

11

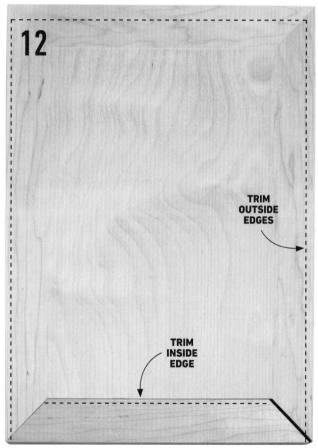

12

TRIM OUTSIDE EDGES

TRIM INSIDE EDGE

12 LENGTHEN A BOARD

Ever cut that last part just a bit too short? There's a solution for that: First, trim off the inside edge of the too-short part. By cutting off the short edge, you effectively make the mitered part longer. Then trim the same amount off the outer edges of the other three sides. Your edging will be a little thinner than you had planned, but nobody will notice.

13

13 BOND JOINTS INSTANTLY

Trim carpenters have used this system for years: Apply a few dabs of cyanoacrylate adhesive (aka "superglue") to one surface and apply activator (or "accelerator") to the other. Immediately press the parts together and they'll bond in seconds. No waiting, no complicated clamping setup. Activator is sometimes sold separately (about $5 and up), sometimes with the glue. Look for it at home centers or shop online; *rockler.com* carries a good selection of glues and activators.

SUCCESS WITH MELAMINE

11 HINTS TO WORKING WITH THIS POPULAR MATERIAL

"Melamine" is the common name for particleboard that's coated with a thin layer of plastic finish. The melamine finish is similar to the plastic laminate on countertops, but it's not as thick. The advantages of building with a melamine-coated product are its durable finish and its relatively low cost. But it can be frustrating to work with. The particleboard can be hard to fasten, and the brittle finish is tricky to cut. Here are 11 tips to make your next melamine project a success.

1 BUY A SPECIAL BLADE

The melamine finish chips easily when cut, especially if you're using an everyday saw blade. But you can largely avoid chipping by investing in a special blade that's designed to cut plastic materials. The teeth on these blades are less angled, which helps prevent chipping. One example is the Freud LU79R007 7¼-in. blade. If you can't justify spending this much, you can still get good results with a less expensive blade that has at least 40 carbide teeth. But be sure to use the chip-free cutting technique that we show in Tip 4.

2 ORDER THE COLOR YOU WANT

You'll typically find melamine products in white at home centers, but many colors are available. Depending on the brand, you'll find 10 to 20 or more colors available for special order. Check with your local lumberyard or home center for your options.

3 WEAR SAFETY GEAR

You should always wear safety gear when you're using power tools. There are particular safety concerns when you're working with melamine. For starters, the plastic finish tends to chip off as it's cut. The chips are as sharp as glass, creating a real hazard for your eyes. Safety glasses are a must.

The fine dust created by cutting the fiber core is bad for your lungs. If possible, cut outdoors. Indoors or out, wear a dust mask. Wear gloves when you're handling large sheets of melamine. The edges can be razor sharp. And don't forget hearing protection.

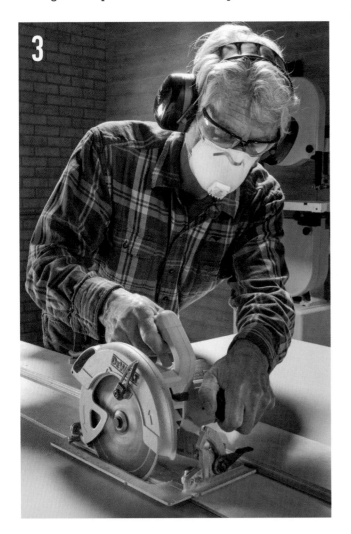

MELAMINE BASICS

Look around and you'll find melamine furniture, melamine shelves, melamine wall panels and even melamine slatwall. It's usually labeled as melamine, but you may also see terms such as *thermally fused laminate* or simply *prefinished panels* or *prefinished shelves*.

You can buy 4 x 8-ft. sheets of melamine in ⅛-, ¼-, ½-, ⅝- and ¾-in. thicknesses and melamine shelves in various lengths and widths. Home centers may stock only ¼-in. and ¾-in. thicknesses. Melamine sheets cost about 60¢ to $1.25 per square foot. Shelving costs about $1.40 to $2 per linear foot depending on the width.

4 CUT WITHOUT CHIPPING

Making a scoring cut before the final one will result in a chip-free edge. First, use a straightedge as a saw guide. Without the straightedge, the saw might wobble slightly as you cut, and this twisting will contribute to chipping. Clamp your straightedge guide in position and set the saw to cut ⅛ in. deep. Run your saw along the straightedge and cut a groove in the melamine panel. This shallow cut shouldn't produce any chipping.

Now reset the saw so the blade extends about ½ in. past the bottom side of the panel and make another pass. The resulting cut will be perfectly chip-free on both sides. You can use the same technique on a table saw. Make one shallow cut. Then run the panel through the saw a second time to complete the cut. If only one side of the panel will be visible in the finished project, you don't need to use this technique because chipping occurs only on the side where the saw blade teeth exit. Just make sure to place the "show" side down if you're cutting with a circular saw and up when you're using a table saw.

SHALLOW SAW KERF

5 PIN PANELS, THEN ADD SCREWS

The melamine finish is slippery, making it difficult to hold the panels in alignment while you drill pilot holes for the screws. Solve this by first pinning the panels together using an 18-gauge brad nail gun. The small holes left by the brads are nearly invisible, and you'll save yourself a lot of time and frustration.

6 DRILL AND COUNTERSINK FOR SCREWS

Particleboard, whether it has a melamine finish or not, doesn't hold screws as well as solid lumber or plywood. Plus, it tends to split if you drive screws without drilling first. The key to fastening it with screws is to drill pilot holes for the screws and countersinks for the screw heads. A combination bit that drills and countersinks in one operation saves time. Choose a countersink bit that's labeled for use with No. 8 screws.

COUNTERSINK BIT

WOOD BISCUIT

SOLID WOOD NOSING

7

7 STRENGTHEN SHELVES WITH NOSING

Melamine shelves will sag over time, especially if they're more than a few feet long. Strengthen shelves by gluing a solid wood nose to one or both edges of the shelf. Here we've slotted the nosing and the melamine shelves with a biscuit joiner to allow the use of wood biscuits. The biscuits add strength and help align the edging perfectly. No nails needed; just apply wood glue, insert the biscuits and clamp the edge to the shelf until the glue sets.

8

SCREW DRIVEN TOO CLOSE TO END

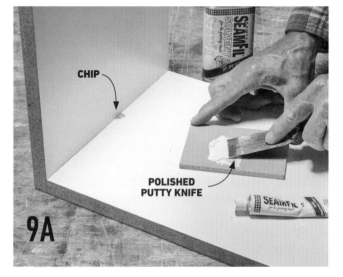

CHIP

POLISHED PUTTY KNIFE

SEAMFIL

9A

9B

8 PREVENT SPLITTING

The particleboard core is rather brittle and can split if you drive screws too close to the edge. Prevent this by positioning screws at least 2 in. from the edges of panels when possible. Drilling a pilot hole also helps prevent splitting (Tip 6).

9 REPAIR CHIPS WITH A SPECIAL FILLER

SeamFil plastic filler paste comes in a tube and is commonly used by pros who work with plastic laminate to repair chips. And since the surface of melamine panels and shelves is also a type of plastic laminate, the repairs blend in well.

SeamFil paste is available for about $5 per 1-oz. tube online or where plastic laminate (used for countertops) is sold. It's available in 20 standard colors that can be mixed to create custom colors.

To use the SeamFil paste, first clean the area with the special SeamFil solvent (available for about $9 per half pint where the paste is sold). Then spread a small amount of the paste on a scrap of wood or plastic laminate. Work the paste around with a polished putty knife until some of the solvent starts to evaporate and the paste starts to thicken. Then press the thickened paste into the area to be repaired and smooth it with the putty knife. It may take a few coats to get a flush surface. Clean off excess paste using a rag dampened with the solvent.

10   HIDE SCREW HEADS

To conceal screw heads, you have a couple of options. You can buy plastic caps that snap onto or over your screw heads. These work fine but leave a protruding cap.

The other option is to cover the screws with FastCap self-sticking plastic screw covers ($3 to $5 for 56 ½-in. covers). These are available at some retailers, online or directly from FastCap. Go to *fastcap.com* to see the huge variety of sizes and colors. If you're really picky and want to install a nearly invisible, flush screw cover, you can buy a special FlushMount drill bit system that makes a perfect-depth recess for the plastic screw covers.

11   FINISH RAW EDGES WITH EDGE BANDING

When the edge of a melamine panel is visible but you don't want to add solid wood nosing, apply edge-banding tape. You can buy iron-on edge banding at most home centers. But an even easier solution is to apply self-adhesive or peel-and-stick edge banding. FastCap is one company that supplies peel-and-stick edge banding in a wide variety of colors, widths and lengths. Called Fastedge, it's available online and at woodworking stores.

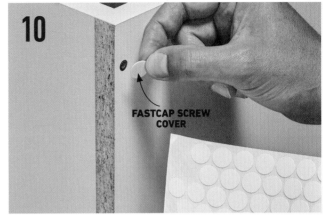

10

FASTCAP SCREW COVER

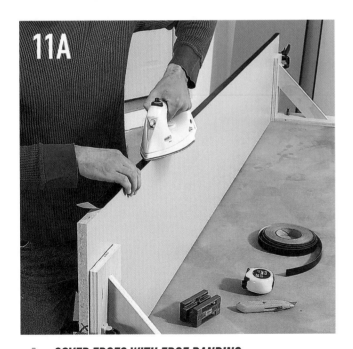

11A

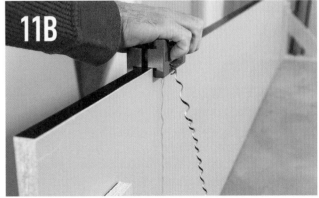

11B

A   COVER EDGES WITH EDGE BANDING

Move a hot iron quickly over iron-on edge-banding tape to melt the glue. If you're using self-adhesive edge banding, you can skip this step and simply peel off the paper backing and stick the edge banding to the particleboard edge.

B   TRIM THE TAPE TO FINISH THE EDGE

Trim the overhanging edges of the tape flush to the melamine surface with a special tool called an edge-banding trimmer. You'll find edge-banding trimmers at home centers, woodworking stores and online for about $20.

ALL ABOUT EURO HINGES

//
THEY MAKE CABINET DOORS A SNAP

3 REASONS TO LOVE EURO HINGES

Euro hinges—also called "cup hinges" or "concealed hinges"—look complicated. But they're actually much easier to install than traditional hinges.

1 ### EASY TO INSTALL
Traditional hinges are fussy to install. And if you get it wrong, you're stuck. With Euro hinges, you just bore one large hole and drive some screws. Get that hole in the right spot and the rest is goof-proof.

2 ### SIMPLE TO ADJUST
With traditional hinges, you can spend hours getting the fit right: planing or sanding the door, shimming or moving hinges ... With Euro hinges, you can move a door in and out, up and down, or side to side just by turning screws.

3 ### INSTANT ON AND OFF
With traditional hinges, you have to remove screws or hinge pins to remove doors. Euro hinges like this one just snap onto mounting plates so you can instantly check the door's fit. Then pull a release lever to remove the door for finishing.

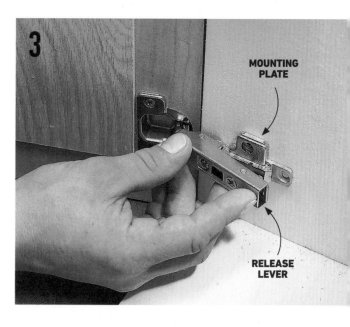

MOUNTING PLATE

RELEASE LEVER

MEET THE EXPERT
Tom Caspar is a professional furniture maker and the former editor of *American Woodworker* magazine.

CHOOSING THE RIGHT HINGE

YOU NEED TO ANSWER 4 BASIC QUESTIONS

Most Euro hinges cost about $2 each, though some specialty hinges cost $10 or more. To get hinges that suit your cabinet, you need to answer these questions:

1 FACE FRAME OR NOT?
A frameless or "Euro-style" cabinet is basically a box. A face frame cabinet has a frame surrounding the opening of the box.

2 INSET OR OVERLAY DOORS?
Inset doors are flush with the front of the cabinet; overlay doors cover all or part of the front. Some doors, called "partial inset" (not shown) are a combination of both. We show frameless cabinets here, but the same terms apply to face frame cabinets.

3 HOW MUCH OVERLAY?
If you choose overlay doors, you'll have to decide how much. With some frameless hinges, the amount of overlay is determined by the thickness of the mounting plate; a thicker mounting plate results in a lesser overlay.

4 HOW FAR DO YOU WANT YOUR DOORS TO OPEN?
The simplest, smallest and least expensive hinges usually open to 105 or 110 degrees. If you want your doors to open farther for easier access inside the cabinet, the hinges will be bulkier and more expensive.

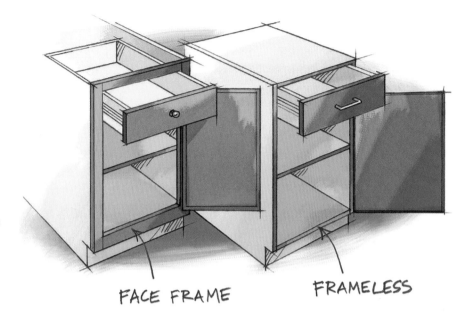

FACE FRAME   FRAMELESS

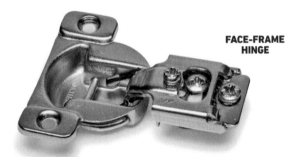

FACE-FRAME HINGE

Hinges like this one mount onto the face frame, typically with a single screw.

FRAMELESS HINGE   **MOUNTING PLATE**

Hinges like this one attach to a mounting plate that's screwed to the cabinet. They're made for frameless cabinets but can be used with face frame cabinets if you buy special mounting brackets.

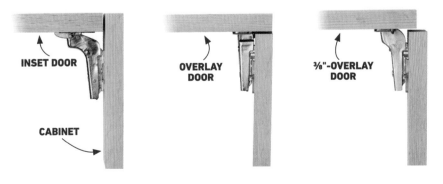

INSET DOOR   OVERLAY DOOR   ⅜"-OVERLAY DOOR

CABINET

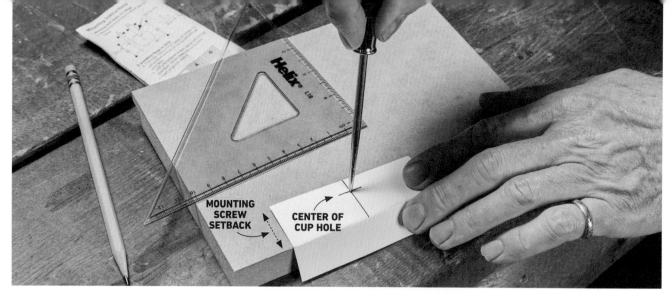

MOUNTING SCREW SETBACK

CENTER OF CUP HOLE

INSTALLING EURO HINGES

No matter what type of hinge you choose, the hinges are mounted on the door first and then the cabinet. You'll be drilling two sets of holes in the door. First, there's the "cup hole," the large hole that the hinge drops into. This hole is 35 mm (1⅜ in.) diameter for all Euro hinges. You'll need a Forstner bit to drill it (about $20 at home centers or online).

Second, you'll drill two pilot holes for the screws that fasten the hinge to the door. The instructions will tell you what bit to use.

Some Euro hinges come with a full-size template for marking both sets of holes, but many hinges don't. In that case, the instructions will include a scale drawing in millimeters (not inches) and you'll have to make a template yourself.

Make the template from an old business card. Fold the card around the edge of a scrap of wood **(Photo 1).** Measuring from the fold, draw a line indicating the mounting screw locations. Cut the card along this line.

Draw a centerline on the card, then measure the distance from the folded edge to the center of the cup hole. Poke a hole here using an awl.

INSTALL THE HINGE ON THE DOOR

Determine the location of the hinges on the door. The distance from the top or bottom of the door to the hinge's centerline is usually about 2 to 3 in. Draw centerlines for the hinges using a square or a wood scrap.

Align the template with the centerline, then trace the edge of the card **(Photo 2).** Use the awl to mark the center of the cup hole.

Drill the cup holes **(Photo 3).** These holes must be at least ½ in. deep. Most Forstner bits are about ½ in. thick, so it's easy to use the bit itself to judge how deep you've drilled.

1 MAKE A TEMPLATE
Fold a business card around a scrap of wood, then cut the card to match the setback of the hinge's mounting screws. Poke a hole in the card to mark the distance to the center of the hinge's cup hole.

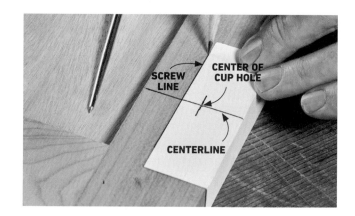

SCREW LINE

CENTER OF CUP HOLE

CENTERLINE

2 MARK THE DOOR
Align the template with a centerline indicating where the hinge will go. Trace the edge of the card to mark the mounting screw line, then use an awl to mark the center of the cup hole.

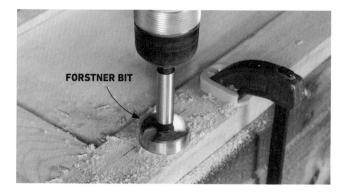

FORSTNER BIT

3 DRILL THE CUP HOLE
Using a 35-mm (1⅜-in.) Forstner bit, drill until the top of the bit is about level with the wood. Close is good enough.

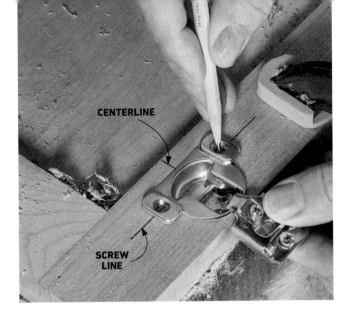

4 MARK SCREW HOLES

Place the hinge in the cup hole, then mark the locations of the mounting screws. Drill pilot holes and install the hinge.

5 FACE FRAME: FASTEN THE HINGE

For a face-frame cabinet, simply position the door and screw the hinge to the face frame.

Place the hinge in the cup hole, then mark the hinge's mounting screw holes **(Photo 4).** Drill pilot holes (making sure you don't drill through the door), then fasten the hinge to the door.

INSTALL THE HINGE ON THE CABINET

To install hinges on face-frame cabinets, turn your cabinet on its side, then place the door alongside it. Rest the protruding parts of the hinges on the face frame. Center the door.

Make sure the tabs on the hinges are butted up to the face frame, then use an awl to mark the centers of the mounting screw pilot holes. Drill the holes and install the screws **(Photo 5).** Stand up the cabinet and fine-tune the door's position by turning the hinge's adjusting screws.

Hinges for frameless cabinets have a separate mounting plate. The instructions will show you the correct distance from the front edge of the cabinet to the screw line. Draw screw lines inside the cabinet.

Attach the mounting plates to the hinges. Place the cabinet on its side, then butt the door to the cabinet. Center the door side-to-side. Align the mounting plate's holes with the setback lines. Mark the centers of the holes.

Pull the door away from the cabinet and remove the mounting plates. Drill pilot holes, then fasten the mounting plates to the cabinet **(Photo 6).** Snap the hinges onto the plates, then stand up the cabinet and adjust the hinges as needed.

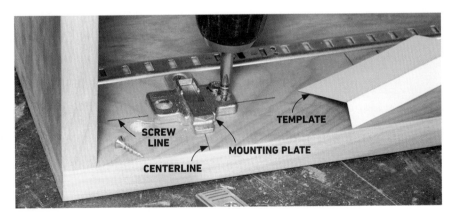

SHOP ONLINE

Home centers carry a limited selection of Euro hinges, so it's smart to browse online as well. Sources like *rockler.com* and *wwhardware.com* carry hinges with features like soft-close or cover plates to hide screws. They also have experts available to help you choose the right hinge system.

6 FRAMELESS: INSTALL A MOUNTING PLATE

For a cabinet without a face frame, make a second template to mark the screw line. Fasten the plate to the cabinet, then snap the door hinge onto the plate.

1 MARK YOUR TEMPLATE

Store-bought templates like this one include lots of holes to accommodate various hinges. It's all too easy to use the wrong holes. To prevent that, mark the holes you need with paint or a marker.

1

BUY BEFORE YOU BUILD

Having your hinges on hand makes the planning and building details much easier and prevents major mistakes.

2 GET BEST RESULTS WITH A CORDED DRILL

You can bore cup holes with a cordless drill, but that strains the drill and drains the battery fast. A corded drill does the job faster and better.

2

3

4

3 DRILL SHALLOW STARTER HOLES

The tiny screws that come with Euro hinges often strip out in softwoods or plywood. So instead of drilling a full-depth pilot hole for screws, just create a divot using a drill bit, awl or even a nail to position the screw.

GO METRIC

In the world of Euro hinges, everything is metric. You will need a metric ruler to make your own marking template, for example. Pick up a metric ruler at any store that carries school supplies.

4 DON'T FORGET THE BUMPERS

Most Euro hinges are self-closing, which means doors slam hard and loud. Pick up sheets of adhesive-backed cabinet bumpers at any home center for a couple of bucks.

5 MARK GOOF-PROOF CENTERLINES

To mark perfect centerlines for the hinges, lay the cabinet box on its side and center the door against it. Then trace along a marking block (2 to 3 in. wide). Use masking tape labels to match doors to their locations.

6 LEAVE ADJUSTMENTS FOR LAST

Euro hinges allow for perfect alignment. But don't bother with that until cabinets are installed. Fussing with adjustments before your cabinets are squared up and level is a waste of time.

MARKING BLOCK

CENTERLINE

INSTALLING CABINET HARDWARE

FINISH CABINETS WITH FLAIR ... AND WITHOUT MISTAKES OR EXTRA HOLES

There's more to installing kitchen hardware than drilling holes and screwing on knobs and pulls. Whether you're installing hardware on brand-new cabinets or replacing the hardware in a 100-year-old kitchen, think before you drill. Cabinets are expensive, and they look a whole lot better without extra holes. We asked Jerome Worm for some tips on how he installs the "jewelry of the kitchen." Use these tips to help your next install go quicker, with fewer mistakes.

1 USE THE DOOR RAIL AS A GUIDE

The location of knobs and pulls isn't written in stone, but there are some "standard practices." One good rule of thumb is to line up a knob with the top of the bottom door rail. If you're installing door pulls, line up the bottom of the pull with the top of the door rail. Always center them on the door stile.

2 MAKE THE JOB EASIER WITH TEMPLATES

If you have more than a few knobs or pulls to install, use a template. A template makes the job go faster, increases uniformity and reduces the chance for mistakes. The Liberty Cabinet and Drawer Installation Templates cost about $8 at a home center.

If you install a lot of hardware, buy a professional version like the one seen on p. 90. The best ones are adjustable and have steel grommets where you insert the drill bit. You can get one for about $40 at online retailers.

1

TOP OF RAIL

RAIL   STILE

2

3 TEMPORARILY ATTACH THE HARDWARE

Ultimately, the person paying for the hardware has the final word on where the knobs and pulls are to be installed. If Jerome's customers don't like his suggestions, he sticks a piece of reusable putty adhesive to the hardware and lets them put it wherever they want. He marks that spot with a pencil and installs the rest of the hardware accordingly. DAP makes a reusable adhesive called BlueStik. You can buy packages at home centers.

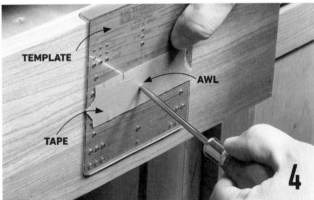

TEMPLATE

AWL

TAPE

4

4 COVER UNUSED HOLES WITH TAPE

Store-bought templates and well-used homemade templates have a bunch of holes you won't use on every job. Avoid using the wrong hole by sticking masking tape over the jig and poking through only the holes you need. Instead of using a pencil to mark the location of the hole on the cabinet, use an awl. Your drill bit won't skate off in the wrong direction when you drill the hole.

3

ADHESIVE PUTTY

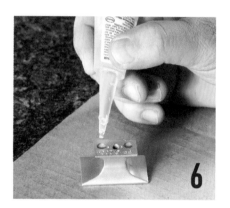

5 HIDE OLD HOLES WITH BACK PLATES

If you're switching from a pull to a knob or you'd prefer to select pulls with a different hole pattern, you can cover the old holes or hide damaged surfaces with back plates. Home centers don't have a huge selection, so consider buying yours from an online source like *myknobs.com*. You'll find hundreds to choose from.

6 SUPER-GLUE THE KNOB

Oblong and rectangular knobs that fasten with a single screw are notorious for twisting over time. Thread sealant will keep a screw from coming loose from the knob, but it won't necessarily stop the knob from twisting. Jerome avoids callbacks by adding a drop of super glue to the back of these types of knobs before he installs them.

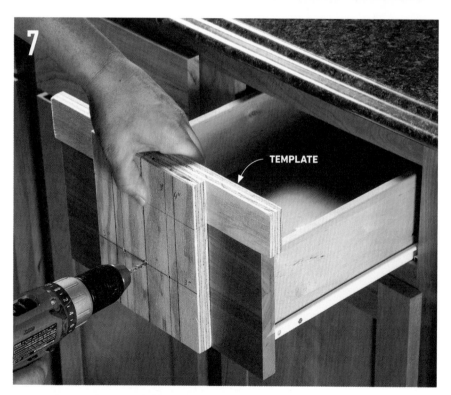

7 MAKE A SIMPLE DRAWER TEMPLATE

If you don't have a template, make one. This simple template consists of two pieces of wood and takes only a few minutes to make. This same template can be used for almost any size door and most hardware sizes.

8 PREVENT TEAR-OUT WITH TWO-SIDED TEMPLATES

If you're having problems with the wood on the back side of the cabinet doors tearing out every time you drill a hole, make a two-sided template. Make sure the spacer wood is close to the same size as the cabinet doors. The tighter the fit, the less chance of tear-out.

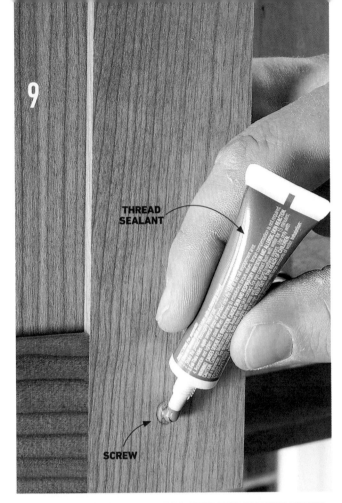

9

THREAD SEALANT

SCREW

9 USE THREAD SEALANT TO KEEP THE SCREWS TIGHT

Every time the screw in a knob works itself loose, the owners of those cabinets are going to think unflattering thoughts about whoever put them in. Keep your customers happy—add a dab of removable thread sealant to every screw you install. Loctite is one brand.

10 INSTALL HARDWARE HIGHER ON THE LOWEST DRAWER

Most drawer pulls are centered on the drawer fronts, but if the cabinet you're working on has two or three drawers the same size and one larger one at the bottom, install the bottom knob (or pull) higher than the center of that drawer front. Install it so all the knobs on the cabinet are spaced evenly. This configuration is pleasing to the eye—and you don't have to bend over as far to open the bottom drawer.

DON'T INSTALL HARDWARE IN FRONT OF THE SINK

The false drawer directly in front of the sink may look naked without any hardware, but it's not very comfortable getting poked by a knob in your midsection every time you lean over the sink.

11

11 MIX PUTTY TO MATCH

If back plates won't cover the old holes, use putty to fill them. The wood grain on cabinet doors and fronts usually varies in color, so take one of the doors to a hardware store or home center and buy three different colors of putty. Buy one that matches the darkest grain, one that matches the lightest grain and one halfway between. Use the three to mix a custom color to fill the holes.

10

HIGHER THAN CENTER

CHAPTER 3

FLOORS, CEILINGS & WALLS

Install a New Floor in One Day 96

Tiling Tricks 102

Choose Self-Leveling Underlayment 106

Spray-Texture a Ceiling 111

Taping Drywall 114

Living with Plaster Walls 119

Plaster & Lath Tear-Off 124

Rock-Solid Handrails 128

INSTALL A NEW FLOOR IN ONE DAY

LUXURY VINYL IS TOUGH AND GOOD-LOOKING—AND THE EASIEST FLOORING TO SET

Editor Mark Petersen has installed just about every type of flooring the world has ever known. So when his wife chose luxury vinyl planks for their new dining room floor, his first thought was: *Why couldn't she pick something I already know how to do?* Now he'd have to muddle through the installation of an unfamiliar product, hoping to avoid costly mistakes.

But it turns out that there was nothing to worry about. Mark was able to install 150 sq. ft. in less than a day without any problems. It was the fastest, easiest floor he's ever installed. And the next time we need new flooring, our vote will be for luxury vinyl. This article will walk you through the process Mark followed and show you some key tips along the way.

LAMINATE

LUXURY VINYL PLANK (LVP)

WHAT IS LUXURY VINYL?

LV flooring is similar to sheet vinyl, but it's thicker, tougher and easier to install. It comes in tiles and planks, but this article covers planks only. Mark used a product called Adura LockSolid. It's a "floating floor," which means it isn't fastened to the subfloor but just lies there. Luxury vinyl is the fastest-growing category in the flooring industry.

LVP (luxury vinyl plank) is similar in price to medium-grade laminate. It's available at flooring stores and home centers.

SOFT AND PLIABLE

LVP flooring feels softer underfoot than most other flooring. And because LVP flooring is pliable, it's a lot easier to install in tight quarters than rigid planks. Other floating floors need cushy underlayment to prevent noise, but LVP flooring doesn't because its flexibility makes it inherently quiet.

NEEDS NO EXPENSIVE TOOLS

You can install LVP flooring using only basic hand tools and a few inexpensive specialty tools.

WATER RESISTANT

Some manufacturers actually refer to their products as "waterproof" rather than just "water resistant." LVP flooring is not damaged by water. Mark was skeptical, so he cut off a chunk and stuck it in a pail of water overnight—it was completely unaffected.

THIN, WITH NO UNDERLAYMENT

LVP is thinner than ceramic tile, wood and other types of flooring, and it doesn't require an underlayment, so it's possible to go over existing flooring without raising the floor much (see "Watch Your Floor Height" on p. 100). It does need to be installed on a smooth surface, so don't lay it on tile, and most manufacturers do not recommend LVP over other floating floor systems. These particular planks are about ⁵⁄₃₂ in. thick.

EASY TO CUT

The real beauty of this flooring is that it's super easy to cut. All you have to do is score it with a utility knife and snap it off. You can make curved cuts with a pair of aviation snips. You won't have noisy saws, caustic sawdust to inhale, or a need to run back and forth to your cut station. It really is a dream to work with.

START WITH A SMOOTH SURFACE

LVP flooring can be installed over most surfaces as long as those surfaces are smooth. Rough and uneven spots will telegraph through the new flooring, causing noticeable high spots that will wear faster than the rest of the floor. Concrete subfloors must be at least six weeks old, dry, and free of powder and flaking. Large cracks and expansion joints should be filled and troweled smooth. Home centers sell mixable and premixed products that work on most surfaces.

Find the high and low spots on wood subfloors with a straightedge. The floor height should not rise or drop more than ⅛ in. over the span of 4 ft. Sand down the high spots with a belt sander equipped with a coarse-grit belt **(Photo 1).** This is a dusty job, so turn off your furnace to avoid spreading dust all over the house, and wear a dust mask. Fill the low spots in the plywood with floor patch **(Photo 2).** Avoid self-leveling floor patch. The floor doesn't have to be level; it just has to be smooth. Some older houses would require a cement truck full of self-leveling floor patch to do the job. Check your installation manual about any other subfloor specifics.

PULL BAR

TAPPING BLOCK

SHIMS

The LVP flooring in this story can be installed with the same tools as laminate flooring. A basic kit costs about $20 at home centers.

1 SAND DOWN THE HIGH SPOTS
Grind down any humps, lumps or bulges in the subfloor. Use the coarsest sanding belt you can find, such as 40- or 60-grit.

BEGIN AND END WITH A HALF PLANK OR MORE

If you lay the planks parallel to the longest wall, you'll end up making fewer cuts. But don't start that first row with full planks without figuring out how wide your last row is going to be. Neither the first nor the last row should be ripped down much smaller than half a plank.

Measure the width of the room, and divide it by the width of the exposed portion of the plank. For example, if your room measures 123 in., and your flooring is 5.75 in. wide, you'd divide 123 by 5.75, which is 21.39. That is, it would take 21.39 planks to complete the floor. Because this 0.39 represents less than half the width of a plank, you would want to cut down the first plank by an inch or so to increase the size of the last plank.

START WITH A PARTIAL PLANK

END WITH A PARTIAL PLANK

2 FILL IN THE LOW SPOTS
Fill the low spots with floor patch, and feather it out with a trowel. Don't worry about the screw heads.

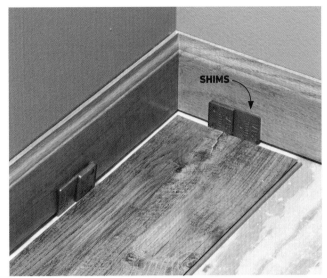

3 UNDERCUT DOORJAMBS
Trim jambs and casing so you can slide the flooring underneath. An oscillating multitool works great. Use a small scrap of flooring as a guide.

4 LEAVE GAPS ALONG WALLS
Insert shims to create gaps. These gaps allow the flooring to expand freely with temperature changes.

UNDERCUT DOORJAMBS AND CASING

Cut the doorjambs and casing so the flooring can slide under them **(Photo 3)**. Mark used an oscillating multitool to cut down jambs and casing, but a small pull saw would work too. Grab a scrap plank of flooring and use it as a guide to get the proper height. You need to cut only the casing and the doorjambs— a shoe molding will eventually be installed to hide the gap between the flooring and the base trim.

LEAVE AN EXPANSION GAP

To allow for the expansion and contraction of both the flooring and the house itself, you'll need to leave about a ¼-in. to ⅜-in. gap between the flooring and the walls. After you install the first row (see "Begin and End with a Half Plank or More" on p. 98), insert shims to maintain this gap **(Photo 4)**.

Keep in mind that extremely heavy items such as fully loaded bookshelves or pool tables will pin the flooring down. One heavy item per room is usually not a problem, but one at each end of the room may cause the flooring to buckle between them.

JOIN THE PLANKS

The planks in the first row are snapped together end to end. Slide the tongue of the first plank on the second row into the groove of the first row at a low angle and lay it on the floor. The second and subsequent planks in each row are installed by locking the

5 SNAP THE PLANKS TOGETHER
Join a plank into the end of the previous plank first, and then work your way down the side of the plank, snapping it into the previous course as you go.

ends together, and then you work your way down the plank, pushing the tongue into the groove as you go **(Photo 5)**.

This is where the flexibility of LVP flooring really shines. It helps to be able to twist and bend each plank into place. Several different laminate products are "supposed to" install the same way (plank by plank), but instead you are forced to snap together a whole row end to end and try to finagle it all in at once, which is a slow process.

STAGGER THE SEAMS

On this floor, the partial plank left over from the first row worked as a "starter" for the second row, and the plank left over from the second row worked as a "starter" for the third row, and so on. Stagger the seams at least 6 in., and don't start or end any row

with a plank less than 6 in. wide. Open several boxes at once and mix them up to ensure a varied pattern. Mark set a bunch of planks in the area where he was working to reduce the number of trips needed to get more material.

TAP IN STUBBORN PLANKS

When a plank is installed properly, the seams should be smooth to the touch and almost invisible. Every now and again, individual planks need a little "convincing" with a tapping block to seat properly. To avoid marring the edge of the plank, lock in a scrap chunk of flooring, and rest the tapping block up against the scrap.

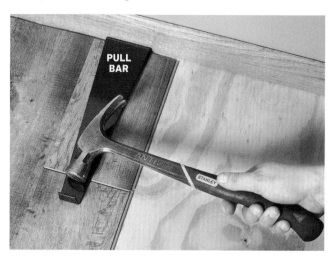

6 TAP IN THE END PLANKS
Hook the pull bar onto the end of the piece, and tap stubborn seams closed.

7 INSTALL SHOE MOLDING
Cover the expansion gap between the flooring and the base trim. Don't nail into the flooring—that will prevent the floor from expanding freely.

WATCH YOUR FLOOR HEIGHT

New flooring raises or lowers the final height of the floor, which can create unexpected problems. Here are some things to keep in mind:

GAP

Jambs

If you're pulling out flooring that is thicker than your new stuff, you'll end up with gaps under the doorjambs. To prevent that, you could cover the subfloor with a layer of ¼-in. underlayment to raise the height of the entire floor.

Dishwasher

In most cases, there's enough space above the dishwasher so that you can raise the floor level a little and still reinstall the dishwasher. But check the gap between the top of the dishwasher and the countertop first just to be sure.

Stairs

Be careful when changing flooring that butts up to a flight of stairs. Building codes allow no more than a ⅜-in. difference between the heights of the lowest and tallest stair risers. Changing the floor height at the top or bottom of stairs will alter riser heights and could create a trip hazard.

Existing sheet vinyl and carpet

If your kitchen floor is sheet vinyl and the dining room is carpet, don't forget that the sheet vinyl will have ¼-in. underlayment beneath it, but the carpet won't. If you want to install LV flooring in both, you'll have to remove the underlayment in the kitchen or add some to the dining room.

If you're having trouble closing the last butt seam in a row, use the pull bar from your installation kit to pull it tight **(Photo 6)**. Make sure you have a shim against the wall on the opposite side of that row or you could end up pulling the whole row tight up against the wall, losing your expansion gap in the process.

ADD SHOE MOLDING

Once your flooring is down, install shoe molding to cover the expansion gap between the flooring and the base trim **(Photo 7)**. Shoot 1¼-in. finish nails through the shoe and into the base trim. Be careful not to pin the flooring down in the process. Finish the molding to match the trim, not the flooring.

WORK AROUND THE DOORJAMBS

PLANKS PARALLEL TO OPENING

Land the seam in the door opening

It's easier to work away from door openings than into them, but sometimes that's not an option. When working parallel to a door, make sure the seam on the row that intersects the jamb lands inside the door opening. Mark and cut the first plank, then tap it into place using a scrap of flooring and a tapping block.

Bend the second plank into place

Mark and cut the second plank to fit, and then slide it under the jamb. Bend it up in the middle so you can lock it into place. This is another situation where the flexibility of this product comes in handy. The larger this second plank is, the easier it is to work with.

PLANKS PERPENDICULAR TO OPENING

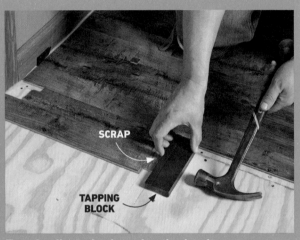

Tap the first plank under the jamb

Sometimes you'll have to cut around jambs while laying the planks perpendicular to a door opening. This is easy if the door opening falls on the same side as you started your rows. Simply mark and cut the first plank to size and tap it under the jamb with a tapping block.

Tap the end plank in sideways

If the opening is located at the rows' end, mark and cut the end plank to size, and tap it in along the end groove of the previous plank. You may have to remove the bottom lip on the previous plank. If you remove more than 6 in., use seam sealer to glue the planks together.

TILING TRICKS

LEARN HOW TO SET AND GROUT YOUR TILES, WHETHER LARGE SQUARES OR SMALL MOSAICS, WITH NO ISSUES

Tile just keeps getting bigger and bigger—in popularity and in size. The materials have changed too: Ceramic is still around, but porcelain and glass are now almost as common. Our tile guru, Dean Sorem, has had to change how he works to keep up with the trends. Here are some of his tips.

1 PICK A LARGE-NOTCHED TROWEL FOR BIG TILE

Tiles as large as 2 ft. square have become more popular, and these monsters require a deep layer of thin-set to allow for adjustments. To get the right amount of thin-set, use a ½ x ½-in. notched trowel for tiles up to 16 in. square, and a ¾ x ¾-in. notched trowel for larger tiles. Don't forget: Using large notched trowels means you'll need a lot more thin-set. As a general rule, a 50-lb. bag of thin-set will cover about 40 to 50 sq. ft. using a ½ x ½-in. notched trowel, and about 30 to 40 sq. ft. using a ¾ x ¾-in. notched trowel. When you use large notched trowels like this, look for thin-set labeled "medium bed," "large tile" or "large format."

¾" X ¾" NOTCHED TROWEL

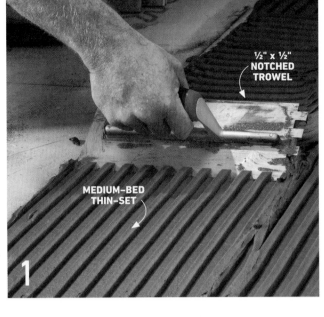

½" x ½" NOTCHED TROWEL

MEDIUM-BED THIN-SET

2 CUT WITHOUT CRACKING THE TILE

You'll need a diamond wet saw to cut large porcelain tiles. Dean recommends renting a contractor-quality saw for about $75 per day rather than buying a cheapie. But even with such a saw, tiles larger than about 8 in. square have a tendency to crack before you finish the cut, often ruining the tile. You can help prevent this by pressing the two pieces of the tile together as you near completion of the cut. Holding the tile like this stabilizes it and dampens vibration, resulting in a cleaner cut.

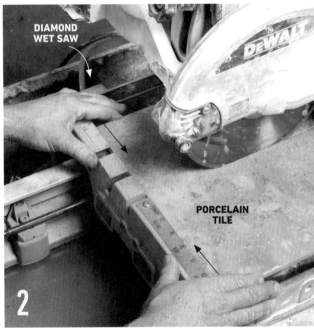

DIAMOND WET SAW

PORCELAIN TILE

3 UPGRADE YOUR GROUT SPONGE

It's hard to get the last bit of grout haze off using a grout sponge. After the grout dries, you usually have to come back and polish off the remaining cloudy layer with a rag. But if you finish your grout cleanup with a microfiber sponge, you'll end up with a job so clean you may not have to do anything more.

Start your cleanup with the plain side of the sponge after the grout firms up. Then when the joints are nicely shaped and most of the grout is off the face of the tile, switch to the microfiber side of the sponge. You'll find microfiber sponges for about $3 at home centers and tile shops.

MICROFIBER SPONGE

GROUT HAZE

FLATTEN THE FRAMING

4 Old-school tile setters made up for wavy walls by installing wire lath and floating a layer of mortar over it. But modern tile backer boards simply follow along the crooked wall, and if you don't fix the wall, you'll have a wavy tile job.

The best solution is to straighten the walls before you install the backer board. Lay a straightedge against the walls to find high and low spots. In most cases, you can fix problems by adding shims to the faces of the studs until the faces all line up. But if you have just one protruding stud, then it may be quicker to plane it down with a power planer or replace it if you can.

Dean prefers thin paper shims as shown (available in the drywall section of some home centers) because they provide precise control over shim thickness and can be offset to create a tapered shim. You can make your own thin shims from heavy felt paper or thin cardboard. Staple the shims in place.

BACK-BUTTER LARGE TILE

5 The increased surface area of tiles larger than about 8 x 8 in. makes it critical that you butter the back to ensure a strong bond. It takes only a few extra seconds per tile to spread a thin layer of thin-set on the back of the tile with the flat side of the trowel. Then when you set the tile, this thin layer bonds easily with the layer you've troweled onto the floor or wall, and it creates a strong connection.

Dean also butters the backs of larger transparent glass tiles to provide a consistent color. Otherwise you'll see air bubbles and other imperfections in the thin-set through the transparent glass.

FLATTEN THIN-SET BEFORE INSTALLING MOSAIC TILE

6 Mosaic tile is typically thin, and it has a lot of grout joints. If you simply apply thin-set with a notched trowel and embed the sheets of mosaic in it, the ridges of thin-set will squeeze out of all those grout joints and you'll have a real mess to clean up.

The way to avoid this is to flatten the ridges with the flat side of the trowel before you set the mosaic tiles in it. Use the notched side of a ¼ x ¼-in. V-notched trowel first to apply the right amount of thin-set. Then flip the trowel over to the flat side and, holding the trowel fairly flat to the surface and using medium pressure, flatten the ridges. Now you can safely embed the sheets of mosaic tile without worrying about thin-set filling the grout joints.

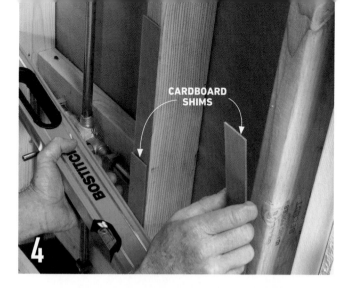

CARDBOARD SHIMS

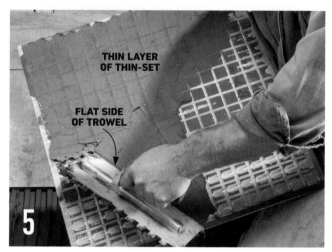

THIN LAYER OF THIN-SET

FLAT SIDE OF TROWEL

CLEAN GROUT JOINTS WITH A TOOTHBRUSH

7 No matter how careful you are, you're bound to end up with some thin-set in the joints between tiles. And if you allow it to harden, it'll interfere with your grout job. A toothbrush works great to clean excess thin-set from grout joints, especially for the skinny joints between mosaic tiles. Let the thin-set get firm, but not hard, before you start the cleanup process. If you try to clean up thin-set too soon, you risk disturbing the tiles.

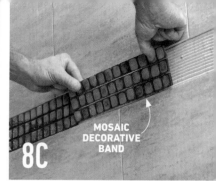

8 MAKE A CUSTOM TROWEL

Dean has discovered that inexpensive auto-body filler spatulas, available at home centers and auto parts stores, are perfect for making custom trowels for special circumstances. One way Dean uses a custom-made trowel is for insetting thinner tiles into a field of thicker tiles. After finishing the field tile installation, he cuts notches on each edge of the spatula with a utility knife to create a mini screed. He cuts the notches about ¹⁄₁₆ in. deeper than the thickness of the decorative tile to allow for thin-set. Then he uses this trowel to add a layer of thin-set that acts as a shim when it hardens (8A). After this layer hardens, he cuts ³⁄₁₆-in.-deep teeth in the spatula to make a notched trowel and uses it to apply thin-set (8B). Now when he sets the decorative tile, it's perfectly flush with the field tile (8C).

9 FINISH YOUR JOB WITH PREMIUM GROUT

There's been a revolution in grout technology in recent years, and all of the big-name grout producers have updated grout that's easier to apply, denser, more stain resistant and more colorfast than standard grout. These new grouts also cure faster and are resistant to mold and mildew.

You no longer have to mix in latex additives, worry about uneven or blotchy grout joints, or decide between sanded and unsanded grout. Power Grout, Custom Building Product's Prism and Fusion Pro grouts, and Laticrete's PermaColor are a few examples of premium grout. You may have to visit a specialty tile store to find them, though. The formulas vary, but all of these will outperform standard grout. And some, such as Power Grout and Fusion Pro, don't even require sealing, saving you time and money.

Premium grouts are more expensive, of course, and might add about $20 to $50 to the total cost of your project. But considering all the other costs (and all your hard work), premium grout is a bargain.

10 LEVEL MOSAIC TILE WITH A BLOCK

Mosaic tiles are so small and numerous that getting their faces flush using just your fingers is nearly impossible. But tamping them with a flat block of wood creates a perfectly aligned surface in no time. Make a tamping block out of any flat scrap of wood. An 8-in. length of hardwood 1x6 or a 6 x 8-in. rectangle of plywood is perfect. After you set several square feet of mosaic tile, pat the tile into the thin-set with the tamping block. Hold the block in place and bump it with your fist to flatten the mosaic. Repeat the tamping process on each new section of tile you install.

MEET THE EXPERT

Josh Risberg is a certified tile installer. He also has 10 years under his tool belt as a lead carpenter for high-end home builders and remodelers.

CHOOSE SELF-LEVELING UNDERLAYMENT

ACHIEVE A FLAT AND LEVEL SURFACE THAT'S AS SMOOTH AS GLASS

Whether you're installing ceramic tile, laminate planks or carpet, self-leveling underlayment is a great choice for floors that are rough, uneven or out of level. And it's the absolute best choice for tile installations over an in-floor heating system.

Self-leveling underlayment is easy to work with

and doesn't require a lot of fancy tools or years of training. However, there is a fair amount of prep work that needs to be done—and done right—because once the pouring starts, you'll need to work fast. Josh Risberg will show you the step-by-step process to achieve a perfectly flat and level underlayment.

1 SEAL EVERY HOLE AND CRACK WITH CAULK

Thoroughly sweep and vacuum the entire floor, and then seal all the holes and seams in the plywood with caulking. The self-leveler will drain through any opening as small as a nail hole, so make sure you are thorough. Get the type of caulk that goes on white but turns clear when it dries so you can tell when it's done setting up.

Taping over the caulk with packing tape isn't required, but it's a terrific way to avoid stepping in a glob and then tracking it around the rest of the house. When working on an older house with floor planks instead of plywood, cover the whole floor with self-adhering roofing underlayment.

2 BUILD DAMS AROUND BIG OPENINGS

Isolate large holes like heating vents and floor drains with pieces of cardboard. Just shape a cardboard piece to each hole and tape it in place. Then caulk the cardboard pieces to the floor.

3 MAKE THE WALLS LEAKPROOF

Sill sealer (a foam gasket that carpenters use to seal between the foundation and the bottom wall plates) makes a great barrier to keep the self-leveler from escaping into other rooms or into the basement. Hold it in place with staples from a staple gun. Keep the staples low enough so the staple holes will be hidden by the base trim.

Sill sealer that's either 3½ in. or 5½ in. wide will work, but the wider sealer definitely does a better job of protecting painted walls from splashes.

Caulk the sill sealer to the floor. Smear the caulk with your finger to make sure it adheres to both surfaces. Once the pour is complete, the seal sealer can easily be cut flush with a razor. The small void near the wall won't affect any finished floor installation.

COST
One 40-lb. bag of self-leveling underlayment costs about $40 and will cover about 20 sq. ft. at ¼ in. thick.

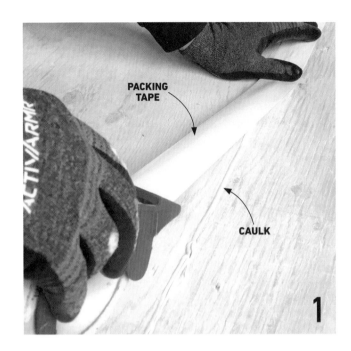

PACKING TAPE

CAULK

1

2

3

SILL SEALER

4 STRENGTHEN THE FLOOR WITH LATH

Lath adds strength to the underlayment in the same way rebar adds strength to concrete. Use plastic lath instead of metal when working with in-floor heating. Check with the manufacturer of the heating system as to whether the lath should be installed over or under the mat/cables.

Overlap the lath at least 3 in., and secure it with a hammer tacker stapler. Keep the lath an inch or so away from the walls so it doesn't poke through the sill sealer when you're installing it. Try to keep the lath as flat as possible; you don't want any part of it projecting through the leveler after it's placed.

Always check the continuity of the heating cables or mats before you start mixing. If you accidentally sever or nick a cable, it's easier to repair it before the underlayment is poured ... that's an understatement!

5 BUILD DAMS IN DOORWAYS

Dam up doorways with strips of wood. Make sure you seal the wood to the floor with caulk, as well as caulk the area where the wood strip meets the sill sealer. Think through the placement. For the best look, the joint between the newly finished floor and the adjoining floor in the next room should typically fall directly under the middle of the door.

6 PRIME THE WOOD

Covering the floor with two coats of primer will prevent the plywood from absorbing water. Waterlogged wood swells. It shrinks back down when it dries, which could create cracks in the underlayment and in the tiles above. Floor primer can be rolled on or brushed, but our expert prefers spraying it on because it's fast and easy and there are no brushes or rollers to clean up. He uses a pump-up sprayer on larger jobs and a simple spray bottle on smaller ones. No primer is needed if you use self-adhering underlayment.

7 KEEP BAGS DRY

Bags of self-leveler can be ruined by wicking up moisture from concrete in the garage or on the basement floor. Keep your bags dry by setting them on a pallet or a sheet of plywood resting on scrap 2x4s.

PLASTIC LATH

4

5

DAM

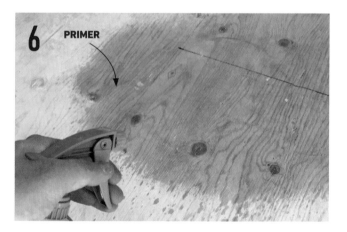

6 PRIMER

7

PREP THE BAGS

Most bags filled with dry cementitious mixes have a vent in the top. It's there so the bags don't break open when they're handled. Minimize the mess by keeping the vent side up. Line the open bags up next to buckets. Mixing is a messy business, so do it outdoors whenever possible, or protect the floor. Extreme temperatures can affect the time it takes the leveler to set up, so store the bags at room temperature before use.

FILL A SEPARATE BUCKET FOR THE MIXER

Keep the paddle mixer in a bucket of water between pours to prevent the paddle from getting crusty. Fill the bucket at least three-quarters full so the mixer won't tip over.

PULL WATER FROM A GARBAGE CAN

Drill holes in your fill bucket at the fill line so the bucket will drain to the proper level. For fast filling, dip a bucket into a barrel or garbage can filled with water. At this stage of the game, speed is important.

GARBAGE CAN

ORDER 20% EXTRA

Running out of self-leveler before a pour is finished is a big hassle, so don't let that happen. Buy 20% more than you think you need. A large room poured even 1/16 in. thicker than planned can gobble up several additional bags. You can return any unused bags.

11 MIX A LOT AT ONCE

Mixing self-leveler in 5-gallon buckets is a messy proposition. Get yourself 6-gallon buckets if you can. Many flooring stores carry them. Fill all your buckets with the recommended amount of water first, and then add the self-leveler. Keep the buckets close to each other to reduce the mess when moving the mixer from one bucket to another, and keep all the bucket handles facing out so they're easier to grab (every second counts).

Once you've mixed all the buckets, go back to the first and mix it up again for a few seconds in order to stir up the sand that has settled. After dumping a bucket, fluff the sand in the next one before hauling it in. Set the mixer in the next bucket to be hauled in, and then store it in the bucket of water between batches.

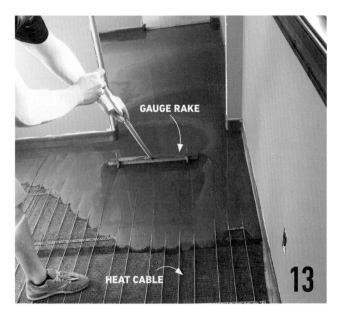

12 SPREAD AS YOU POUR

Move the bucket along the floor as you pour. Keep the bucket low to minimize splashing. If you do splash on the wall, try to resist the temptation to wipe it off right away because small drops can quickly become large smudges. You'll have better luck letting it dry and scraping it off.

Completely cover the heating cables/mats with self-leveler to avoid damaging them with a trowel while installing the thin-set. The depth of your pour may vary depending on your project, but shoot for a thickness between ½ in. and ¾ in. Anything over ¾ in. will likely require two pours, but confirm that by reading the instructions printed on the bag of the product you're using. Check the thickness with a gauge rake, a junky tape measure or just a stick with the desired thickness marked on it.

> **WASH BUCKETS RIGHT AWAY**
> Wash your buckets as soon as you're done pouring, and never dump the dirty water down a drain.

13 MOVE SELF-LEVELER WITH A GAUGE RAKE

A gauge rake is a metal squeegee that rides on two adjustable depth guides. This tool isn't absolutely necessary, but it does work well at spreading the self-leveler, and it helps gauge how thick the self-leveler is. It's especially useful for large pours. Be careful to work the rake very gently near the heating cables or mat. Gauge rakes cost about $45 at flooring stores and online.

Start at the far end of the room and work your way to the door. If you pass other entry points along the way, lock the doors and hang "keep out" signs.

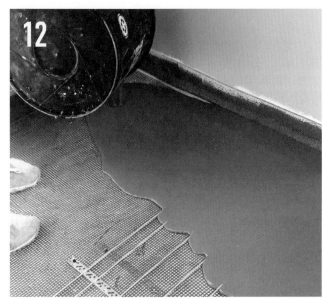

GAUGE RAKE

HEAT CABLE

SPRAY-TEXTURE A CEILING

REFRESH YOUR ROOM WITH A NEW COAT OF TEXTURE

If your spray-textured ceiling is dingy or stained, you can renew it with one coat each of sealer and paint. But if the texture is falling off or missing in spots, the best way to fix the problem is by respraying the entire ceiling. It's a messy job, but it's not hard. In fact, after you spray one room, you may want to keep going. The key is in the prep work, which is the time-consuming part. Once the room is prepped, it'll take you only about 15 minutes to spray the ceiling.

If any of the paper drywall tape is loose or the drywall is soft or damaged, repair and sand these areas first. In addition to the putty knives and drywall joint compound for the repairs, you'll need a wide putty or taping knife for scraping, a roll of 1½-in. or wider masking tape, enough painter's plastic to cover the walls, a gallon or two of primer/sealer, a bag of spray texture (enough to cover 300 to 400 sq. ft.), and a compressor and hopper gun. You can buy coarse, medium or fine texture. If you're matching existing ceilings, take a sample of the material and ask for help matching it. Medium is usually the best choice to match most ceilings. You can rent a compressor

Buy a hopper gun like this for about $90 and connect it to any 2.5-cfm or larger air compressor.

1 Speed up and simplify your masking job by applying the tape along the ceiling first. Leave the lower edge of the tape loose. Then roll out a length of lightweight poly along the floor, pull one edge up to the ceiling and stick it to the tape.

and hopper gun for about $50 for a half day or buy a hopper gun for about $90 and connect it to any average-size or larger compressor. If you use a small compressor, you may occasionally have to stop spraying to let the pressure build up. Minimize rental costs by getting all the prep work done before you pick up the compressor and hopper gun.

Start by removing what you can from the room. If you must leave furniture in the room, stack it in the center and cover it with plastic. Cover the floor with sheets or a canvas drop cloth. Then cover the walls with thin (1-mil or less) poly sheeting **(Photo 1)** such as painter's plastic. Leave an opening with overlapping poly at the doorway so you can get in and out. Turn off the power to lights and remove any ceiling fixtures. Cap bare wires with wire connectors. Stuff newspaper into the electrical box to keep out the spray.

Next, scrape off the old texture **(Photo 2),** but first test it for asbestos. If it hasn't been painted, it'll usually come off easily with scraping. If that doesn't work, wet the texture with a pump-up garden sprayer. That might make it easier to scrape, but it'll leave a sticky mess on the floor; cover your drop cloths with 4-mil plastic so you can dispose of the wet texture and not track it all over. Texture that's been painted over can be a lot harder to remove. Try to knock off the high spots and flatten it as much as possible. The ceiling doesn't have to be smooth, but it's easier to get a nice-looking job if most of the old texture has been removed.

When you're done scraping, paint the ceiling with stain-sealing primer **(Photo 3).** Use an aerosol can of solvent-based sealer to spot-prime severe stains. Then paint the ceiling with a water-based primer/sealer.

The key to success is mixing the texture to the right consistency—not too thick. Use the amount of water recommended on the bag, and adjust the thickness

2 Suit up with goggles, a dust mask and a hat before you start the messy job of scraping texture. Popcorn spray texture comes off easily if it hasn't been painted.

3 Paint the ceiling with a fast-drying primer/sealer. Let it dry before applying the spray texture.

4 Mix the powdered spray texture and water thoroughly. Lumps will clog the spray tip and could mess up your spray job. Let it rest 15 minutes and remix, adding water if necessary.

by adding water or powder. Mix slowly using a mixing paddle mounted in a ½-in. drill **(Photo 4).** Add water until the material reaches the consistency of runny yogurt—or thick paint—with tiny lumps. Let it sit for 15 minutes, then remix; add more water if necessary.

Set both the mechanism that controls the diameter of the pattern and the trigger control that governs the volume of spray to the middle position. Then load the hopper about half full with texture material and practice on a piece of cardboard or drywall scrap **(Photo 5).** Adjust the spray pattern and trigger until you can get a nice, even pattern without runs or excess buildup. When you're comfortable, start on the ceiling.

Start by spraying the perimeter **(Photo 6).** Hold the gun about 18 to 24 in. from the ceiling and aim so about two-thirds of spray hits the ceiling and the rest hits the wall. Move quickly around the room, paying special attention to inside corners. Remember, you can make another pass if it's too light. The goal is to cover the ceiling with an even layer of texture, and it will become more pronounced as it dries. If you mess up and get a puddle or a thick buildup, stop and scrape off the texture with a wide putty knife. Then try again. Move the gun back and forth while backing up across the room. After you've covered the ceiling, turn 90 degrees and apply another light coat at a right angle to the first. Concentrate on filling in light spots to create an even texture.

When you're satisfied with the texture's consistency, clean up the gun, hopper and hose with water, and pull down the poly. If there's texture on the wall or flooring, wait for it to dry. Then carefully scrape it off and remove the white residue with a wet sponge.

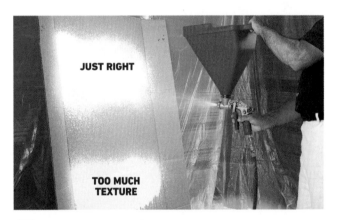

5 Practice on cardboard or a piece of drywall to get a feel for spraying. Adjust the gun's tip and trigger until you get a consistent spray pattern that's easy to control.

6 Start by spraying the perimeter, then fill in the middle. Avoid heavy buildup—you can always add more.

TAPING DRYWALL

FOLLOW THESE STEPS FOR SMOOTH WALLS AND CRISP CORNERS

Drywall taping is one of the most important jobs on any construction project. A skilled taper can hide a lot of mistakes left behind by framers and drywall hangers. But a poor taping job can frustrate trim carpenters and it can make the painters seem as if they were a bunch of hacks.

A quality outcome requires the proper tools and materials (a steady hand doesn't hurt either). We asked pro taper Scott Pauly to show us his three-day, step-by-step taping routine. If you want to end up with even walls and well-defined corners, Scott's tips are sure to help.

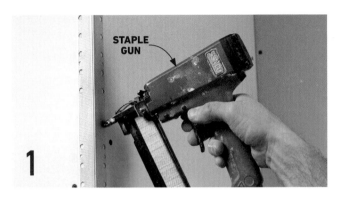

1 TACK ON CORNER BEAD

Scott installs the outside corner beads with a staple gun that shoots 1-in., 18-gauge staples with a ¼-in. crown. Drywall nails also work, but using a staple gun frees up one hand to place the bead exactly right. Outside corners take a lot of abuse, so securely fasten the corner beads to the framing. Nail or staple each side of the bead every 10 to 12 in.

2 ROLL OUT THE FIBER MESH

Installing fiber mesh saves time because it is self-adhering and allows mud to pass right through it, so you don't need to fill cracks and gaps in the drywall before you install the tape. Just roll it on and trim it off with a 6-in. taping knife. Tape over all joints, large gaps, holes larger than ⅛ in. and both sides of the outside corner beads. On inside corners, only gaps larger than ⅛ in. need mesh. Other inside corners will get covered on Day 2 with paper tape.

3 MIX UP THE SETTING COMPOUND

Setting compound shrinks less than regular joint compound and dries rock hard, making it ideal for filling big holes and gaps. But setting compound doesn't sand easily, so thinner coats are better. The number on the bag of powder indicates how many minutes it takes to set up. The bigger the job, the longer working time you'll want. Scott mixes his with a mixing paddle bit in a ½-in. drill. He keeps a bucket of water close by to clean the paddle right away.

4 COVER THE TAPE AND FILL THE GAPS

Cover all tape with setting compound using a 6-in. taping knife. Apply enough mud to fill the gaps under the tape, but setting compound is much harder than the joint compound you've yet to apply, so you want just a thin coat covering the tape. If you sand through the joint compound into the setting compound, the result may be noticeably different textures.

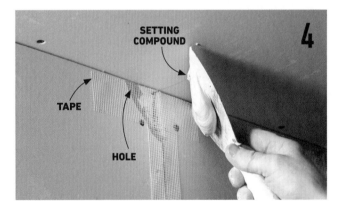

DAY 1 TOOLS

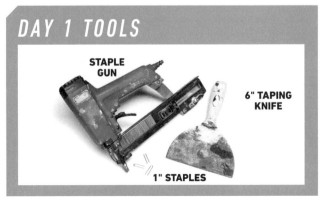

14" TAPING KNIFE

BUTT JOINT

5

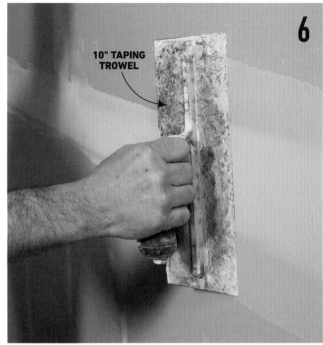

10" TAPING TROWEL

6

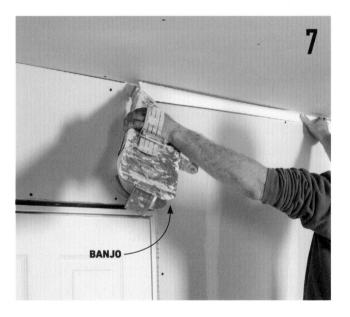

7

BANJO

5 COAT THE BUTT JOINTS WITH A KNIFE

Use a lightweight joint compound on Day 2. Knock off any crumbs or ridges left over from the day before with a clean 6-in. taping knife—Scott always has one in his back pocket. Spread a thin coat of joint compound on the butt joints with a 14-in. taping knife.

6 COAT THE TAPERED JOINTS WITH A TROWEL

Each of the long sides of drywall is tapered to allow room for the mud. The goal is to fill this recessed area with mud so the wall ends up smooth. Taping knives are flat but flexible. If you press one too hard against a tapered joint in the wall, it could bend into the recess and you could squeeze too much mud out, creating a trough. Taping trowels have a little bend in them, so when you press them against the wall, they flatten out to form a straight bridge across the tapered joint. Scott uses a 10-in. trowel on Day 2. Be careful when you buy one: A taping trowel might look like a concrete trowel but it's not—a concrete trowel is bent in the opposite direction.

7 TAPE THE INSIDE CORNERS

Paper tape is more flexible than fiber mesh and has a crease in it, which makes it easier to push into corners. Scott uses a banjo to install paper tape on all the inside corners. He holds the tape secure with one hand as he moves the banjo along the corner. Once a long section of tape is

pulled out, he pushes it into the corner with a corner trowel. If you don't own a banjo, lay down a thin coat of mud and push the tape into the mud. Make sure there's mud under every square inch of the tape or you'll end up with bubbles. Banjos do a great job of applying the proper amount of mud to the tape, but when you're using one, regular joint compound will have to be watered down. This usually requires about 1 cup of water for every gallon of mud, but it depends on the moisture content of the mud you're working with, so just keep adding a little water until it's roughly the consistency of yogurt. You can buy a mid-quality banjo for about $100.

8 TOP-COAT THE CORNER TAPE

A banjo applies mud only on the bottom of the tape, so once the tape is laid down, it will need to be top-coated. Scott uses a corner trowel. Corner trowels can be tricky to work with—the secret (as with much of taping) is not to lay down too much mud. This is especially true where inside corners meet the ceiling and floor. Too much mud will round out the corners, making it difficult to install trim and moldings. Start at the top of an inside corner an inch or so down from the ceiling because a lot of mud will ooze out the top side of the trowel when you first press it to the walls. Then go back for another pass and smooth out the excess left behind.

Once the tape has been covered, Scott goes back with his 6-in. knife and cleans up each side of the tape. This step takes skill and practice. An easier (but more time-consuming) method is to top-coat one side of the tape and do the other side after the first side has dried.

9 FILL THE SCREW HOLES

Make two passes over every screw hole with a 6-in. taping knife. Hit all the screws that line up vertically in the field of each panel of drywall at the same time. To eliminate voids, each pass should come from a different direction. One efficient method is to lay out a thick coat in an upward motion and then come back down, scraping off the excess as you go. Don't forget about the screws on the ceiling. Save yourself a lot of walking by covering all the joints, corners and screw holes in one area of a room at a time. Then it's time to set up some fans and call it a day.

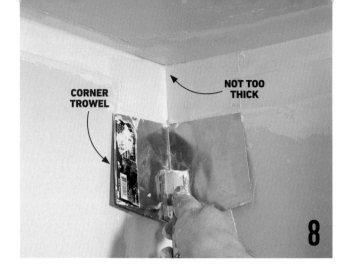

CORNER TROWEL

NOT TOO THICK

8

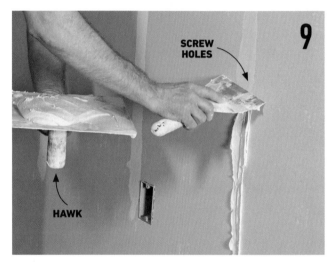

SCREW HOLES

9

HAWK

DAY 2 TOOLS

10" TROWEL

14" KNIFE

6" KNIFE

CORNER TROWEL

MUD MANAGEMENT

Scott's tools are caked with mud, but he works mostly on new homes where water is usually unavailable. He also burns through most of his tools in months, not years, so he focuses only on keeping the edges clean—a must for smooth mud lines. Here are some tips for managing your mud.

- Scrape and wipe out the bucket sides to remove mud before it dries and crumbles into the good mud.
- Clean lids after opening new buckets for the same reason.
- Never return unused mud to the bucket. Throw it away.
- Keep a wet rag or sponge on hand to clean tools and buckets.
- Add a little water to the top of your mud between jobs to keep a crust from forming.

10

11

10 MAKE YOUR OWN TOPPING COMPOUND

The same lightweight joint compound you used on Day 2 will also work for your final coat on Day 3, but topping compound works better. Topping compound is easier to sand and doesn't leave behind as many tiny air pockets. You could buy a bucket of topping compound or you could make your own. Scott pours in about ½ cup of dish soap (any brand will do) into a 4½-gallon pail of lightweight joint compound. He's found that this concoction works every bit as well and is cheaper and a lot more convenient.

DAY 3 TOOLS

24" KNIFE

12" TROWEL

14" KNIFE

CORNER TROWEL

6" KNIFE

11 COVER EVERYTHING ONE MORE TIME

Scott applies the final coat on the inside corners the same way he did on Day 2, laying down the mud with a corner trowel and smoothing each side with a 6-in. knife. He covers all the recessed joints with a 12-in. trowel (2 in. larger than the one used on Day 2). The farther the mud is feathered out, the less noticeable the joint will be, especially on butt joints. That's why after Scott lays down a layer of mud on the butt joints with his 14-in. knife, he immediately follows with a monster 2-ft. knife—no need to add more mud on the second pass. That's it. You're done. Now set up some fans so you can move on to sanding.

LIVING WITH PLASTER WALLS

TIPS AND TRICKS FOR REPAIRING CRACKS, HANGING ART AND MUCH MORE

You may view plaster in an old house—much like the original floors, windows or architectural millwork—as a blessing or a curse, but it's a valuable part of the fabric of an old home that needs special considerations for you to keep it looking its best. Writer Alex Santantonio learned how to repair, restore and maintain the traditional lath and horsehair lime plaster in his home. Whether you're a plaster purist or someone just trying to hang a picture, if you want to live with your plaster walls, we hope Alex's tips help you have an easier time. (And if you end up deciding to remove the plaster, see page 124.)

1 SAVE BADLY DAMAGED PLASTER

How often have you heard "That plaster is too far gone; it has to go!" Alex has dealt with plaster that's "beyond repair," only to bring it back from the brink. Restoring badly damaged plaster involves three crucial phases.

1. STABILIZE: Using an adhesive product such as Plaster Magic allows you to resecure both cracked areas and loose plaster to sound lath. To resecure lath that's pulled away from the studs, use plaster buttons. The goal is to ensure the plaster is sound instead of bouncy.

2. PREPARE AND REPAIR: Remove any loose or peeling paint, or strip the surface bare. If the plaster has any large holes or missing sections, repair it using lime plaster. You are preparing the plaster for the skim coat.

3. ADD SKIM COATS: Use a three-coat process of LimeWorks.us Takcoat with embedded fiberglass screen, Master of Plaster base coat and Master of Plaster finish coat. The Takcoat adheres without a bonding agent and is the decoupling layer that prevents future cracks. The final coats are to achieve a smooth finish. Best of all, no sanding means no dust.

2 FIND A STUD IN YOUR PLASTER WALLS

Electronic stud finders simply don't work on plaster walls. Stud finders use a magnetic sensor to find screws holding drywall to the studs just below the wall's surface, but thick plaster on wood lath is held to the stud by small nails that are well beneath the surface. Standard stud finders just aren't sensitive enough to detect the smaller nails through the plaster.

So, rather than an electronic stud finder, use a magnetic one. This simple device uses a super-strong magnet that is more able to detect those little lath nails deep below the surface. The magnets are able to cling to the small nails as you drag it across the wall, letting you know exactly where a stud is. Hands down, this is the best thing to use when locating a stud in a lath-and-plaster wall.

3 PRACTICE SAFETY FIRST

As much as lime plaster is a traditional building material, fresh plaster must be handled carefully. Lime can be a caustic irritant, and gloves are necessary when handling new plaster. The recipes for plaster have changed some in modern times, as have the paints used to cover plaster surfaces. In the mid-1900s, unsafe manufacturing additives were used as binders and lead paint was used to cover plaster surfaces.

If you plan to disturb your plaster and it was applied in the mid-1900s, sending off a small sample for lab testing before you begin demo is an important consideration. Likewise, if your walls were painted before 1978, testing for lead paint and taking proper precautions are necessary if you'll be disturbing the paint. Visit *epa.gov/lead/lead-test-kits* for more information.

HEPA filtration and vacuums, negative air machines, plastic containment coverings, approved hazardous waste disposal practices and proper particulate respirator masks all play an important role in safety.

4 DEAL WITH A VISIBLE LEAK

Many of us have encountered a discolored area on a plaster wall or a ceiling caused by a leak. Well, you identified and stopped the leak, but then what? Does the damaged plaster need to come out?

The beauty of lime plaster is that it's not nearly as fragile as paper-faced drywall or gypsum plaster. A little water infiltration is no match for lime plaster. Lime plaster inhibits mold growth that traditionally impacts damp paper on drywall because plaster can dry completely without mold or compromise.

The key is to remove any sagging, failed or affected paint so the plaster can breathe and release that moisture. Use a moisture meter to determine when the readings are similar to dry sections of your plaster, then refer to Step 10, "Paint Plaster Walls," to finish your repair.

2

5 STRIP PAINT/WALLPAPER FROM PLASTER WALLS

Plaster that's been around for 100 years or more has likely been covered by wallpaper, paint or both, many times over. If you're fully restoring your plaster and want it to stand the test of time, you must return your plaster to its raw base.

Plaster is resilient and unaffected by applying steam to the surface. A wallpaper, garment or heavy-duty steamer softens old layers of wallpaper and applied texture, such as popcorn ceilings, for removal without damaging the underlying plaster.

While steam also works for paint removal, you may have the most luck with chemical strippers, specifically SmartStrip and Peel Away 1. SmartStrip tends to work well on modern latex paints and is less aggressive. Peel Away 1 will remove a dozen or more layers of paint with a single application and is great for older paint. Peel Away 1 also keeps the paint in a paste or liquid form, so airborne particles are less likely. These chemical strippers work while wet, so cover them up with waxed paper or a product like Peel Away paper to keep them working longer.

6 CUT INTO PLASTER FOR JUNCTION BOXES

For many electrical projects, adding a receptacle or switch in a plaster wall often results in an area that looks as if an animal chewed its way through the wall. Not to worry—there's a better way.

After outlining an "old work" style junction box, use an oscillating tool to cut the plaster (not the lath). Then pry the plaster out of the hole, using a small pry bar to expose the lath **(Photo 6A)**. Switch to a jigsaw to cut the lath about 95% through on either side of each piece, leaving a little wood to stabilize the lath.

Next, place a drywall screw in the middle of the lath and hold it with pliers while you make the rest of the cut. This keeps the jigsaw from causing vibration damage.

Finally, secure any loose or floating lath to the plaster using Plaster Magic adhesive. Let the adhesive cure, then place your old work junction box **(Photo 6B)**. If your plaster and lath are thick and the tabs won't clamp, swap the box's screws with No. 6 pan-head screws that are 2 or 3 in. long to extend the clamping tabs.

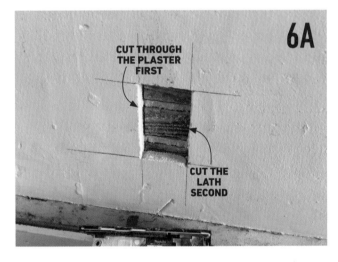

CUT THROUGH THE PLASTER FIRST

CUT THE LATH SECOND

OLD WORK BOX

DRYWALL PATCH

7

7 REPAIR/PATCH PLASTER WALLS

There are two ways to repair a large hole in plaster: one traditional and one that's a modern compromise.

OX PRO PLASTERER'S SCARIFIER 12"

The traditional method uses lime plaster with goat hair, which is applied to the strips of wood (lath) that are attached to the framing. When applied, the plaster pushes through the gaps between the lath strips in lumps that harden to create the new "plaster keys." This "scratch coat" is the plaster's first coat, and its keys establish the bond with the lath. Before the first coat fully hardens, it's also scratched in zigzag patterns using a scarifier to give it a rough surface to bond with the next coat. Following a cure time of several days, applying the second coat, called the brown coat, will completely fill the hole and bring the patched-up area to the level of the old surface.

Finally, applying a finish coat of lime putty to blend the patch with the old plaster will make the wall sound again. The advantages are material compatibility and longevity, while the drawbacks are the work's complexity and the plaster's expense.

A modern repair/patching approach is to use modern gypsum-based material for the patch. First, cut the drywall patch and screw it to the lath. Before applying plaster over the patch, use a bonding agent, such as Plaster-Weld, to prep the surface. You may use gypsum plaster—such as Structo-Lite, joint compound or Plaster Magic patching plaster—along with a fiber drywall tape to bridge any gaps and bring the patched surface flush before applying a finish coat of joint compound. The advantages here are the ease of sourcing materials, but the drawbacks could be future cracks caused by using gypsum materials with lime plaster.

8 HANG PICTURES WITH CARE

Picture this: You're admiring a new picture you just hung on your home's antique plaster walls. Fast-forward a few minutes. Your picture is not on the wall, and in its place is a bent nail, a large hole and a new crack. Spare yourself more agony and try one of these methods.

8A

Use an Angled Hanger

On a normal gypsum wall, these types of hangers **(Photo 8A)** are simple to use, but you need to approach this differently with plaster walls. Use your drill and a 1/16-in. drill bit to create a pilot hole for the hook's nail. Drill your pilot hole(s) to match the angle of the nail. Gently tap the hook and nail into the wall. If the nail encounters a piece of lath, the pilot hole will allow it to pass without damage. If no lath, the nail's angle and the plaster's structure should be sufficient to hold the frame.

Install Picture Railing

If you don't want to put holes in your walls, consider installing picture rail molding around the upper perimeter of the room **(Photo 8B)**. To hang artwork, suspend wall hangings from the picture rail molding with hooks and wire. Then when your preferences change, you can replace or move things with no nail holes to repair.

PICTURE RAIL

8B

9 BE PROACTIVE IN HOME MAINTENANCE

Like many old house features, plaster is maintainable and can be repaired rather than replaced when a problem occurs. Plaster cracks or other common failures are often caused by underlying structural or water intrusion issues that have been neglected and must be addressed. The most significant aspect of caring for your plaster is maintaining your home proactively and on a regular basis.

Beyond issue resolution, ensuring plaster can remain breathable is the next most important step. Nonpermeable insulation (such as closed-cell spray foam) behind plaster walls and a solid painted surface creates a plaster sandwich that results in eventual failure. Caring for plaster means choosing the right building materials for wall coverings and insulation that will maintain the vapor permeability of lime plaster.

The final aspect of caring for your plaster is to limit unnecessary vibrations and impacts that could damage the plaster. Hammering nails, broken door stops, slamming doors and running in the house are all enemies of plaster. Do you think your grandparents yelled at you about those activities to improve your manners? No, it was probably to protect their plaster!

10 PAINT PLASTER WALLS

You can't beat the immediate gratification of paint, but painting plaster requires some considerations not encountered when painting drywall.

Because old plaster is often lime-based, it naturally absorbs and releases ambient moisture, which can cause modern acrylic latex paint and primer to bubble and fail. And you may be painting over existing layers of paint that may have already been compromised. Preparation is key.

If the prior paint is thick and failing, remove it. If the paint is mostly adhered, remove any peeling portions. Take safety precautions if dealing with lead paint.

Apply a thin coat, aka a skim coat, of an appropriate plaster, such as Master of Plaster restoration plaster, over any heavily textured surface. Then select and apply an alkyd or oil primer before applying your chosen paint color. As long as you're following these steps in priming, you can topcoat with your preferred paint.

If your plaster is bare, select a paint that will let lime plaster breathe. Whether we're talking clay paint—such as those from Earthborn Paints or Fenwick & Tilbrook—or a traditional limewash finish, the goal is a permeable surface covering that does not inhibit the plaster's ability to release moisture.

10

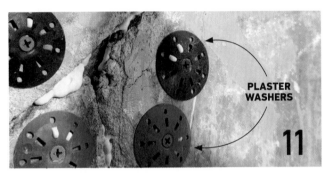

PLASTER WASHERS

11

11 REPAIR CRACKS

Repairing cracks in plaster can be intimidating. But it's not difficult—just a bit tedious. The first step is to correct any underlying issue that caused the crack or, unfortunately, the crack will return. Plaster tends to crack because of stress, resulting in the plaster "keys" breaking and no longer supporting the wall properly. To resolve this issue, the plaster needs to be re-adhered to the lath with a stabilizing adhesive such as Plaster Magic.

Begin by drilling holes through the surface of the plaster but not through the lath. Spray the Plaster Magic Conditioner into the hole you've drilled, then inject Plaster Magic Adhesive into the hole and between the plaster and lath. Finally, screw large plastic washers through the holes and lath to clamp the plaster back onto the lath. After 24 hours, your wall will be stable. Remove the washers and the crack can be corrected.

Next, use a taping knife to remove any loose portions of plaster or high spots. Fill the gaps with a plaster patching compound and reinforce the crack with fibered seam tape. Then smooth out the wall using lime putty to keep material consistency. You can also use sandable joint compound if you have chosen to use gypsum products to repair your plaster.

MEET THE EXPERT

Gary Wentz is a carpenter and former editor-in-chief of *The Family Handyman*. He claims to have torn out more than 2 acres of plaster and lath.

PLASTER & LATH TEAR-OFF

DO IT FASTER, SAFER AND BETTER

We've shared with you how to live with the plaster in your old home (see p. 119), but what if you want to remove the plaster altogether? Removing plaster and lath is an ugly ordeal, but carpenter Gary Wentz's tips will save you time, frustration *and* blood.

1 TURN OFF THE POWER!

Old walls hold hazardous surprises like wires without insulation and devices without junction boxes. In one wall Gary tore out, the wiring was embedded in the plaster! So turn off the circuits inside the wall and check any outlets or switches with a noncontact voltage tester before starting the tear-out.

2 PREPARE FOR A DUST STORM

Demolishing plaster and lath is a dusty, filthy job. Wear a dust mask, cover doorways with painter's plastic, turn off the furnace or central air conditioning, and cover HVAC grates.

3 PROTECT FLOORS

Lath nails and plaster chunks really tear up flooring. The best protection is ⅛-in. hardboard taped together at seams. With wood floors, use hardboard even if you plan to refinish the floor later. Lath nails can leave deep gouges that are hard to sand out.

4 CUT THE PLASTER

As you break up plaster, cracks can spread to adjoining walls and ceilings. To prevent that, cut the plaster where you want the demolition to stop. Make perimeter cuts with a grinder and a diamond blade. A diamond blade can also cut through metal lath, which was sometimes added over wood lath at corners and archways.

Cutting with a grinder whips up tons of dust. You can also use an oscillating tool equipped with a diamond or carbide-grit blade; it will cut slower but with less mess.

5 CUT THE LATH

After cutting the perimeter of the plaster, cut the wood lath to prevent cracking the adjoining walls and ceilings. An oscillating tool with a round blade is perfect for this.

OSCILLATING TOOL

ROUND BLADE

DIAMOND BLADE

GRINDER

6A

SCRAPE OFF THE PLASTER

6 Chip away a small starter hole with your hammer claw. Then get to scraping. Gary's tool of choice is a bent pole scraper (**Photo 6B**, Hyde No. 12070; about $15) that screws onto a broom handle. Some home wreckers prefer an ice scraper or a square shovel. Whatever you use, scrape parallel or diagonal to the lath (**Photo 6A**). If you scrape perpendicular to the lath, your scraper will break through.

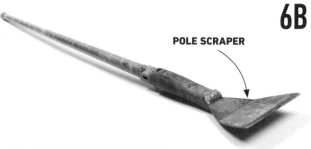

6B

POLE SCRAPER

SCOOP UP THE PLASTER

7 Shovel the plaster into buckets or heavy-duty trash bags. If you choose bags, don't fill them too full; plaster is heavy!

DON'T MIX PLASTER AND LATH

8 You could tear off plaster and lath at the same time—that's a little faster than attacking them separately. But cleaning up a mountain of mixed debris is painfully slow. You can't shovel the plaster until you fish out the lath, one stick at a time. So tear off the plaster, clean up and then strip off the lath.

7

8

9 YANK OFF THE LATH

Lath nails come out easily, so you can often pull off two or three rows at a time. Use the hook of a wrecking bar. Try to remove full lengths of lath; they're easier to pick up and haul out than a million splintered sticks.

10 WATCH WHERE YOU STEP

When you step on a big nail, you can often feel the pressure and shift your step to avoid an injury. Not with lath nails. Those sharp, skinny buggers will puncture your shoe and foot before you know what's happened.

11 HIT THE OTHER SIDE FROM BEHIND

If you're removing plaster and lath from both sides of a wall, completely strip one side of the wall, then attack the other side from behind. Stab at the lath with a square shovel, right next to studs. As the lath loosens, the plaster breaks away and falls off. After that, the lath will pop off with a few more shovel whacks. Karate kicks work too!

DOES PLASTER CONTAIN ASBESTOS?

Adding fiber to plaster, for extra strength and crack resistance, was standard practice for centuries. The wall shown here contained horsehair. But at least one major plaster manufacturer used asbestos instead and did so from the 1920s until the '70s. You can't be sure unless you test. Just search online to find a testing service and send in a sample. You'll get the results in about two weeks and pay less than $100. If the plaster does contain asbestos, check with your local inspector for demolition regulations.

MEET THE EXPERT

Jerome Worm has installed a couple miles of handrails in his 35-plus years as a trim carpenter.

ROCK-SOLID HANDRAILS

PREVENT A MISSTEP WITH A BEAUTIFUL ADDITION TO YOUR STAIRWAY WALL

Handrails can prevent nasty tumbles down the stairs, so it's important that they be sturdy. Looking good is also important because of their prominent place in the house. We asked trim carpenter Jerome Worm for some tips on installing handrails. He demonstrated a fast and foolproof way to measure, showed us a great way to assemble the rail, and specified what hardware he likes best and explained why. This advice will help you hang an attractive, rock-solid handrail that will last as long as the house.

1 MEASURE FROM THE BOTTOM STAIR NOSE TO THE TOP STAIR NOSE

The handrail needs to run the entire length of the stairs to make sure it's safe and code compliant. The easiest way to determine that distance is to hook a tape measure onto the bottom stair nose and measure up to the top. Our expert prefers to add 6 in. to that measurement to provide a 3-in. buffer on each end.

2 MARK THE STUDS

Handrail brackets should be secured to the studs; drywall anchors aren't strong enough. These brackets need to be fastened a maximum of 48 in. apart, but check the specifications on the hardware you're using. Space the brackets 32 in. apart for round and oval handrails because they aren't as sturdy as the beefy, oak "bread loaf" style rail we're installing. Install a bracket on the studs closest to the top and bottom of the handrail. Mark the studs with painter's tape so you don't have to make pencil marks on the wall.

3 FIND THE BRACKET HEIGHT WITH A CARPENTER'S SQUARE

Mark the location of the bracket screw hole on the wall, not the top of the handrail. To find that measurement, set the handrail upside down on the stairs. Set a rafter square on a stair tread, right up to the edge of the stair nose. Next, set a bracket on the bottom of the rail where the screw hole lines up with the edge of the square. That dimension (5 in. in this case) is the distance to subtract from the desired height of the top of the handrail. We want the top of our handrail to be 36 in. high, so we'll mark the wall at 31 in. high.

STUD FINDER
STUD LOCATIONS

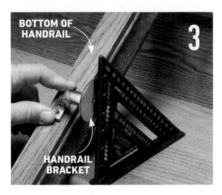
3
BOTTOM OF HANDRAIL
HANDRAIL BRACKET

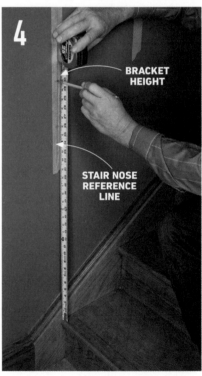
4
BRACKET HEIGHT
STAIR NOSE REFERENCE LINE

4 MARK THE STARTING POINT AND BRACKET HEIGHT

Use a 4-ft. level to plumb up from the nose of the bottom step, and mark a vertical line on the wall that will indicate where the bottom end of the handrail should start. Next, measure up from the nose of the steps and mark an intersecting line representing the height of the bracket screw.

5 SET OTHER BRACKET LOCATIONS WITH A SQUARE

Set a framing square on the skirt board, line it up with the mark indicating the bracket height, and note that number (see Step 4). Move the square up to the next stud that will support a bracket, and mark that number on the wall. If there's no skirt board, lay a 2x4 on the stairs and slide the framing square on that.

5
BRACKET HEIGHT
SKIRT BOARD

6 AVOID 90-DEGREE RETURNS

Handrails need to meet the wall (or a newel post) at each end. These "returns" alert people that the railing has ended. Returns also protect folks from bumping into a sharp edge of the rail. Jerome cuts his returns so they die into the wall at a 45-degree angle instead of a 90-degree angle. This method looks good and prevents clothing, purses and other items from getting hooked on the end of the rail.

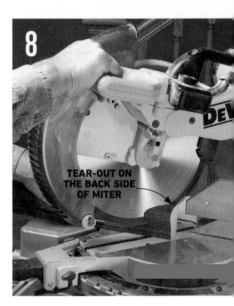

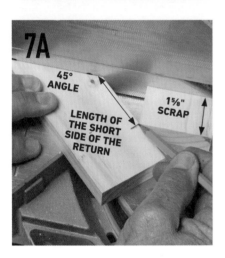

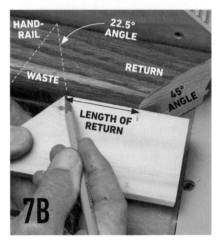

7 FIND THE LENGTH OF THE RETURN WITH A BLOCK

Code requires a space that's at least 1½ in. between the wall and the handrail. To find the length of the return piece, cut a 45-degree angle on a scrap of wood, and then cut a block of wood to the thickness of the desired gap between the wall and the railing (1⅝ in. in this case). Place the 45-degree angle up against the fence and slide the 1⅝-in. block up to that. Mark the point where the two intersect (**Photo 7A**). That mark represents the short side of the handrail return. Transfer the mark onto the handrail (**Photo 7B**). Cut the return off the same side of the rail where it will be installed. That way the wood grain will carry seamlessly through on the front of the railing.

BUILDING CODE REQUIREMENTS

- Handrails must run the entire length of the stairs.
- The top of the rail should be between 34 in. and 38 in., measured directly up from the stair nosing.
- There needs to be at least 1½ in. between the wall and the rail.
- Handrails must die into a wall or newel post.
- Circular handrails must have a diameter between 1¼ in. and 2 in.
- Custom shapes are acceptable but may have a specific size requirement (check with your building official).

8 CUT WITH THE "SHOW" SIDE TOWARD THE FENCE

Miter saws cause wood to tear out and splinter more on the side that rests against the fence. This may sound counterintuitive to woodworkers, but when cutting a handrail, it's better to have the tear-out occur on the "show" side of the rail, or the side that faces away from the wall. Tear-outs on the wall side of the rail will show up on the inside of the miter and are difficult to sand out. Rough wood on the outside of the miter can be sanded and rounded over much easier. Minimize tear-outs with a sharp blade and by cutting slowly and letting the blade stop spinning before raising it.

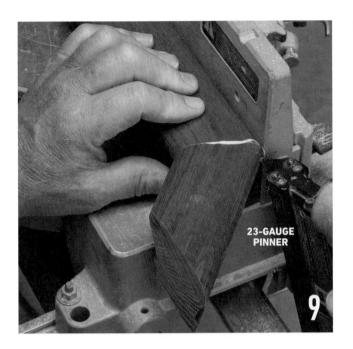

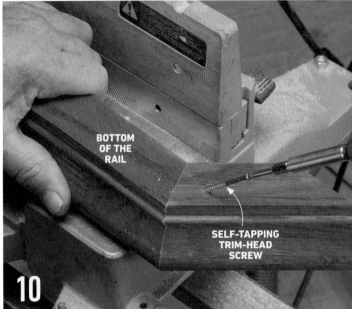

9 GLUE AND PIN RETURNS

Glue and pin the return pieces before screwing them together. Line up the two glued ends as accurately as you can before pushing them together. If you move them around too much, the glue can act as a lubricant, making them difficult to hold in place when you pin them together.

Hold the pieces in place with a 23-gauge pinner while the glue dries. Pinners are nice because they don't leave a big, ugly hole, and the pins are less likely to follow the grain of the wood and veer off course as larger-gauge brads are prone to do.

10 SECURE RETURNS WITH TRIM-HEAD SCREWS

Let the glue set up for 15 minutes or so, and then strengthen the miter with a 2½-in. screw driven in at the bottom. A self-tapping trim-head screw leaves a smaller hole and is less likely to split the wood. But regardless of the screw type you use, predrill a hole all the way through the first piece and about ½ in. or so into the second piece.

11 CHOOSE SINGLE-HOLE BRACKETS

The rail brackets that have one screw hole are easier to attach than the brackets with three because the one screw will still hit the stud if the stud line is a little off.

12 USE TAPE TO ALIGN THE HANDRAIL

Fasten the brackets to the wall, but leave them loose enough so you can twist them into perfect position with the handrail. This rail runs 3 in. past the top and bottom stair nose. Our expert wrapped tape 3 in. from the bottom of the rail in order to line up the rail with the tape that represents the bottom stair nose. Predrill holes into the handrail for the bracket screws, and finish tightening the brackets to the wall after all the brackets are secured to the rail.

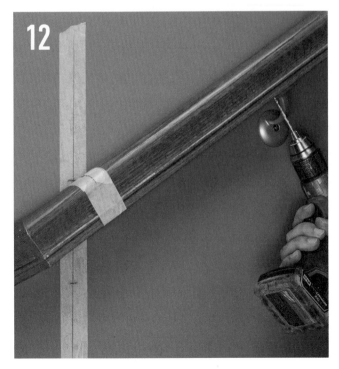

CHAPTER 4

DOORS, WINDOWS & TRIM

Install an Interior Door 134
How Much Does Window Replacement Cost? 138
Restore Your Old Windows 140
Working with Trim 147
Finishing Trim 154
Essential Caulking Tips 158

MEET THE EXPERT

Jerome Worm has installed thousands of interior doors, but he no longer hangs them the same way he did when he started. He uses a system that has evolved over his decades-long trim carpentry career.

INSTALL AN INTERIOR DOOR

HANG A DOOR THAT WILL WORK WITHOUT ISSUES, AND STAND THE TEST OF TIME

Nobody pays much attention to doors that work the way they should. They open—they close. But doors that were improperly installed can bind, swing open by themselves or rattle in a breeze even when shut.

We asked longtime trim carpenter Jerome Worm to show us his best door-hanging tricks. Whether

you have hung a hundred doors or you are installing your first nb , we're confident that Jerome has a tip or two that will result in your door operating properly, lasting as long as it is needed, and enduring the occasional slam from an emotional teenager.

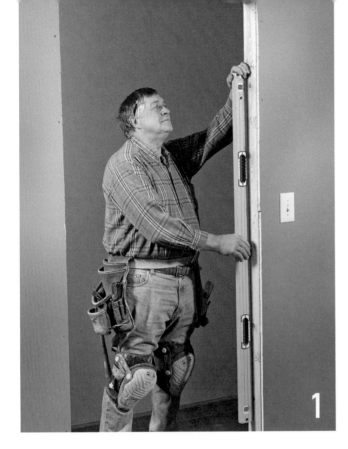

1 CHECK THE ROUGH OPENING

Make sure your door is going to fit into the opening. Measure the height of the opening, and then measure the width at both the top and the bottom. Next, check each side with a level. The sides don't have to be perfectly plumb (they rarely are), but they do have to be close enough to allow adequate room for your door.

If your rough opening is ½ in. bigger than your door but the sides of the opening are each ½ in. out of plumb, that opening is not big enough to hang your door properly. Finally, check to see if the walls are plumb.

2 LEVEL THE FLOOR

For Jerome, the most critical step of any door installation is making sure the bottom of each doorjamb is at the proper height. If you're installing a door on a finished floor and the floor isn't level, cut a little off the bottom of one of the jambs.

Use a level to check the floor. Rest a level across the opening, and level it with one or more shims. Mark the shim at the thickest point, and measure the thickness of the shim at the mark. That's exactly how much you'll need to cut off the jamb at the opposite side of the opening.

3 USE BLOCKS TO LEVEL JAMB BOTTOMS

If you're installing a door on an unfinished floor and need space under the jambs for carpet, just rest the jambs on temporary blocks while you're hanging the door. Adjust the size of the blocks so the bottoms of the jambs are on a level plane. Jerome leaves a space under his jambs of anywhere from ⅜ in. to ⅝ in., depending on the thickness of the carpet and pad.

4 CHECK THE PLUG

Make sure the plug that holds the door slab in place is the type that can be removed after the door is installed. If it's not, sometimes you can cut off the plastic strap and insert the plug back in through the doorknob hole. It's difficult to move the door when the slab is flopping all over the place, but it's worse to install a door that won't open.

5 CUT DOWN THE HIGH SIDE OF THE JAMB

Jerome prefers a circular saw to cut down jambs when they need it. He installs an 80-tooth blade in his saw to prevent tearing out the wood veneer. It's easy to cut off the wrong jamb, so make sure you cut the jamb that rests on the high side of the floor. It's the one on the opposite side of the opening where you marked your shim. A rafter square works great as a saw guide.

6 ATTACH TEMPORARY BLOCKS TO THE JAMB

To hold the doorjamb flush with the drywall before permanently fastening it, Jerome attaches temporary blocks to both sides of the jamb. He uses scrap lumber to make five 4-to-5-in. blocks. He attaches each with 2-in. 18-gauge brads. He nails three blocks on the latch side and two on the hinge side (the door slab keeps the middle of the hinge side rigid). Keep the blocks away from the hinges so they won't interfere with shimming. The casing will cover up the nail holes when the blocks are removed.

7 NAIL THE BLOCKS TO THE WALL

Set the door in the center of the opening. Make sure you have a consistent gap between the door slab and all three sides of the jamb. If the bottoms of the jambs were properly cut beforehand, the gaps will be consistent, the top jamb will be level and the sides will be plumb.

Double-check the hinge side for plumb before nailing the blocks to the wall with a couple of 2-in. 15-gauge finish nails. Nail the hinge side first, and then recheck the gap around the door slab before fastening the blocks on the latch side. The blocks will allow enough wiggle room for fine-tuning before the jamb is shimmed and nailed to the framing.

8 SHIM THE TOP JAMB

It's not always necessary to use shims on the top doorjamb—the casing will hold it in place. And on new homes and additions, walls can compress as they settle and push down on the top shims, causing the jamb to bow down. Jerome shims the top jamb only if he's working with a 3-ft.-wide door and the top jamb arrives bowed from the factory.

9 CHECK GAP AT DOOR STOPS

Before installing any shims, remove the plug that holds the door slab in place, and make sure the door opens and closes properly. The door should come in contact with the door stop evenly along the whole length of the stop. If one side of the door hits the stop first, you will have to adjust the jambs by moving either the top side or the bottom side of the jamb in or out, depending on which part of the door hits first.

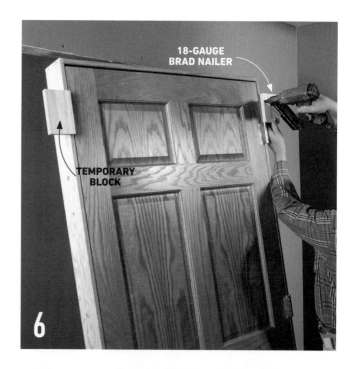

18-GAUGE BRAD NAILER

TEMPORARY BLOCK

6

HINGE SIDE

15-GAUGE FINISH NAILER

7

DOOR STOP

GAP

9

10 SHIM BEHIND HINGES

Remove the center screw from all three hinges, and slide shims behind the empty screw hole, starting with the top hinge. Fill the whole gap evenly between the jamb and the framing or you'll pull the door out of alignment when you drive in the screw.

If the framing on the rough opening seems to be twisted one way or the other, position your shims so the jamb stays perpendicular to the wall. Once the shims are in place, make sure the jambs are still flush with the drywall (if your walls are plumb).

Recheck the gap between the slab and the jambs. Recheck the gap between the door slab and the door stop. If this gap is more than ⅜ in., it's best to split this adjustment between the hinge-side and the latch-side jambs; adjust the jamb so it's only halfway corrected. And finally, nail the shims into place using three 2-in. 15-gauge nails.

11 INSTALL LONGER SCREWS IN EACH HINGE

Replace one factory screw in each hinge with a longer screw. Drive the screw in very slowly the last few turns, and pay close attention to the jamb. You don't want to suck the jamb in and throw off the alignment of the door. Check all the gaps, and open and close the door after you install each screw.

Make sure the screws penetrate the framing a minimum of 1 in. The gap between the framing and this doorjamb was about ½ in., so Jerome installed 2½-in. screws. Don't use drywall screws—they're brittle and won't hold up to years of abuse. Buy construction screws instead, and try to find screws that are close to the same color as your hinges.

2½"
CONSTRUCTION
SCREW

12 SECURE THE LATCH SIDE

Insert and secure shims 4 in. down from the top of the door and 4 in. up from the floor. Nail the shims the same way that you did on the hinge side.

Jerome has repaired doors that were slammed shut so violently from the wind that the jamb on the latch side was knocked several inches out of place. To prevent this problem, he installs a long construction screw behind the latch plate. He predrills and countersinks a hole in the corner of the latch plate space so it won't interfere with the latch plate screws. He doesn't use longer screws in the latch plate holes because they are too close to the edge and can split the framing lumber.

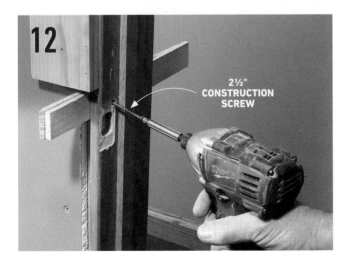

2½"
CONSTRUCTION
SCREW

HOW MUCH DOES WINDOW REPLACEMENT COST?

SAVE MONEY AND ENERGY WITH THESE TIPS FROM A WINDOW EXPERT

New windows are appealing for a lot of reasons: transforming the look of your house, getting rid of old windows that are hard to open and close, eliminating drafts and more. Another big motivation is energy savings. Contemporary windows feature double- and triple-pane glass and thermally insulated frames.

In part because of the energy-saving benefit, window replacement could save you money in the long run and can increase home value. HomeLight estimates an 81% return on investment.

On average, it costs about $7,500 to professionally replace 10 double-hung windows in a typical 2,500-sq.-ft. home. High-end wood windows cost more. But there are ways to lower window replacement costs.

FACTORS AFFECT COST

Unlike new windows, replacements fit inside existing window frames. Wayne Owczarzak, owner of Mr. Handyman, a Neighborly company, calls these "pocket windows." Several factors influence the cost of window replacement:

- **Frame Material:** Most common are vinyl, fiberglass and wood.
- **Window Type:** All have different price tags and installation requirements.
- **Window Opening Size:** Larger windows obviously cost more.
- **Window Opening Condition:** Severe rot and deterioration drive up labor costs.
- **Window Placement:** Upper-story windows may call for extra skill and equipment.
- **Home Age:** Older homes often have nonstandard window openings that require custom-made replacements.
- **Glass Type:** Most new windows have double-pane, but triple-pane, tempered or laminated (safety), and UV-resistant glass panes are available.

DIY VS. PRO WINDOW REPLACEMENT

Replacing windows isn't all that complicated, and in many cases it requires minimal exterior work. You can often remove old sashes from indoors after prying off the molding, pop in pocket windows and replace the molding. Some homeowners may have the DIY skills to install their own windows, depending on window type and placement. However, experts like Owczarzak say most shouldn't attempt it.

It takes a contractor from two to four hours, on average, to install a replacement window. Unless you are skilled, it will likely take you longer. Consider the following before you decide to DIY:

- Contractors get a discount on replacement windows unavailable to homeowners.
- Contractors are better equipped to handle problems, such as windows that don't fit exactly and crumbling or out-of-square window frames. Owczarzak says window replacement won't improve efficiency if air is coming through the gap between the window and the framing. It often takes professional skill to resolve issues like this.
- Replacement windows can be heavy, and it often takes two people to lift one and set it in the window opening. If you drop the window, you pay for a replacement. But if a contractor happens to drop one, that contractor is the person who pays, not you.
- Poor installation practices, such as improper sealing or omitting weatherproof frame lining, shorten the life of the window and negate the insulation benefits. A contractor guarantees work against such defects. If you do the job yourself, you assume the liability.
- DIY installation may void the product warranty.

REPLACEMENT COSTS OF DIFFERENT WINDOW TYPES

For cost estimation, you can classify windows by frame material and window type.

FRAME MATERIAL

■ **Aluminum:** Aluminum frames are cheap, but they don't insulate well. They're usually reserved for utility and commercial windows. Each window unit costs from about $100 to $400.

WINDOW TYPE

■ **Vinyl:** This is the second-least expensive frame material. It runs about $200 to $500 for a standard double-hung window.

■ **Wood:** This traditional material never falls out of favor. A double-hung wood window costs about $300 to $600.

■ **Fiberglass:** Fiberglass can be molded to look like wood and offers the best durability and energy efficiency. A double-hung window costs about $800 to $2,000.

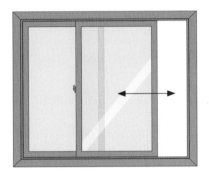

SLIDING: These open and close along a horizontal track. Quality varies, and so does cost—from about $200 to $2,000.

PICTURE: These are fixed but often nonstandard sizes. Costs range from about $300 to $800.

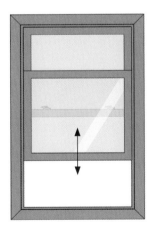

CASEMENT: The sash on a casement window pivots on a vertical axis, operated by a crank. An awning window is similar but pivots from the top on a horizontal axis. Replacement costs are about $300 to $600.

SINGLE-HUNG: Found in older homes, these feature a lower sash that slides up and down and a fixed upper sash. A replacement single-hung window costs about $100 to $400.

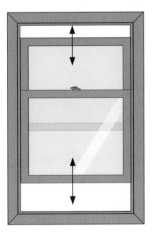

DOUBLE-HUNG: These have two sliding sashes that tilt inward, making it safe and easy to clean the outside glass. They cost about $300 to $600.

TIPS FOR SAVING MONEY

Over and above doing the installation yourself, you can control window replacement costs in these ways:

▥ Install windows with a simpler design than the ones you're replacing, such as solid panes instead of panes with grids.

▥ Stick with standard colors and sizes.

▥ Replace several windows at once so you can buy them in bulk.

▥ Pay by cash or check. A window supplier who incurs a 3% swipe fee for a credit card usually passes that fee on to the consumer.

▥ Look around for seconds. Builders often sell unused windows on *craigslist.com* or at Habitat for Humanity's ReStore.

▥ Choose Energy Star windows, which qualify for any applicable energy-efficiency tax credits. The federal Residential Energy Efficiency tax credit expired in 2021, but some state and local governments still offer incentives for energy-efficient windows.

RESTORE YOUR OLD WINDOWS

///

IMPROVE THE VIEW BY GETTING THEM BACK IN SHAPE

Sash windows are beautiful features of many homes built in the early 20th century—even going back as far as the 17th century. When these old windows need TLC, is it possible to salvage them? Will they work as efficiently as new windows? Yes and yes, if you restore them properly.

For an expert view, we spoke with Quaint Milwaukee Window Restoration in Milwaukee, Wisconsin, which specializes in the historic preservation of windows, repairing everything from scratches to sash cord malfunctions. Owner Norbert Rodriguez says the most common issues are windows not opening properly, broken glass, windows painted or caulked shut, and broken sash cords. The good news? Most of the time the windows can be restored and don't need to be replaced.

Follow Rodriguez's step-by-step instructions to do the most common fixes.

MEET THE EXPERT
Norbert Rodriguez is the owner of Quaint Milwaukee Window Restoration.

REPLACING SASH CORDS

Replacing sash cords is a common old window restoration project. There are two sash cords—one on each side of the window that connects each sash to a weight. The weight is located in a cavity inside the wall. Over time, these cords get brittle and break,

and it's important to replace them with the correct type of cord.

Rodriguez recommends using ⅜-in. cord in most situations. But if your window is heavy, about 60 to 80 lbs., then you'll want to use a ½-in. cord or chain to support the weight.

The two weights already there are probably correct for your

sash window. To double-check, place the weights separately on a scale, and make sure they weigh the same as the sash. For example, if your sash is 14 lbs., each weight should be about 7 lbs. Now, let's get down to the job:

1 REMOVE SASH

Start by removing the front stops, which are usually screwed in. Score paint lines or any caulk with a utility knife. Remove the front stops by using a molding pry bar. You may need a rubber mallet to get the pry bar between the sash and the stops.

2 DISCONNECT SASH CORDS

Detach the sash cords from the sash, then remove the lower sash from the window frame before removing the upper sash.

FRONT STOPS

BROKEN SASH CORD

WHAT IT TAKES		
TIME 1 day	**COST** $40	**SKILL LEVEL** Intermediate

TOOLS
Utility knife, screwdriver, carbide paint scraper, molding pry bar, rubber mallet, hammer

MATERIALS & SUPPLIES
Safety glasses, gloves, nails, ⅜" sash cord, HEPA filter vacuum, shop vac with HEPA filter

3 ACCESS THE SASH WEIGHTS

Use a screwdriver to open and remove doors on each side of the cavities to access the weights. Remove both weights from the cavities.

4 ATTACH SASH CORDS TO WEIGHTS

To feed new sash cord through the pulley system down the weight cavity, attach something small with weight to the end of the cord so it does not get stuck in the cavity. Pull cord through and tie the end to the weight. Let the remaining end of the cord hang to about the meeting rail and cut it. Repeat this on the other side. Close the doors of the weight cavities with a screwdriver.

5 ATTACH CORDS TO SASH

Pull on the cords to lift the weights up near the very top. Line up the cords to the sash, and attach both cords to the sash by tying knots at the ends of the cords. Then place them into the two sash cord slots located on each side of the sash. Drive a nail or staple through the knot so the cords won't move out of the cord slots. Cut off excess cord.

6 MOUNT FRONT STOPS

Reinstall the front stops with screws and test the window.

SASH WEIGHT DOOR

3

SASH WEIGHT

4

NEW SASH CORD

SASH CORD SLOT

5

6

FREEING UP WINDOWS

Carelessness is often the reason windows become painted shut. The paint buildup gets between the sash and frame, making it impossible to open. Some people have even caulked windows shut, thinking it would help with efficiency.

If you're going to paint your windows, Rodriguez recommends coming back to a freshly painted window every 30 minutes after you paint it and wiggling it up an inch to make sure the paint doesn't dry it shut. Or to avoid this situation, remove the windows before you paint them and reinstall them when they are dry. If you do get stuck windows, follow these steps:

SCORE PAINT LINES
Score the paint lines or caulk with a utility knife between the sash and front stops (also known as parting beads).

BREAK DRIED PAINT
Saw through the dried paint on both sides of the sash by using the CRL Window Zipper Deglazing Tool (or sash saw) between the sash and wood stops. Repeat this process on the top and bottom of the sash, and make sure the window is unlocked.

REMOVE STOPS
Remove front stops (**Photo 1**, p. 141) on the left and right sides of the sash. Unscrew any screws and remove stops with the pry bar. You may need a rubber mallet to get the pry bar between the sash and the stops.

1

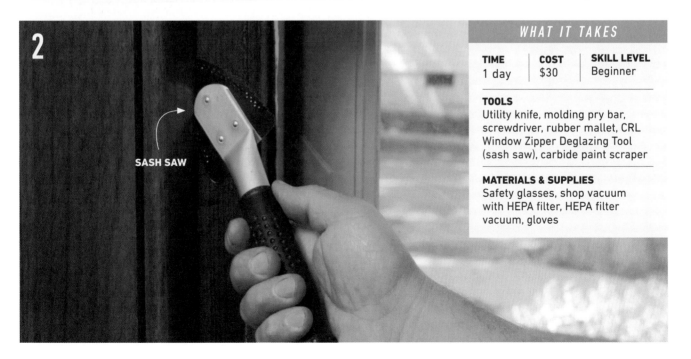

2

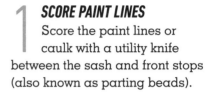

SASH SAW

WHAT IT TAKES		
TIME	**COST**	**SKILL LEVEL**
1 day	$30	Beginner

TOOLS
Utility knife, molding pry bar, screwdriver, rubber mallet, CRL Window Zipper Deglazing Tool (sash saw), carbide paint scraper

MATERIALS & SUPPLIES
Safety glasses, shop vacuum with HEPA filter, HEPA filter vacuum, gloves

4 FREE THE MEETING RAIL

Use a paint scraper to free the meeting rail if dried paint seems present. Gently tilt the sash toward you, and the window should break free from dried paint.

5 CLEAN OFF EXCESS DEBRIS (NOT SHOWN)

Using a carbide scraper or chisel, scrape off any extra paint or debris on the casing or frame of the window. Vacuum paint chips and debris as needed. (Rodriguez and his team use a paint scraper that is directly connected to a vacuum hose; this type is available at some hardware stores and online.)

SAFETY CAUTION:
Be sure to wear gloves, a paint respirator/mask and eye protection. If the windows were made before 1978, assume you are working with lead-based paint and take proper precautions. To learn how to safely remove lead paint, go to *familyhandyman.com/project/how-to-remove-lead-paint-safely/*.

MEETING RAIL

REPLACING GLASS

Replacing glass in old windows can be challenging. You can pick up a new glass pane from your local hardware store to either cut yourself or have the glass cut for you. If your window contains antique glass and you want the replacement glass to match it, you can reach out to a local window repair store. Rodriguez said it's important that the replacement glass pane is of similar thickness to the window's original pane of glass to keep the weight of the sash balanced properly. Now let's get started:

1 CLEAN OFF OLD GLAZING COMPOUND

Chip out the old glazing compound carefully with a window zipper deglazing tool or glazing putty knife. A heat gun or torch can be helpful to soften the putty for easy removal.

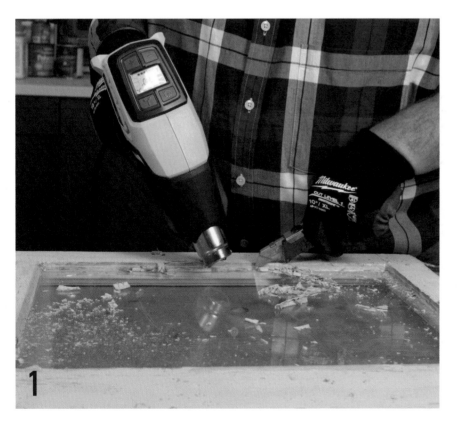

WHAT IT TAKES

TIME	COST	SKILL LEVEL
1 day	$60	Intermediate

TOOLS
Utility knife, carbide paint scraper or chisel, glazing putty knife, screwdriver

MATERIALS & SUPPLIES
Safety glasses, gloves, replacement antique glass pane, glazing points, glazing compound, cloth

GLAZING POINT

2

3A

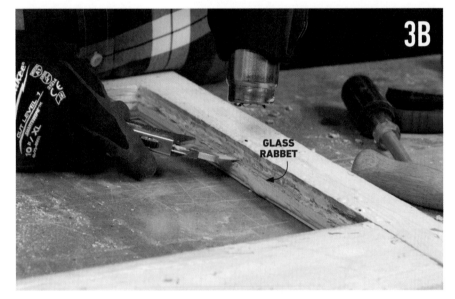

3B

GLASS RABBET

GLAZING PUTTY IN RABBET

6

2 REMOVE BROKEN GLASS

Use a putty knife or pliers to remove the glazing points that hold the glass in place. Pull out the old glass carefully.

3 CLEAN GLASS RABBET

Remove any remaining glazing compound on the glass rabbets using a carbide scraper or chisel, making sure not to damage or scrape the wood.

4 MEASURE THE OPENING AND GET NEW GLASS (NOT SHOWN)

Measure the glass opening and subtract about ⅛ in. to ¼ in. for the replacement glass. If you don't feel comfortable cutting the glass yourself, take your measurements to a local window repair shop and they will cut the glass for you for a small fee. Clean the replacement pane of glass and make sure there are no cracks or flaws.

5 APPLY GLAZING PUTTY TO RABBETS (NOT SHOWN)

Apply glazing putty with a putty knife to the glass rabbets that the glass pane will rest on. Rodriguez recommends using Sarco Linseed oil-based glazing compound, but it can be expensive. There are less expensive options, such as DAP glazing compound.

6 INSERT THE NEW GLASS

Carefully tilt the new pane of glass into place, and verify that it fits and that it's completely flat against the glass rabbets. Apply a small amount of pressure around the perimeter where the putty touches the glass to make sure there is complete contact.

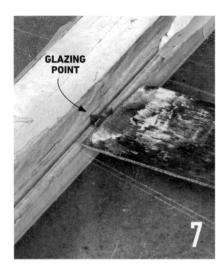

GLAZING POINT

7 ADD THE GLAZING POINTS

Install the glazing points with a putty knife to secure the glass pane. The points secure the glass in place while the putty dries; depending on the size of the glass pane, about two or three points on each side will be enough.

8 CLEAN EXCESS PUTTY (NOT SHOWN)

Allow the excess putty to ooze out under the glass and carefully scrape it off.

9 APPLY GLAZING PUTTY

Add new glazing putty (Sarco Linseed oil-based glazing compound) around the new pane of glass by rolling the putty with your hands and placing it around the perimeter of the glass in a heavy layer. Push the putty down with pressure, and be sure to not leave any gaps or hollow spots. Use a putty knife to create a beveled profile and smooth out the new glazing compound. Remove excess putty by dragging the putty knife away from the finished joint without harming the smoothed putty. TIP: Spray your putty knife with silicone for smooth application and so the compound won't stick to the knife.

9A

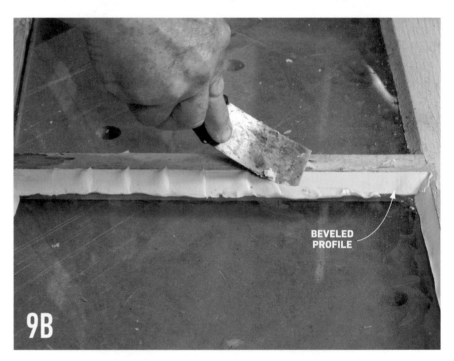

9B

BEVELED PROFILE

10 CLEAN THE GLASS (NOT SHOWN)

Continue to use the putty knife to clean up the edges. Remove putty oils with a microfiber cloth and mineral spirits, or paint thinner if the window is very messy. If you wait for the putty to dry and skin before cleaning, it may be easier to remove.

11 WAIT TO PAINT (NOT SHOWN)

Prime and paint the putty after it skins. That typically takes about one week, depending on temperature. (Rodriguez recommends using primer before you paint and not using paints that are "primer and paint in one.") It is mandatory to paint the putty or it will not be effective.

WORKING WITH TRIM

GREAT RESULTS, EVEN IN BAD SITUATIONS

Wavy walls, crooked studs, uneven floors and out-of-square corners are the norm in most houses, and they all add to the challenge of getting your moldings to fit just right. To help you out, we've collected problem-solving tips from three veteran carpenters with a wide range of trim carpentry experience.

TIGHTEN UP OPEN MITERS

Uneven walls or misaligned jambs make it hard to get tight-fitting miters. If your miter has a consistent gap at the front, there's a good chance that putting a slight back bevel on both moldings will fix the problem. If you own a compound miter saw, you could tilt the saw about a half-degree, but that requires fussy adjustments.

The quickest and easiest way to cut a slight back bevel is to shim the molding so it's resting at an angle to the saw blade. A pencil makes a handy shim and is just about the right thickness. You can adjust the position or thickness of the shim to compensate for all kinds of wall variations. You can even shim just the back or the front to mimic how the trim rests on uneven drywall.

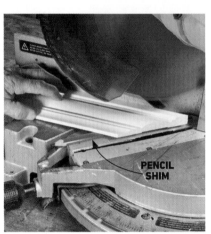

PENCIL SHIM

PROBLEM: *AN OPEN MITER*

This doorjamb protrudes a bit beyond the wall, and the result is that the trim can't lie flat and the front of the miter joint can't close.

SOLUTION: *CUT A "BACK BEVEL"*

You could tilt the saw blade to back-bevel the miters, but tilting the trim is faster and easier. Slip a pencil or shim under the molding, just behind where the cut will be. Cut both sides of the miter with shims in the same position. Then test the fit and make adjustments as needed.

CUT STEEP ANGLES ON YOUR MITER SAW

It's not common, but occasionally you'll run into a situation that requires miters greater than the 45- or 50-degree angle available on miter saws. The photo at right shows one solution.

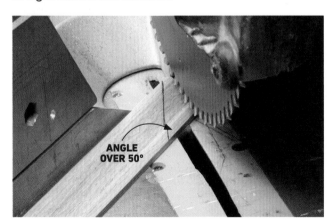

ANGLE OVER 50°

SUPPORT BLOCK

PROBLEM: *MITER SAWS DON'T CUT STEEP ANGLES*

This miter saw won't cut the 60-degree angle we need.

SOLUTION: *CLAMP TO AN ANGLED BLOCK*

Cut a block of wood at a 45-degree angle and cut a flat spot for the clamp. Clamp the molding to the block and line up the miter saw with the mark to make the cut.

SCRIBE TRIM TO FIT UNEVEN WALLS

Learning how to scribe moldings to fit tightly to uneven surfaces is a vital trim carpentry skill. And once you get the hang of scribing, you'll find all kinds of situations where it'll come in handy. Here we show how to fit a casing against an out-of-plumb wall. You can also scribe door bottoms, inside corners of wainscoting, and even shelving or cabinets that abut crooked walls.

There are several types of scribing tools, but the simple compass with a wing-nut lock shown is a favorite with many trim carpenters. The photo at right shows how to use the compass to scribe a line. Then finish up by cutting and trimming to the line for a perfectly fitting piece **(Photo Solution, Step 2)**.

SCRIBING TOOL

SOLUTION, STEP 1:
SCRIBE A LINE ON THE CASING

Set the scribing tool to the distance between the wall and the mark on the casing. Scribe a line by running the point of the tool against the wall, being careful to keep the tool perpendicular to the wall.

PROBLEM: *THE TRIM WON'T FIT*

This casing is wider than the space between the door and the wall, so the casing needs to be cut. That cut will need to fit tightly against an uneven wall.

SCRIBE LINE

PINNED DOWN

SOLUTION, STEP 2:
CUT ALONG THE LINE

Next, remove the molding and tack it to a board. Carefully saw along the line with your circular saw. Stay a little outside the line. Then finish up by belt-sanding or planing up to the line.

ANGLE A NAIL TO CLOSE BASEBOARD GAPS

Sometimes you can't force a baseboard tight against the wall because there's no stud behind the gap. This is especially common at outside corners if there's a buildup of joint compound. But you can reach a bottom plate with a well-placed nail. For the best control and maximum hold, set aside your nail gun for a minute and reach for a hammer and an 8d finish nail. The photo at the right shows how the angled nail catches the plate.

PROBLEM: *UGLY GAP, NO STUD*

This gap seems impossible to close because there's no stud to nail into. This is common near outside corners where there's a buildup of joint compound.

SOLUTION: *NAIL INTO THE PLATE*

If there's no stud where you need to pull in the molding, drive an 8d finish nail at an angle into the bottom plate. In hardwood trim, drill a pilot hole. Use a hammer and a nail to set the nail head slightly below the surface.

MAKE BLOCKS FOR TOUGH TRANSITIONS

Used tastefully, transition blocks can be a real problem solver. Rather than struggling to align moldings or fudging to match profiles, you can make a nice transition with a decorative block. You can buy ready-made blocks, but it's easy to make your own. Cut the block to the height and width you think look good. Then cut or rout the top or add a small molding to complement your trim style. Use transition blocks where stair skirts intersect baseboards, where floor levels change, or at the bottom of door casings where the baseboard is thicker than the casing.

TRANSITION BLOCK

PROBLEM: *MOLDINGS DON'T LINE UP*

A change in floor heights creates an ugly jog in the baseboard.

SOLUTION: *CUT A DECORATIVE BLOCK*

Cut a block of wood that's a little thicker than the baseboard. Then finish the top with a bevel or a routed profile.

PERFORM SURGERY ON BIG HUMPS

Careful framing is the key to easy trim installation. But in the rush to get the walls put up, framing carpenters sometimes get a little sloppy. A stud that's not lined up with the plate causes a big hump in the wall, making it difficult to get the baseboard tight. But if you're courageous enough to cut into your wall, the fix is simple. Start by cutting out a little chunk of drywall right at the hump to see what the problem is. There could just be a chunk of drywall or other debris trapped between the drywall and the bottom plate. Or the stud could be misaligned. If this is the case, see the bottom photo for the solution.

CLEAN OUT CORNERS BEFORE YOU START

Even careful drywall tapers can end up with an accumulation of joint compound near the bottoms of inside corners. The problem is that all that extra mud prevents the baseboard from fitting well. The trick is to scrape off the buildup before you start installing the base. You can use a small pry bar with a sharp edge, a dull chisel or a stiff putty knife scraper. Before you start scraping, mark the top of the baseboard on the wall. Then scrape below the line where it won't show.

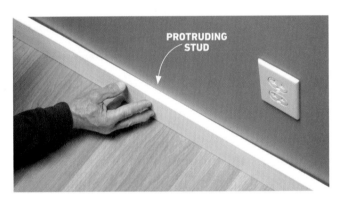

PROBLEM: *A HUMP CAUSES BASEBOARD GAPS*
Even if we could draw the baseboard tight to the wall on both sides of this hump, the baseboard would still look wavy. It's better to get rid of the hump.

PROBLEM: *SLOPPY MUD IN CORNERS*
Lumps and ridges will lead to a gapped or tilted baseboard and open joints.

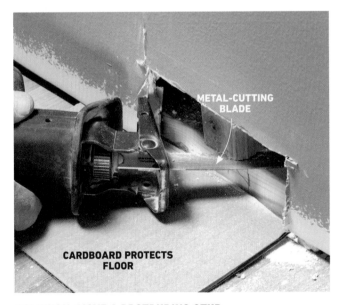

SOLUTION: *MOVE A PROTRUDING STUD*
Cut the nails that hold the stud to the plate. Then push the stud back until it's lined up with the plate and reattach it with an angled screw.

SOLUTION: *SCRAPE OUT THE CORNERS*
Mark the top of the baseboard on the wall. Then scrape away any excess mud below the line.

KEEP AN OSCILLATING MULTITOOL HANDY

On every trim job, there's at least one situation where an oscillating multitool can save the day. Whether it's trimming the bottom of an installed casing or notching a transition piece, an oscillating tool with a woodcutting blade is the perfect choice. And now that you can buy one for as little as about $40, it's a tool every trim carpenter can afford.

FLOOR TRANSITION

BASEBOARD SCRAP

PROBLEM: *TRANSITIONS GET IN THE WAY*
You could notch the base to fit over this transition piece. But it would be easier and look better if you cut the transition instead.

SOLUTION: *NOTCH TRANSITION WITH AN OSCILLATING TOOL*
Mount a fine-tooth blade in the oscillating tool. Then use a scrap of baseboard as a guide to cut the wood transition.

KEEP BASEBOARD FROM TILTING

Most drywall is installed with the tapered edge parallel to the floor and with at least ½ in. between the drywall and the floor. The combination of the space along the floor and the drywall taper can allow the baseboard to tilt at the bottom. This isn't a big problem along the length of walls, but at inside corners, the tilt can make fitting coped corners difficult. The photo at right shows a simple fix.

TILTED BASEBOARD

PROBLEM: *TILTING BASE CREATES A GAP*
The tapered drywall edge allows the baseboard to tilt—and that means a gap in the corner.

SOLUTION: *PREVENT TILTING WITH SPACER BLOCKS*
Cut strips of wood to the thickness of the drywall and cut small pieces to use as spacers at inside corners or wherever they're needed. The spacers prevent the trim from tilting and make fitting inside corner joints much simpler.

JOIN MOLDINGS WITH BISCUITS

Strengthening trim joints with biscuits may seem like overkill, but it's a great way to keep miters tight and prevent misalignment when you nail moldings to the wall. This tip is especially useful for larger casings, which are harder to hold in alignment. But you can add biscuits to just about any joint that's wide enough to accommodate them. The photos below show how.

You'll need a biscuit joiner and biscuits. If you're not familiar with the tool, go to *familyhandyman.com* and search for "biscuit joiner" for tips and operating instructions.

Cut and fit the miters first, then cut the biscuit slots. The photo below left shows how to cut biscuit slots in a profiled molding. On new doors and windows that are perfectly square, some carpenters cut and assemble the casings with biscuits and then nail the assembly to the wall after the glue dries. Or you can use the technique we show here and add the biscuits as you go.

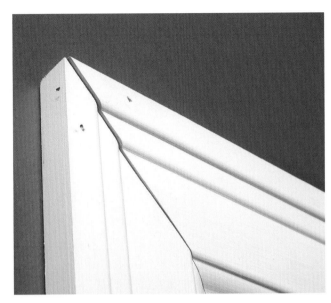

PROBLEM: *JOINTS OPEN WHEN NAILED*
Perfect-fitting miters can become misaligned as you nail them to the wall.

BACK OF MOLDING

SOLUTION, STEP 1:
CUT BISCUIT SLOTS
Clamp the molding (face down if it has a profile) and cut a slot with the biscuit joiner. Cut a biscuit slot in the same location on the other molding.

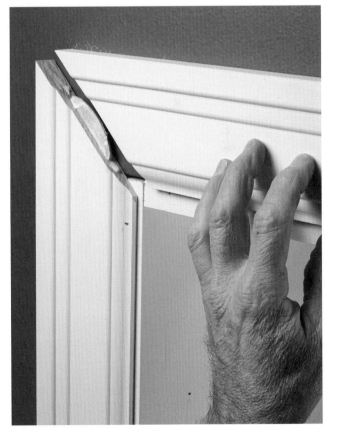

SOLUTION, STEP 2:
JOIN MOLDINGS WITH A BISCUIT
Nail one casing to the jamb and wall. Spread glue on the miter and the biscuit, and assemble the miter.

MEET THE EXPERT

Gary Hakkinen, the sole proprietor of Empire Painting in Lake Elmo, Minnesota, has been painting, staining and varnishing residential homes and commercial buildings for more than 40 years.

FINISHING TRIM

FOLLOW THESE STEPS TO AVOID MISHAPS AND ACHIEVE A BRILLIANT OUTCOME

A beautiful finish is all about proper preparation, a suitable workspace and the right products. We asked Gary Hakkinen, a painting veteran of 40-plus years, to show us his best practices for perfection. Here are a few of his favorite staining, sanding and finishing tips to help you create rich, silky-smooth trim.

1 SAND WOOD FOR EVEN FINISHES

The trim you bought may look perfect, but it likely has imperfections from machining that won't show up until you stain it. Sand every contour and flat area in the direction of the grain with a combination of medium-grit sanding sponges and pads. When necessary, fold 120-grit paper to get into tight cracks.

2 TEST STAIN COLORS FIRST

Try out the stain on a sample of the same wood you plan to finish. You can create your own custom color by mixing two or three stains (of the same type) together. If you go this route, it's important to mix up a batch big enough to finish all the wood. The odds of achieving identical results on the second batch are slim. Keep a little extra on hand for touch-ups and repairs.

3 DRY-BRUSH CREVICES

Stain will pool in cracks. Use a dry paintbrush to remove stain from each piece after it's been completely wiped. Wipe the brush on a clean rag or dab it on newspaper to clean off the stain between strokes.

4 STAIN ONE PIECE AT A TIME

Saturate the wood with a liberal coat of stain using a natural-bristle brush. Wipe off the stain with clean cotton rags in the same order you put it on. That will enable the stain to soak into all areas of the wood for about the same amount of time. Wipe with light, even pressure. Refold the wiping rags frequently so you have a dry cloth for most of the strokes, and grab a new rag whenever one gets soaked. Work on one piece of trim at a time to keep the stain from drying before wiping.

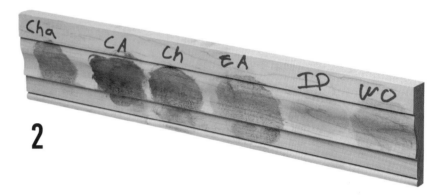

5 APPLY SANDING SEALER FIRST

Sanding sealer is the perfect foundation for the clear coat. It is formulated to dry quickly and has more solids than conventional clear coats, making it very easy to sand. And varnish adheres better to a well-sanded, sealed surface. Pick a sealer that's designed for the overlying finish, preferably the same brand. After the sanding sealer dries, sand it with fine-grit sandpaper and sanding sponges. Remove dust with a tack cloth.

6 USE LONG STROKES FOR A SMOOTH FINISH

If you can, arrange your trim boards in such a way that after you brush on the desired amount of finish, you can make your last couple of strokes in one continuous pass. That will ensure no overlap marks. If you do end up with imperfections after the finish dries, sand them out before the next coat.

7 CLEAN THE ROOM

If possible, do your sanding and finishing in different rooms. All that sanding dust will affect the clear coats. If you have to sand and finish in the same area, do whatever you can to clean the room before applying the sanding sealer and clear coat. If you're in a garage, open the overhead door and use a leaf blower to blow dust outside. Use a shop vacuum on the floor, and damp-mop it so your feet don't stir up dust.

8

9

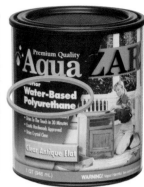

10

Cleanup is easier with water-based products, and the odor isn't nearly as strong.

10 DISPOSE OF THE RAGS

Rags soaked with oil-based products can spontaneously combust and burn down your house. Spread out stain-soaked rags away from other combustible items, and let them dry before disposing of them.

11 POLYURETHANE VS. VARNISH

What's the difference between polyurethane and varnish? The quick-and-dirty answer is that varnish contains a resin and a solvent (oil or water). Once varnish is applied to wood, the solvent evaporates and the protective resin is left behind. Varnish can contain one of a few different resins, and polyurethane is one of those resins.

Varnish that contains polyurethane just goes by the name polyurethane. The upside to polyurethane is that it is tougher than the other varnishes, almost like a plastic coating. The downside is that it can appear cloudy when it's applied too thick, and it's harder to sand between coats.

8 DON'T SKIMP ON THE BRUSH

Buy a 2-in. or 2½-in. brush, and don't buy something cheap. If you take care of it and clean it well, a top-quality brush will last a long time. A cheap brush is more likely to leave brush marks and shed bristles that could get stuck in the finish. China (natural) bristle brushes are the top choice for oil-based products; synthetic are the top choice for water-based.

9 OIL VS. WATER-BASED TOPCOATS

Oil-based finishes are a little more durable than water-based, but the difference isn't nearly as great as it was years ago. Oil will yellow unstained wood more than water-based products will, which can be good or bad depending on the look you're after. Yellowing isn't an issue with stained wood.

Water-based products dry faster, which helps keep dust from settling into the finish, but fast drying may be a disadvantage for slower, meticulous workers.

11

ESSENTIAL CAULKING TIPS

MAKE THE TEDIOUS JOB MUCH EASIER (AND LESS MESSY) WITH THESE 12 POINTERS

Former editor Mark Petersen has emptied at least 5,000 tubes of caulk in his career—that's a bead about 20 miles long! He's filled in gaps so flawlessly that the caulk was virtually imperceptible, but there also have been plenty of times he globbed things up pretty good. To help you get a top-notch caulking job with less frustration, here are a few tips he learned along the way.

1 CHOOSE THE RIGHT CAULK FOR THE JOB

The selection in the caulk aisle at home centers is mind-boggling, but actually choosing the right caulk is pretty simple. Most of the caulk on store shelves is one of four types: elastomeric, polyurethane, latex or silicone. Here's how to make the right choice:

1. **SIDING, WINDOWS AND DOORS:** Polyurethane is the hands-down favorite. It's paintable. It doesn't shrink. It stays flexible. It adheres better than silicone, and it doesn't attract dust and dirt the way silicone does.

2. **ROOFING:** An elastomeric or rubberized product won't dry out in extreme conditions, and it sticks to everything.

3. **INTERIOR TRIM:** If you're sealing gaps and nail holes in trim that's going to be painted, always use latex. It cleans up easily and dries fast. It's also easy to tool—and it's cheap.

4. **KITCHEN AND BATH:** This is where silicone products shine. Silicone tools well. It can be purchased with antimicrobial additives, and it can be easily removed and replaced when it gets grungy.

2 BE PREPARED FOR CLEANUP

Some tubes have air in them and "burp" at the worst possible moment. Some continue to run after you set them aside. The bottom line: There's going to be cleanup. Use mineral spirits to clean up elastomeric and polyurethane. Latex cleans up great with just a wet rag. Silicone is another story. It seems to get on everything. Mark's only tip for cleaning up silicone is that when it does get all over your gloves (and it will), just consider the waterproofing it provides as a bonus.

3 BUY A GOOD GUN

The most expensive gun on the rack isn't necessarily the best. Mark looks for a gun with a cradle. Tubes seem to fall out of the guns with the rails. Also, Mark prefer guns with ratchet action rather than friction action and won't even consider a gun that doesn't have a hook. Forget about gun-mounted tube cutters—they just don't do a good job. Use a utility knife. And if all other things are equal, buy the gun with the longer tube poker. Some aren't long enough to work on every kind of tube.

4 PICK THE RIGHT COLOR

When you're caulking gaps between prefinished siding and trim, use the color of the siding. When working with stained or natural wood, choose

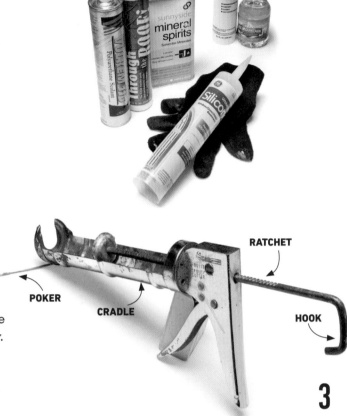

a color a little darker than the wood. A darker color will blend in with the knots and other imperfections.

5 PUSH, DON'T PULL

Always try to push the caulk into the gap rather than drag it over the gap. This greatly increases the odds that the caulk will adhere to both surfaces, because pushing forces caulk into the gap—pulling doesn't. One exception to this rule is when both surfaces are flush. When caulking flush surfaces, if you try to push the tip too hard, it will skate all over the place and you'll have a big mess on your hands.

6 RIDE THE SMOOTH SIDE

When one of the surfaces you're caulking is rougher than the other, always try to ride the tip on the smoother surface (the brick mold in this case). If you ride the middle or the rough surface (siding), the caulking will duplicate the bumps, sometimes in an exaggerated way.

7 CUT TIPS OFF STRAIGHT

You probably learned to cut the tip at an angle. That works OK in some situations, but an angled tip limits the position the caulking gun has to be in. With a straight tip, you can swivel the gun out of the way of obstacles and you're able to caulk right up to an inside corner. And if you have various-size gaps to fill, cut the tip small and do the small gaps first, then cut it bigger for the larger gaps. It won't work the other way around.

8 TOOL IF YOU MUST

Mark isn't a huge fan of tooling. He tries to get the bead right the first time. But sometimes tooling is a necessary evil. Elastomeric and polyurethanes don't tool well—a finger dipped in soapy water is your best bet. Latex is easily tooled, and even if you screw it up, you can wipe it off with a wet rag and start over. The only time Mark tapes off an area is when he is using a silicone product, and the only time he uses a tool other than his finger is when he's working with tape. The DAP Pro Caulk Tool Kit (No. 09125) shown at right is available at home centers for less than $20. And if you get your bead close to the way you want it, Mark's best advice is to leave it alone. It seems the more a bead is messed with, the uglier it gets.

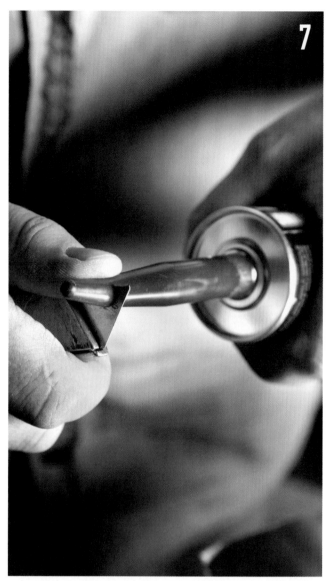

8

9 DON'T USE YOUR WRISTS

Every golfer knows that the best way to keep a putter moving in a straight line and at a consistent speed is to control it with the upper body. It's the same with caulking. Use your upper body, or even your legs, to move the tube along as you caulk. Do not use your wrists.

10 SALVAGE A WET TUBE

The new guy left the case of caulking out in the rain again (it's always the new guy). Those soggy tubes are now going to split open under pressure. Before that happens, wrap some duct tape around the tube. You can also salvage tubes with house wrap tape, masking tape, stretch wrap, shipping tape—it all works. Just use whatever's handy.

11 PULL THE PLUG

It seems you can never seal the cut tip of a partial tube of caulk well enough so that a plug doesn't form in the tip. To remove the plug, try using a large screw with aggressive threads. This method works best with silicone products.

12 MEET IN THE MIDDLE

When you have a long bead to run and you know that you can't get it done in one shot, don't start again where you left off. Instead, start at the other end and meet in the middle. It is hard to continue a bead once you've stopped without creating a glob. Also, try to keep the point where the two beads meet somewhere other than eye level.

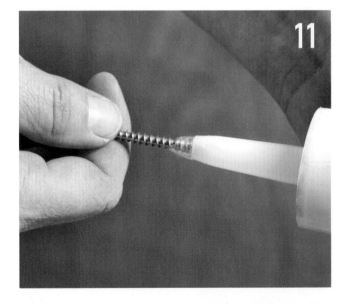

CHAPTER 5

REMODELING, ENERGY SAVING & ELECTRICITY

Do's and Don'ts from Home Inspectors 164
Avoid Framing Mistakes... 167
Leveling 101 172
Replacing a Refrigerator 176
Toilet Shopping Tips 180
A New Tub & Surround.. 182
9 Things Electricians Do in Their Own Homes........ 189
Fire-Blocking Basics 192
Prevent Fires & Cut Your Energy Bill! 196

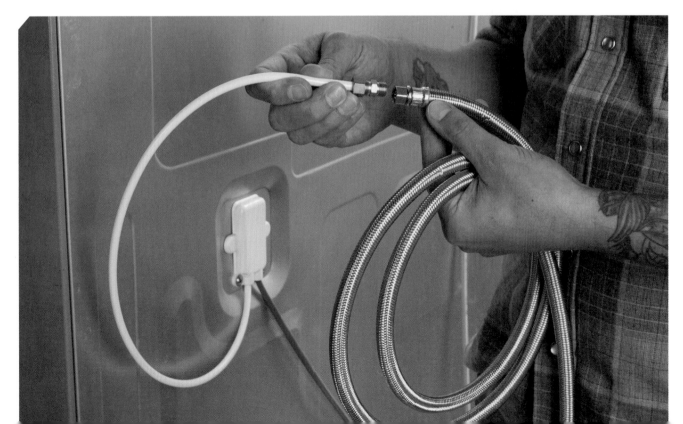

DO'S AND DON'TS FROM HOME INSPECTORS

HOMEOWNERS SOMETIMES MAKE INCORRECT FIXES, BUT WE'LL SHOW YOU THE PROPER WAY TO GET THINGS DONE

As you might imagine, home inspectors encounter all kinds of improvised, dangerous and bizarre fixes. And lucky for us, these inspectors often photograph the odder "repairs" they come across. Here are some photos from a home inspection company, along with some advice on the proper fix.

UNPROTECTED CABLE

OLD SPARKY

There are at least two things wrong with this picture (three if you count the dead mouse). Nonmetallic (NM) cable should never enter a metal electrical box or service panel without the protection of a proper clamp. Eventually the sharp edge on the entry hole will cause the cable sheathing to wear through, creating a short and a fire hazard. In addition, an open hole will let in moisture, bugs and critters, leading to havoc like gnawed wire insulation, nests and electrocuted mice.

THE RIGHT WAY: Use cable clamps or snap-in grommets to protect the cable and hold it in place as it enters any type of electrical box. Unused holes should be plugged with box plugs.

MEET THE EXPERT

Reuben Saltzman (pictured above) is the owner and CEO of Structure Tech Home Inspections, a Minnesota home inspection company. He grew up remodeling homes and learning about carpentry, so he knows his stuff. Check out the company's website, *structuretech1.com*.

GROMMET

CLAMP

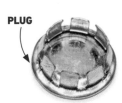

PLUG

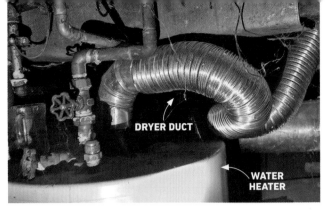

THE PLUMBER'S SOLUTION

This is all too common. The carpenters carelessly placed a floor joist directly under a shower drain that should be marked on the house plans. And then a plumber goes nuts with a reciprocating saw. If you have manufactured I-joists, never, ever cut the top or bottom flanges!

THE RIGHT WAY: You can drill holes up to 1½ in. almost anywhere in the web area (the area between the flanges). Just stay 6 in. away from any end or load-bearing wall. Holes up to 4 in. can be drilled in the middle of the I-joist away from the ends or load-bearing wall.

DR. SEUSS WATER HEATER VENTING

Wow! This looks silly, but it's also downright dangerous. Flexible aluminum dryer duct isn't designed for venting exhaust gases, and this duct doesn't have a continuous upward slope. With this setup, carbon monoxide is likely entering the house.

THE RIGHT WAY: Water heaters must be vented with the solid single-wall or double-wall pipe available in the HVAC aisle at home centers. The vents must always slope upward at least ¼ in. per linear foot and include a draft hood to allow room air to help draw out the exhaust gases.

NOW THAT'S FREEZE PROTECTION!

What you see in the photo below is a freeze-proof sillcock mounted on the *outside* of the house. Not a good idea.

THE RIGHT WAY: In the photo at right, you'll see that the water valve extends inside the house where it's warm. The 12-in.-long pipe "after" the valve is slightly sloped toward the outside so residual water will drain after the valve is closed.

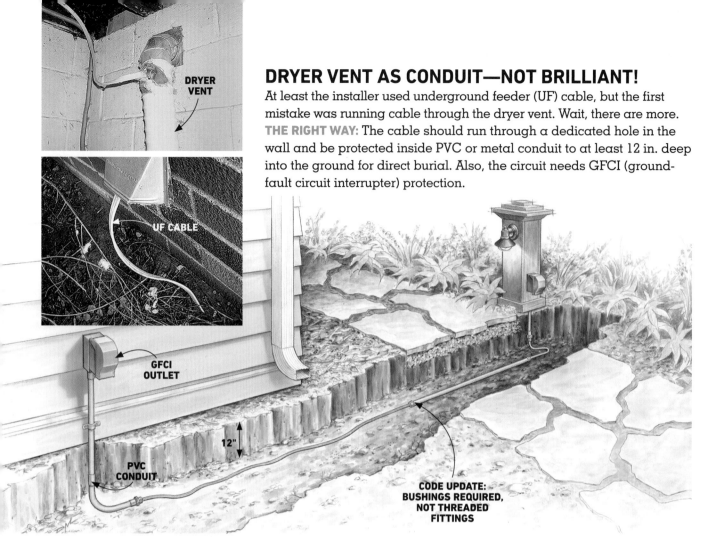

DRYER VENT

UF CABLE

GFCI OUTLET

PVC CONDUIT

12"

CODE UPDATE: BUSHINGS REQUIRED, NOT THREADED FITTINGS

DRYER VENT AS CONDUIT—NOT BRILLIANT!

At least the installer used underground feeder (UF) cable, but the first mistake was running cable through the dryer vent. Wait, there are more. **THE RIGHT WAY:** The cable should run through a dedicated hole in the wall and be protected inside PVC or metal conduit to at least 12 in. deep into the ground for direct burial. Also, the circuit needs GFCI (ground-fault circuit interrupter) protection.

WELL, THAT'S ONE SOLUTION

Before going to the home center to choose a new toilet, know that toilet tanks and bowls vary in height, depth and distance to the wall. Take some careful measurements of the existing toilet while it's still in place. The homeowners here evidently skipped that step.

THE RIGHT WAY: Check the clearance in front of

the bowl and clearances from each side of the tank. Check the distance from the wall to the toilet flange bolts. That's almost always 12 in., but in rare cases you'll find that it's 10 or 14 in. When people run into trouble, it's usually from replacing a standard toilet bowl with an elongated one. They're 2 in. longer than a round bowl and might stop a door or drawer from opening.

WHAT COULD HAPPEN?

Fires caused by dryers occur about 7,000 times in the United States every year, killing 10 people on average. Once a dryer fire starts, the lint inside the duct can ignite, and a vinyl dryer vent line will burn right through and ignite nearby materials.

THE RIGHT WAY: Replace vinyl vents with rigid metal ducts that are less likely than corrugated metal to accumulate lint. Use foil tape rather than screws to join sections because exposed screw shanks also gather lint. Clean the lint from ducts, the exhaust hood and the underside of the dryer cabinet at least once a year.

VINYL DRYER VENT

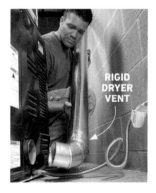

RIGID DRYER VENT

MEET THE EXPERT

Don Sivigny saw a few framing mistakes and code violations in his years as a construction manager, general contractor and building inspector. More recently Don is a construction code representative for Minnesota.

AVOID FRAMING MISTAKES

ROCK-SOLID FRAMING ADVICE FOR A ROCK-SOLID HOUSE

Minor framing mistakes can lead to wavy walls and squeaky floors. More serious mistakes can leave a house vulnerable to high winds, heavy snow loads and earthquakes. We wanted to know which mistakes were the most common and how to avoid them, so who better to talk to than a building inspector? He shared his experiences, his insight and a few horror stories. We walked away with some great tips on how to build a solid house, build it code compliant and build it right the first time.

1 STAGGER THE JOINTS IN THE TOP PLATES

It's best to have one continuous top and tie plate, but that's not possible on longer walls. When multiple plates are necessary, keep top plate end joints a minimum of 24 in. away from tie plate end joints. And keep end joints at least 24 in. from the end of the wall as well. If the two end joints are not kept apart, they create a hinge point, which weakens the wall. But 24 in. is a bare minimum; most conscientious framers prefer at least twice that distance.

2 NAIL TO THE FRAMING

When you're securing the bottom plates of walls to the floor, nail into the floor joists/trusses below. Nailing through the plywood keeps the wall from moving side to side, but expansion and contraction of the roof system could cause the wall to lift if it's not also nailed to the floor joists/trusses. Plus, the nails will be out of the way when contractors need to cut holes in the plates for pipes, ducts and wires. For the same reason, nail top plates to overlying floor joists or roof trusses near studs whenever possible.

3 DON'T FORGET THE CONNECTORS

Structural connectors are designed to hold framing members to the foundation and to one another. They help a building withstand heavy loads, strong winds and earthquakes. Building codes that require structural connectors have been changing as connector technology improves, so make sure to review your local codes and contact your local building department if you still have questions. The foundation straps shown here prevent high winds from blowing these small garage walls off the foundation.

4 INCLUDE FINISHED FLOORING WHEN LAYING OUT STAIRS

The highest riser (step) height cannot be more than ⅜ in. higher than the shortest riser height throughout the entire flight of stairs. Those measurements include finished floor heights. So mock up and plan for the absolute finished floor heights, top and bottom, before you begin doing the math and laying out the stair stringers.

Installing ¾-in.-thick hardwood floors on a ¼-in. subfloor will raise a floor height 1 in. Some carpet, vinyl and laminate flooring options are less than ⅜ in. thick. If you don't account for those height differences, you could fail your inspection, and ripping out stairs is an expensive callback.

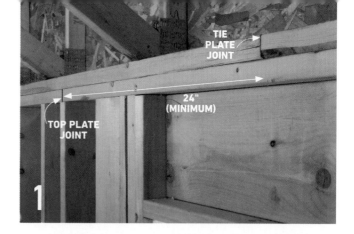

TIE PLATE JOINT
TOP PLATE JOINT
24" (MINIMUM)

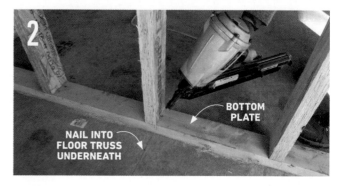

NAIL INTO FLOOR TRUSS UNDERNEATH
BOTTOM PLATE

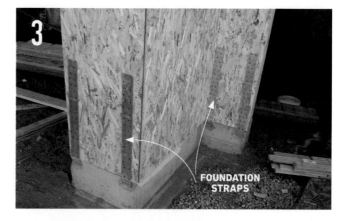

FOUNDATION STRAPS

TEMPORARY TREAD
HARDWOOD FLOOR SAMPLE

TREATED BOTTOM PLATE

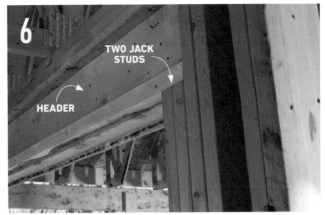

TWO JACK STUDS

HEADER

5 USE APPROVED NAILS ON TREATED LUMBER

Today, treated lumber intended for residential construction is protected with a copper-based preservative system called alkaline copper quaternary (ACQ). Whenever you're working with ACQ lumber, be sure to use only ACQ-approved nails. ACQ treated wood is extremely corrosive to standard framing nails; they will actually dissolve when in direct contact with ACQ lumber. And if there are no nails holding wall studs to a treated bottom plate, foundation bolts/anchors are ineffective. It's also important to use ACQ nails to secure the sheathing to a treated bottom plate.

6 DOUBLE UP JACK STUDS

Jack studs, or "trimmers," are the framing members that support headers. The number of jack studs needed depends on the length (and sometimes the width) of the header. If the blueprints don't specify, a good rule of thumb is to install two on each side if the opening is wider than 6 ft., the typical patio door size.

7 CHECK FOR CROWNS IN THE STUDS

This may seem like a "duh!" tip, but some carpenters don't take the time to check the crown (bow) in every stud before assembling a wall. No one will notice if two studs with a ¼-in. crown are aligned the same way. But if those same studs are installed on opposite sides of the wall, that ½-in. difference will be noticeable on both sides of the wall. Also, the studs may continue to warp as they dry, making the wave even more prominent. When you're assembling walls on the ground, keep the crown side up. If the crowns face down, the studs behave like a rocking chair and make it harder to assemble the wall. Some builders use engineered lumber on walls where cabinets will be located because it's super straight and stable.

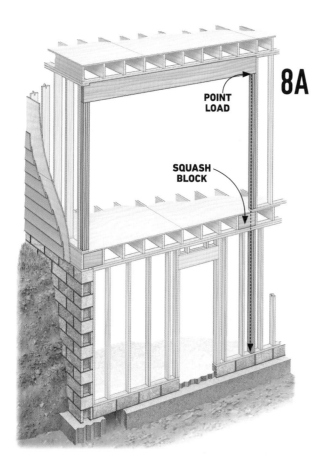

8A

POINT LOAD

SQUASH BLOCK

8B

SQUASH BLOCKS

8 ADD SQUASH BLOCKS TO CARRY LOADS

When a heavy load-bearing beam sits atop a wall, extra studs are needed to help carry that "point load" down to the bottom of the wall. But the story doesn't end there; that load has to be carried all the way down to the foundation. Squash blocks are often required to bridge the gap between a beam-supporting wall and the wall beneath it. Either vertical blocks **(Photo 8B)** or horizontal blocks **(Illustration 8A)** could work.

9

DRYWALL BACKER

9 DON'T FORGET DRYWALL BACKING

Most framing assemblies require extra backers to secure the drywall. Even if you're conscious of installing drywall backers as you build, it's easy to forget a section now and again. Don't treat missing backers lightly; they can be a lot more difficult to install if there are wires, pipes or ducts in the way. Also, a grumpy drywall guy may have to rip off moisture barrier, pull out fiberglass insulation or chip out spray foam in order to hang the drywall. To make sure all the backing is there, one simple trick is to walk from room to room and scan every single wall and ceiling intersection with the thought of hanging drywall. And don't forget the closets.

10

DOOR OPENING

ADHESIVE UNDER PLATE

10 REINFORCE DOORWAY WALLS

A wall that supports a door takes a lot of abuse. Some solid-core doors weigh more than 100 lbs. Add an emotional, door-slamming family member, and you have a door frame that needs to withstand a lot of force. It's important to add extra support to doorway walls, both on the hinge and on the latch side. Do that by applying construction adhesive under the bottom plate on each side of the opening and by adding a couple of 3-in. toe screws.

11 TALK TO THE MASONS ABOUT ANCHOR LOCATIONS

Meet with the masons before they build the foundation. They should know that anchor bolts are required to secure wall plates every 6 ft. on center and within 12 in. from the ends and each side of joints. But sometimes anchors end up where they don't belong, like in door openings or under jack studs. A short meeting to discuss locations of openings and splices could spare you from cutting out misplaced anchors and installing new ones.

12 SHELTER YOUR MATERIALS

A little moisture isn't going to hurt most building materials, but if a project is delayed or you know you're in for a long run of wet weather, cover your materials with a tarp. Long exposure to wet conditions can promote mold as well as cause engineered lumber to delaminate and framing lumber to warp and twist. Plus, no one wants to work with wet lumber! Keep the tarp a little loose at the bottom for air circulation.

PLATE ANCHOR

11

AVOID HEADACHES!
Don't install joists under toilets

All blueprints should indicate the sizes and spacing of floor joists/trusses, but many don't spell out their exact locations. Avoid installing floor joists/trusses directly in the path of large drainpipes and mechanical chases. Toilet locations usually cannot be moved, which means the plumber will have to cut into a joist/truss. This can mean hiring an engineer to design a repair, which takes time and costs money.

12

LEVELING 101

A CARPENTER'S FAVORITE TIPS FOR GETTING THINGS STRAIGHT

Whether you're just hanging a set of pictures or building an entire house, getting things level is an extremely important part of any project. And often there's a tip that will help you get the job done quicker, easier or more accurately. Here are some of our favorites.

USE A SMARTPHONE

This is probably old news to some of you, but your phone can work like a small level. You can download a level app, or your phone may already have a leveling app built into the operating system. You wouldn't want to build an addition with a phone level, but it can for sure come in handy for little leveling tasks around the house.

LEVEL A ROW OF PICTURES

Getting a row of pictures to line up on an invisible line across the top can be tricky, especially if the frames' hanging wires are different lengths. Here's a tip from a professional picture hanger. Hook a tape measure to each wire and pull it tight **(Photo 1 below)**. Measure to the top of the picture frame. On the wall, measure down from a level line and mark the distance at the centerline of your new picture location. Align the hook of the picture hanger with the mark and nail it to the wall **(Photo 2)**. Repeat this process for all of the pictures, and their tops will be perfectly aligned.

MEASURE TO FRAME EDGE

1 MEASURE FROM THE WIRE
Measure the distance from the stretched wire to the top of picture frame.

LEVEL LINE

HANGER MARK

2 MARK FOR THE HANGER HOOK
Measure down from the level line and mark the location for the hanger hook.

TRY A POOR MAN'S LASER LEVEL

If you need to make a long, level line and don't own a laser, try this method. Mark the desired height of your line on the wall. Hold your level at the mark and adjust it until the bubble is centered. Then make a mark at the opposite end of the level **(Photo 1 below)**. Extend the line by stretching a chalk line and aligning it with both marks **(Photo 2)**. If you're working indoors, use dust-off marking chalk, which is easy to erase. Stretch the chalk line and snap it to create a perfectly level line across the wall.

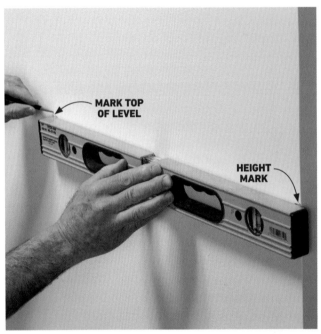

MARK TOP OF LEVEL

HEIGHT MARK

1 MAKE A LEVEL MARK
Align the top of the level with your mark and center the bubble. Mark the opposite end.

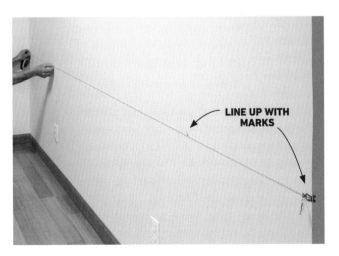

LINE UP WITH MARKS

2 SNAP A LINE
Line up a chalk line with the two marks and snap a line.

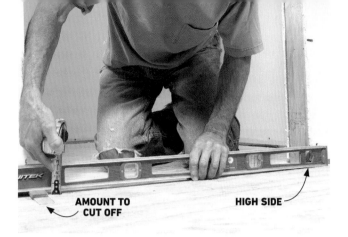

AMOUNT TO CUT OFF · HIGH SIDE

FINE-TOOTH SAW

HIGH SIDE JAMB

1 CHECK THE OPENING
Lay a level across the opening and shim under one end until the bubble is centered. Measure the thickness of the shims.

2 TRIM THE BOTTOM OF THE JAMB
Transfer the measurement to the appropriate jamb and draw a cutting line with a square. Saw along the line to trim the jamb. Now when you set the door in the opening, the top of the jamb will be level.

PRE-LEVEL YOUR DOORJAMBS

If your floors are going to be carpeted, you don't have to worry about a gap under one of the door-jamb sides. In fact, most trim installers raise the doors so they don't drag on the carpet. This is done by resting the jambs on ⅜-in.-thick shims, or temporary scraps of trim. That raises the whole door so it completely clears the carpet. But if the jambs have to fit tight to tile, wood or vinyl floors, you'll have to cut them to fit an out-of-level floor. **Photos 1 and 2** above show how.

CHECK OLD LEVELS BEFORE YOU USE THEM

When levels get beaten up like the one pictured on the right, it's possible that some or all of the vials will be out of whack. And if you have a super cheap and/or older level, don't trust it! Before you do any more level-ing, test the vials for level (horizontal) and for plumb (vertical). Check the leveling vials by placing your level on a flat surface and piling playing cards under one end until the bubble is centered. Now lift the level and rotate it 180 degrees, end for end, and rest it on the cards in the same location. The bubble should still be centered. If it's not, your leveling vial is inaccurate.

To check for accurate plumb vials, rest your level against a wall and note the location of the bubble between the lines **(Photo 1 to the right)**. Then rotate the level 180 degrees, edge to edge, keeping the same end facing up **(Photo 2)**. The bubble should be in the same spot. If not, your plumb vial is off. Levels like the one shown can be adjusted, but many levels can't. In some cases, one set of vials will be good, and you can simply cross out the bad set with a permanent marker to avoid using it. Or toss a bad level and buy a new one.

BUBBLE TO RIGHT

1 REST THE LEVEL AGAINST A CORNER
The bubble on this level is lined up with the right-hand line.

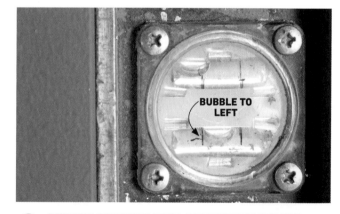

BUBBLE TO LEFT

2 PUT THE OPPOSITE EDGE AGAINST THE CORNER
Now the bubble on this level is lined up with the left-hand line, indicating a bad plumb vial. Adjust the level or mark this vial as bad with a permanent marker.

GET YOUR FIRST ROW OF TILE PERFECTLY LEVEL

Tubs and shower bases aren't always level, so starting your first row of tile against them could throw off your whole job. Instead, make level marks on the wall, line up the ends of a straight board with the marks and screw the board to the wall. Rest the first row of tile on the board for a perfectly level tile job. The distance from the top of the shower or tub to the top of the board should be less than the width of a tile. That way you can custom-cut the tiles to accommodate an out-of-level tub or shower and keep consistent grout lines.

LIFT AN APPLIANCE FOR EASY LEVELING

Here's a two-part tip for leveling appliances. First, use a level with a built-in magnet, like a torpedo level, to free up both hands. Second, lift the front of the appliance with a pry bar to take pressure off the leveling feet. It's much easier to turn the feet when they're off the ground.

FIX CROOKED SWITCHES AND OUTLETS

Here's a handy tip from one of our electrical consultants. The screws that attach an outlet or a switch to the box go in a slot that allows the device to be adjusted. But you don't always have to remove the cover plate to fix crooked switches or outlets. Instead, try pushing a flat-blade screwdriver against the cover plate. Use a screwdriver with a sharp blade. A rounded-over blade will just slip off. You may have to push from more than one corner to fix really crooked devices.

EXTEND YOUR LEVEL

You could use a plumb bob to transfer layout marks from the floor to the ceiling, but extending your level with a straight board works much faster. Just remember to mark on the correct side of the level.

REPLACING A REFRIGERATOR

///

BUY THE REFRIGERATOR THAT FITS YOUR SPACE, NEEDS AND BUDGET

With all the different styles, colors and features available, shopping for a new refrigerator can be fun. But the excitement can turn into a real headache if you get your new refrigerator home and discover that it doesn't fit or that the door won't open far enough to pull out the crisper drawers.

A good appliance salesperson can help you choose the best style and features for your budget and for your family's lifestyle. But here are some tips to consider that probably won't be addressed at the store.

1 *MAKE SURE IT'LL FIT!*

Some appliances, like stoves and dishwashers, are made to fit standard-size openings in your cabinetry, but not refrigerators. You may find one the right width and then discover that it's too tall. To avoid surprises on delivery day, measure the width and height of the refrigerator space and jot it down before you go shopping. Allow at least an inch of extra space on all sides of the refrigerator for easy installation and adequate ventilation. Also make sure the new refrigerator will fit through doorways leading to the kitchen.

CHECK THE ENERGYGUIDE STICKER

Use the EnergyGuide stickers to compare the annual operating costs of the refrigerators you are considering. Also, if you know how much your old refrigerator costs to run, you can figure out how much you'll save by buying a new, energy-efficient model. To do this, multiply the "estimated yearly electricity use" in kWh (kilowatt-hours) from the EnergyGuide sticker by the cost of your electricity per kWh. For example, if the tag shows an annual usage of 630 kWh and your electricity costs 8 cents per kWh, multiply 630 by 0.08 to arrive at an annual cost of $50.40.

SEE IF PARTS ARE AVAILABLE

Before you purchase a refrigerator made in another country, check with your local appliance repair service to see if parts are readily available. Parts for some foreign-made appliances are expensive and hard to get. Also ask about repair costs for the model you're considering.

FIND OUT WHAT YOUR OLD REFRIGERATOR IS COSTING YOU

Buying a new, energy-efficient refrigerator can save you money. But to calculate your savings, you have to figure out what your old refrigerator costs to run.

First, check your electric bill to see what the utility is charging you per kilowatt hour (kWh). This number will likely be 7 cents to 40 cents per kWh depending on

where you live. Next, find out how much electricity your refrigerator is consuming. The most accurate method is to plug your refrigerator into a meter that records how many kilowatt-hours of electricity are consumed while the refrigerator is running. (The Kill A Watt meter shown in **Photo 4** is available at *amazon.com*.)

5

For example, let's say your electricity costs 10¢ per kWh, and your refrigerator consumes 3 kilowatt hours of electricity over a 24-hour period. Multiply the cost of your electricity (10 cents) by the total kWh used (3) to arrive at 30 cents. Your refrigerator costs 30 cents a day, or about $110 a year, to operate. For more accurate results, record usage for a longer period. You can also go to *energystar.gov* and use the Flip Your Fridge Calculator to find the amount of money and carbon pollution you can save with a new model.

5 ASK ABOUT HAUL-AWAY AND DELIVERY

Moving a refrigerator in and out of your house can be a nasty task, especially if stairs are involved. When you buy your refrigerator, check to see if the cost of removing your old refrigerator and delivering the new one is included, and if not, ask what the charges would be. And don't forget that if you have an icemaker, you'll need to connect the water. Be sure to find out if this is included in the delivery cost.

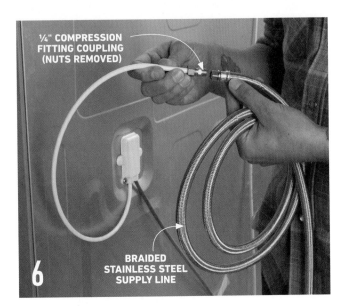

¼" COMPRESSION FITTING COUPLING (NUTS REMOVED)

BRAIDED STAINLESS STEEL SUPPLY LINE

6

6 USE A BRAIDED STAINLESS SUPPLY LINE

Refrigerators with icemakers or water dispensers require a water supply line. Plastic tubing is cheap and easy to install, but it is not rodent-proof and can get brittle as it ages. If it breaks or gets gnawed through, the leak can cause thousands of dollars' worth of damage. Quarter-inch soft copper tubing is a better choice, but it's more difficult to install and prone to kinking.

Braided stainless steel supply lines are the best choice because they're durable and easy to connect. Simply thread the nuts onto each end of your supply valve and refrigerator tubing. Rubber gaskets ensure a leak-free connection, and the stainless steel covering protects the supply line. The cost of stainless steel lines depends on the length. You'll need a ¼-in. threaded male compression fitting at the refrigerator. If your refrigerator doesn't have this connection, you'll have to add a fitting.

7

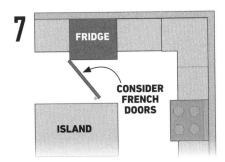

FRIDGE

CONSIDER FRENCH DOORS

ISLAND

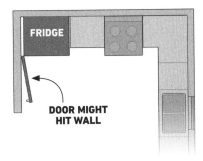

FRIDGE

DOOR MIGHT HIT WALL

7 MAKE SURE DOORS WILL CLEAR

When you're shopping for a new refrigerator, don't forget to plan for how the doors will open within the flow of your kitchen. If you have an island close to the refrigerator, or a narrow kitchen, smaller French doors or double doors may be a better choice. If the refrigerator is against a wall, make sure you have enough clearance so the door can open completely. Otherwise you may have trouble opening interior drawers or removing them for cleaning. And remember that single refrigerator doors can swing in either direction depending on which side the hinges are on. Most refrigerator doors are reversible, but it's much easier to order the refrigerator with the correct door swing than to change it yourself.

8 ASK ABOUT SMUDGE-FREE STAINLESS STEEL

If you hate trying to keep your stainless steel appliances looking shiny, ask about new easy-to-clean finishes. Some brands offer stainless steel look-alikes that have the added advantage of holding refrigerator magnets. Others offer special types of stainless steel that resist smudges and are much easier to clean.

9 DON'T USE A SADDLE VALVE

Most icemaker connection kits include a saddle valve for connecting the icemaker supply line to your home's copper water pipe. Saddle valves are easy to install, but they're unreliable and prone to leaking. Instead, add a tee and a shutoff valve. If the connection isn't concealed in a wall or ceiling, you can avoid soldering by using push-fit connectors and push-fit valves like the ones shown here.

10 PROTECT YOUR REFRIGERATOR

Power surges are fluctuations in voltage that can damage or degrade the electronics in your new refrigerator. Large power surges like those caused by lightning strikes can literally fry electronics, but even small surges originating from motors inside your house can cause cumulative damage to delicate electronics. And, unfortunately, most new refrigerators have expensive, vulnerable circuit boards.

The best insurance against power surges is to replace your refrigerator outlet with a new surge protector outlet. Electrical codes may also require that the new outlet be protected by a GFCI (ground-fault circuit interrupter) and AFCI (arc-fault circuit interrupter). Check with your local inspections department.

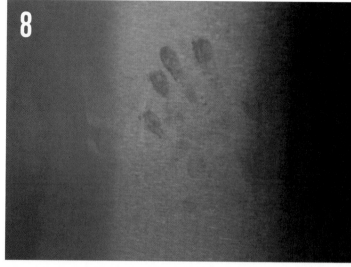

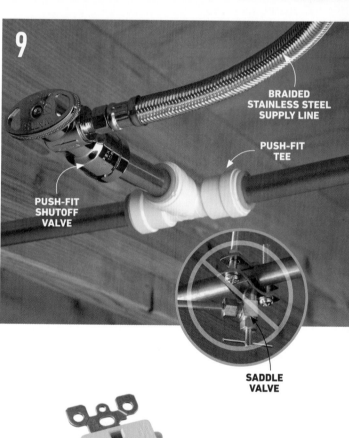

BRAIDED STAINLESS STEEL SUPPLY LINE

PUSH-FIT TEE

PUSH-FIT SHUTOFF VALVE

SADDLE VALVE

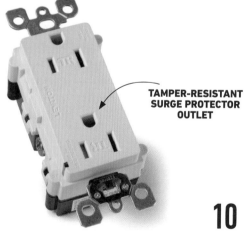

TAMPER-RESISTANT SURGE PROTECTOR OUTLET

10

TOILET SHOPPING TIPS

MAKE THE RIGHT CHOICE FOR YOUR BATHROOM

Sick of your old, leaky, water hog of a toilet and want to buy a new one? You'll find water-efficient toilets with an array of options. Our friends at Maximum Performance (MaP) Testing make a living putting toilets through their paces. John Koeller, a principal at MaP, offers these tips for the next time you go shopping for a toilet.

1 INSULATED TANK

If summers are humid where you live and you don't have air conditioning, you've probably noticed your toilet "sweating" quite a bit. Condensation forms on the outside of the toilet, which can drip down and make a mess or even rot out your floor. Some toilets are available with insulated tanks to prevent condensation problems.

2 BOWL HEIGHT

This is the distance from the floor to the top of the toilet bowl's rim. The standard height for toilets used to be 14 to 15 in. But today you'll find toilets that are 16 to 18 in. high. These are often called "comfort height" or "ADA height" or something similar. The additional height makes getting on and off the toilet easier and is more comfortable for lots of people, especially the elderly. Child heights of 10 to 14 in. are also available.

3 ONE-PIECE VS. TWO-PIECE

A two-piece toilet—with separate tank and bowl—is the most common design found in homes. But one-piece models are available (shown at right is a one-piece toilet from American Standard). While two-piece toilets are less expensive, one-piece toilets often have shorter tanks, are easier to clean and are liked for their smooth, sleek appearance.

4 COST

When it comes to toilets, expensive doesn't automatically mean better performance. In fact, some of the best models tested by MaP are relatively inexpensive, while costlier ones offer only marginal performance.

5 COLOR

Fashion is fickle. Stick with a white or an off-white toilet so you're not stuck with a color you'll hate a few years down the road. (Don't miss the blue one on the opposite page!)

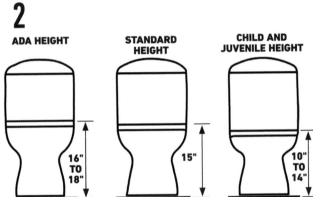

1

2

ADA HEIGHT — 16" TO 18"

STANDARD HEIGHT — 15"

CHILD AND JUVENILE HEIGHT — 10" TO 14"

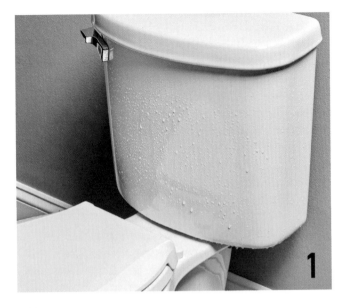

ONE-PIECE TOILET

3

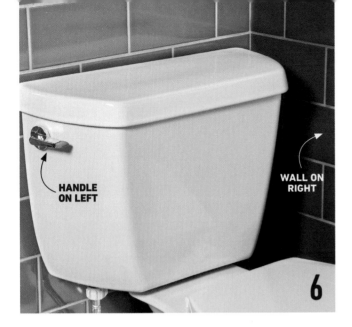

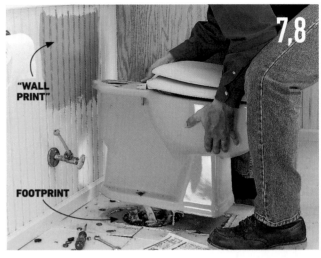

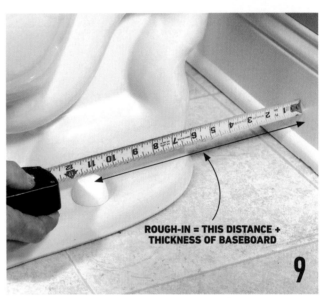

6 FLUSH-HANDLE LOCATION

If you have lots of room above or beside your toilet, this probably isn't all that important. But if your toilet will be right up against a wall or cabinet, choose a toilet with the handle on the opposite side or on the top of the tank.

7 WALL PRINT

If you install a new toilet with a smaller tank, you might have to paint the part of the wall that was covered by the old toilet tank.

8 FOOTPRINT

If you're replacing an old toilet that has a large footprint (the base covers a large floor area), you might have to patch and repair the part of the floor that was covered by the old toilet. You may even have to replace the entire floor before installing a new toilet with a smaller footprint.

9 ROUGH-IN

The distance of the flange bolts—the two bolts that anchor your toilet bowl to the floor—to the wall behind the toilet is known as the "rough-in" dimension (make sure to account for the thickness of your baseboard, paneling or tile). Twelve-inch rough-ins are the most common, but in some older houses you may find 10-in. or 14-in. rough-ins. Be sure to measure your rough-in before you go toilet shopping so you'll know what to ask for.

10 BOWL SHAPE

Most toilets being sold today have either round-front bowls or elongated-front bowls. Round-front bowls are great if space is tight. Elongated bowls have a longer rim—as much as 2 in. longer—and require more space (there have been

cases where doors and drawers couldn't be opened after installation). On the plus side, elongated bowls are generally more comfortable for adult use and help improve hygiene. Check manufacturer websites for dimensions of bowls and measure your space before deciding on the bowl shape.

A NEW TUB & SURROUND

GET A FRESH LOOK AND EASIER MAINTENANCE IN A WEEKEND

You'll be amazed at how a new tub and surround will transform your bathroom. And it's not just about looks: The glossy new surfaces will be easier to clean than an old, worn tub and surround. It's a big job, but if you plan it well, round up all the materials and work hard for a couple of days, you will be able to do it in a weekend.

START WITH AN HONEST ASSESSMENT

Here's the brutal truth about surrounds: It doesn't matter whether your existing walls are in pristine condition or are water damaged; they have to come down before you install a new unit. You simply can't glue or mount a new surround over existing walls. Doing so is a recipe for trouble down the road. And, since you're already investing the effort to rip out the walls, consider replacing the tub and faucet at the same time. It's much easier to replace them when you're already down to bare studs than to tear the walls out a second time years from now. Plus, if you buy a tub/wall combo, the two will match perfectly.

In addition to the cost of a tub/surround combo, plan to spend a bit more for a new brass/chrome overflow and drain kit (plastic/chrome are less expensive). We won't cover the plumbing steps in detail. Go to *familyhandyman.com* and search for "faucet" and "tub drain" to see how to replace a faucet and drain assembly. Most DIYers can easily handle the overflow and drain installation.

MEASURE AND PLAN

Carefully measure the length and width of your existing bathtub. Add about ¾ in. to your measurements to account for the thickness of the old wall surround or tile and cement backer. Then order the new tub/surround combo that's closest to your measurements. Be sure to get a tub with an equally large footprint or plan to replace the flooring. The tub/surround combo we chose is a four-piece design **(Figure A)**.

REMOVE THE WALLS AND TUB

Turn off the water at the main shutoff before removing the faucet hardware. Then remove the faucet handle, trim and spout **(Photo 1)**. If you're leaving the old faucet valve in place, you can turn the water back on after the trim pieces are off.

Next, locate and remove the plumber's tub access panel so you can remove the drain. Find the access

1 REMOVE THE PLUMBING TRIM

From the drain to the showerhead, it all has to come off before you can tear out the old tub and surround. To avoid damage, remove the showerhead even if it's above the surround. You can reuse the faucet, but this would be the perfect time to replace it.

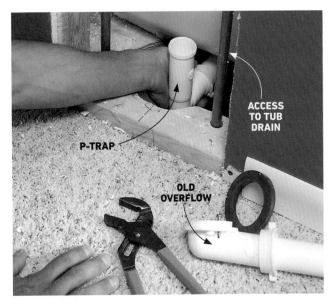

2 DISCONNECT THE DRAIN

Loosen the compression nuts to the overflow and drain assembly. Then remove the overflow pipe from the P-trap. If you can't remove the old compression nuts, cut off the entire overflow and drain with a reciprocating saw. Place tape over the trap opening to keep out demolition debris.

WHAT IT TAKES	
TIME A full weekend	**COST** $100 to $600 for most styles
SKILL LEVEL Medium. The job requires basic plumbing and carpentry skills.	
TOOLS Hand tools, safety gear, reciprocating saw, drill and hole saws, caulk and a caulking gun	

Figure A *Tub and Surround*

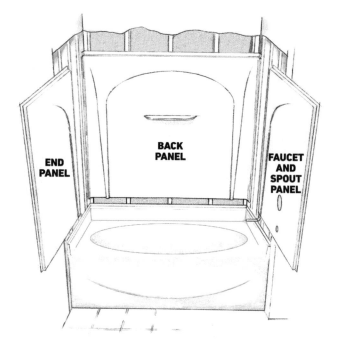

Figure B *Typical Bath Drain*

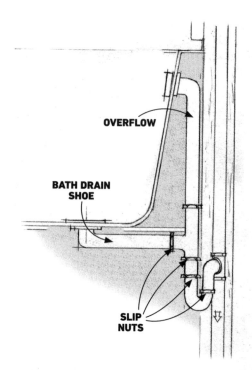

panel in the room or closet directly behind the tub drain. Or, remove the drain from an open ceiling directly below the tub drain. Loosen the compression slip nuts and remove the overflow, P-trap and bath drain shoe **(Photo 2 and Figure B)**. If the connections are stuck, cut them with a reciprocating saw and replace with new plastic drain parts once the new tub is in place.

Spread thick canvas drop cloths over the bathroom floor, sink and countertop. Then don eye protection, leather gloves and a dust mask, because this next part is really messy. Refer to the rough-in measurements for the new surround. Add 1 in. to the measurements, then mark the old drywall and cut through it with a utility knife **(Photo 3)**. Slice through all the caulked seams in corners and where the surround panels meet the tub. You can use a drywall saw as long as you make shallow cuts to avoid hitting water pipes or wiring in the stud cavity.

Next, remove the surround walls and drywall. Start at an outside corner and pry out both the surround and the drywall **(Photo 4)**. Once you get a small section of drywall and surround out, grab just the surround and peel it off the drywall. Then remove the remaining drywall.

Now you're ready to remove the old tub. Slice through any caulk along the edge where the tub meets the bath flooring. Then use a jigsaw or a

3 CUT THE DRYWALL

Score a line about 1 in. larger than the "rough-in" dimensions of the new surround. Then continue slicing through the drywall with a utility knife until you reach the studs.

RIP OUT THE OLD SURROUND

4 Sink a hammer claw into the drywall at a corner and pry the drywall and surround away from the studs. Then pull just the surround away from the drywall to peel it off the drywall.

REMOVE THE TUB

5 Cut an angled piece off the tub apron so you can lift it straight up. Fiberglass or acrylic tubs are easy to cut with a jigsaw. Wear eye protection.

reciprocating saw to cut a chunk out of the plastic/fiberglass tub apron and remove the tub **(Photo 5)**.

If you have an enameled steel tub, remove the remaining drywall from the faucet and end walls. Then get someone to help you roll the tub out and carry it out of the bathroom. If it's cast iron, break it into pieces first—it's too heavy to remove intact. Cover it with a tarp to stop flying shards. Use a sledgehammer and aim for a lower corner of the apron. Once you break the first chunk, the rest of it will be easier to break. Continue breaking away small chunks until you can move the tub.

CLEAN UP, ADD NAILERS AND CHECK THE APRON GAP

Remove all nails and screws left in the studs. Replace any moldy insulation and scrub moldy surfaces with a mold cleaning and remediation product (Concrobium is one brand). Replace any rotten wood. Let the area dry thoroughly before replacing the insulation and vapor barrier. Then add nailer studs to the end wall **(Photo 6)**. Hold off on adding nailers at the drain end until the new tub is in place—you may need the extra stud cavity space to help you maneuver.

Dry-fit the tub; check the area where the tub apron (outer edge) meets the existing floor. Trace the tub apron outline and cut the existing flooring material to get a contoured fit. If the new tub is smaller than the old footprint, cut away just enough flooring to patch in solid-surface material after the tub is securely set in place (use silicone to glue the strips in place).

ADD NAILERS

6 Slide the new nailers behind the drywall. Screw them to the bottom plate and drive screws through the drywall into the nailer. The nailers provide a fastening surface for the new surround and drywall filler strips.

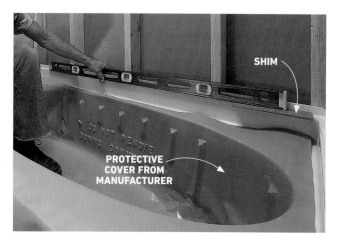

7 LEVEL THE TUB

Place a level on the tub rim and insert shims until it's level. Then move those shims under the tub feet and tack them into place. Recheck for level again and make any final adjustments.

Once you've dealt with the apron/flooring gap, toss a clean canvas drop cloth into the tub to protect the finish (if the new tub doesn't come with a protective covering). Then lay a 4-ft. level on the tub flanges and add shims under the level to determine how much the tub must be shimmed (Photo 7). Tack or hot-glue hardwood or plastic shims under the tub feet to prevent shifting when you set the tub into place. Don't try to level the tub by raising it and attaching the flange to the studs—the flanges aren't designed to bear weight. And don't use softwood shims—they'll crush under the weight of a full tub and you'll wind up with a gap between the tub and the walls.

Apply a bead of clear silicone around the tub drain opening and mount the new drain and drain shoe. Then follow the manufacturer's directions for prepping the floor. Some tubs must be set onto a wet mortar base, while others just install on top of a stapled felt pad. Once you've prepped the floor, move the tub back into place and check for level one last time. Make final adjustments with additional shims. Then secure the tub flange to the studs using the recommended fasteners (Photo 8).

INSTALL THE NEW SURROUND WALLS

Set the back section of the surround on the tub rim, holding it in place temporarily with a nail above the top flange. Then dry-fit the side panels and check for gaps. Shave down any warped or out-of plumb studs so the panels fit squarely on the studs. Shim out any low areas.

8 FASTEN THE TUB

Set heavy cardboard below the nailing flange to protect the tub in case you swing and miss the mark. Then secure the flange with nails, screws or clips as required by the tub manufacturer. To avoid cracking the tub, shim any gaps between the studs and the flange.

9 CUT PLUMBING OPENINGS

Cut the faucet and spout openings from the finished side of the surround with hole saws. Or drill a starter hole on the finished side and cut the hole from the back using a jigsaw.

Next, measure from the back panel or corner stud (depending on the manufacturer's instructions) to the centers of the tub faucet and spout. Then measure up from the tub flange and mark the faucet wall. Repeat your measurements before cutting the holes. Then cut the faucet and spout holes with hole saws or a jigsaw (Photo 9).

BACK PANEL

END PANEL

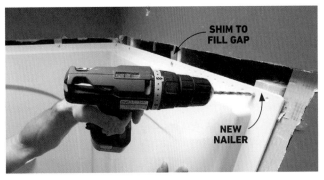

SHIM TO FILL GAP

NEW NAILER

11 SCREW THE PANELS TO STUDS

Secure the wall flanges with the recommended screws. Shim any gaps between the studs and the wall flanges. Don't overtighten the screws or you'll crack the flange.

10 PLACE THE END PANELS

Tip the end panels into place to check how they mate to the back panel. Make adjustments to the back panel. Then secure the panels to the studs.

Some wall surround designs require a bead of caulk where flanges meet; other manufacturers recommend caulking the gaps after the walls are in place. However, some products feature caulkless corner and tub seals. Refer to the manufacturer's installation instructions to determine whether your kit requires caulk, the type of caulk to use, and where and when to apply it.

Center and secure the back wall first. Then apply caulk where needed and set the end panels in place **(Photo 10)**. Tap with a rubber mallet to make final adjustments. Secure all the panels to the studs with the fasteners specified by the manufacturer **(Photo 11)**.

FINISH THE WALLS AND PLUMBING

If you plan to tile around the new surround walls, fill the gap between the wall flanges and the old drywall with either ¼-in.- or ⅜-in.-thick tile backer board **(Photo 12)**. However, if you plan to tape and paint, fill the gaps with water-resistant wallboard and tear-away drywall bead. Then apply joint compound and sand. When you're done, simply tear off the bead and you'll have an attractive edge meeting the surround walls.

Finish the job by installing the drain, trap and overflow. Then reinstall the faucet trim and handle and the tub spout **(Photo 13)**. Caulk any tub and wall gaps as recommended by the manufacturer.

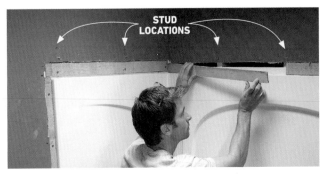

STUD LOCATIONS

12 PATCH THE GAPS

Cut tile backer or water-resistant drywall to fill in along the surround. You can hide the filler strips with tile as we did, or you can cover them with drywall tape, coats of joint compound and paint.

CAULK BEHIND TRIM

CAULK BEHIND SPOUT

13 INSTALL THE PLUMBING TRIM

To prevent leaks, apply silicone caulk under the drain ring and behind the faucet trim and spout.

SHOPPING FOR A TUB AND WALL SURROUND KIT

Tubs and surrounds come in all types of materials and price ranges. They all have a hard shiny surface, but they differ in stiffness, repairability and projected longevity. We divided them into three material categories and price ranges. The first two categories are the most popular.

PREMIUM COMPOSITES AND SOLID-SURFACE: MOST EXPENSIVE

STERLING ENSEMBLE TUB/SURROUND COMBO

Premium composite tub and surround combinations offer caulkless seams and more realistic tile and texture patterns. Solid-surface panels offer the largest selection of styles, including faux granite, quartz and marble. You can order matching solid-surface trim kits that eliminate the need for tile around the edge. The composite units mount directly to studs with screws and clips; the solid-surface panels glue to either walls or studs. Expect a life span of 30-plus years. Some brands include a lifetime warranty.

Two examples are shown here: above is a Sterling Ensemble tile pattern tub/surround combo

and below is a Swanstone tub surround.

PROS:
- Strongest and most scratch- and chip-resistant of materials
- Most realistic tile and texture patterns
- Longer life (30-plus years; some with lifetime warranty)
- Caulkless designs eliminate recaulking
- Scratches and chips can be repaired

CONS:
- More expensive
- Harder to cut
- Some models require a mortar bed under the tub
- Requires a special order at most home centers

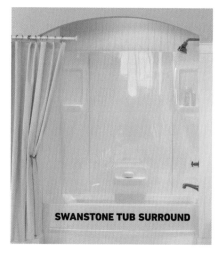

SWANSTONE TUB SURROUND

FIBERGLASS AND COMPOSITES: MIDDLE OF THE ROAD

In this category, you get sturdy shelves and overall stiffness, plus a more durable surface. Fiberglass units are stronger and far more chip- and scratch-resistant than the least-expensive. Composite surrounds are the strongest and have the longest projected life span. Most mount directly to bare studs with screws, nails or manufacturer-provided clips, but a few can be glued to a clean,

smooth surface. Add a few hundred dollars for a matching tub.

PROS:
- Affordable
- Easy to install
- Longer life (15 to 20 years)
- Composite has tighter corner radii, so shelves can be molded right into corners to open space
- Light scratches can be repaired

CONS:
- Fiberglass units have wide radius corners so shelves must be located on the back wall

ACRYLIC-SURFACE PLASTIC SURROUNDS: LEAST EXPENSIVE

These models all have the same surface layer but vary in stiffness. The lowest-priced units are just flat sheets of acrylic-capped polystyrene that you glue to moisture-resistant drywall. Spend a bit more for tile patterns, molded shelves and soap dishes. But since they're made from the same thin material, they can be pretty flimsy.

For more money you can get stiffer acrylic-capped ABS plastic. The best models in this category include fiberglass reinforcement to make the shelves stiff. The lowest-priced units are popular because they fit a tight budget and are fine for low-use showers. But for most bathrooms, we suggest you buy a fiberglass-reinforced unit.

PROS:
- Low cost
- Usually in stock at home centers
- Easy to cut and drill

CONS:
- Scratches and chips happen more readily than on other surfaces and can't be repaired
- Shortest life (10 to 15 years)
- Back shelves intrude into space

9 THINGS ELECTRICIANS DO IN THEIR OWN HOMES

FOLLOW THE SAME UPKEEP GUIDELINES AND BEST PRACTICES AS PRO ELECTRICIANS

Just flipping a light switch, plugging in a toaster and charging a smartphone are simple electrical tasks that are not risky. But your home's electrical system is complex and potentially dangerous, says Christopher Haas, owner of Haas & Sons Electric in Millersville, Maryland. According to him, electrocution occurs more frequently with 120 volts of electricity—the standard in a home—than any other level of voltage.

"And, unfortunately, home electrocution claims lives every single year," Haas says. "So don't think of it as 'just' 120 volts—think of it as something that could permanently injure you."

How can you keep yourself safe while also keeping your lights, outlets and appliances in good working order? Start by following these nine rules professional electricians always follow in their own homes.

1 USE VOLTAGE TESTERS WITH DISPLAYS

Naturally, professional electricians always check the voltage before they start working with wires—and so should you! But they don't use any old voltage tester. "I personally recommend [that] people always use a tester with a display, whether it be digital or analog," says Jake McKusker, general manager of McKusker Electric in Mead, Colorado.

A full display, he says, is better than pin-style testers that only indicate the presence of voltage without giving specifics. If the voltage is low, a pin-style tester might not "read" it—but you could still get shocked. Digital and analog voltage testers with displays will let you know exactly how many volts of electricity are running through wires, so you'll know whether it is safe to proceed. If it turns out your wire is "live," you can stop, troubleshoot and avoid electrical shock.

2 WEAR SHOES WITH RUBBER SOLES WHEN WORKING WITH ELECTRICITY

If you step in water or slip and contact a live wire, it's possible you'll get shocked. To stay safe, electricians wear closed-toe shoes with rubber soles, whether on the job site or while doing electrical upgrades at home. "A thick rubber sole helps insulate you from grounding out," McKusker says. Wear protective gloves and other safety gear too.

3 MAINTAIN THE ELECTRICAL PANEL

If you have stacks of boxes, shelving or stuff stacked in front your electrical panel (also known as a circuit breaker or breaker box), clear the area.

"Your electrical panel should be clean and accessible," says Dan Mock, brand manager for Mister Sparky, a national electrical services franchise. Blocking access to the panel, he says, makes it more difficult if you, or the fire department, need to access the panel quickly. Electrical malfunction results in 51,000 fires each year, according to the Electrical Safety Foundation International. Sometimes those fires originate in the electrical panel.

Furthermore, it's vital to make sure all the switches on your electrical panel are properly labeled and kept "on," Mock says. If you're unsure about the labels, consider calling an electrician to help sort it out. And don't ignore a breaker that is constantly tripping. That's a sign of a short circuit or some other problem that needs to be addressed immediately.

4 TEST GFCIs MONTHLY

You probably know that electricians always use ground-fault circuit-interrupter (GFCI) outlets outdoors and in specific indoor areas of the home, such as bathrooms, kitchens, laundry rooms and crawl spaces. But installing the GFCI is just the beginning.

GFCIs need to be tested regularly to be sure they function properly, says McKusker. He advises testing them once a month or on the manufacturer's schedule. In most cases, to conduct the test, you simply press the "test" button on the outlet. Here are the basic instructions:

■ Plug an appliance into the outlet. A hair dryer or lamp works well for testing.
■ Turn on the appliance and press the (usually red) test button.
■ If the GFCI is working properly, the appliance will "trip"—meaning electricity will stop flowing to the appliance and the test button will pop out. "If it trips, it is working correctly," McKusker says. "If it doesn't trip, that is a big indicator that you shouldn't use it." McKusker says a GFCI that doesn't trip needs to be replaced immediately.

If you have a new GFCI that keeps tripping, the device you are plugging into it could be the culprit. Try another appliance to be sure, then replace that faulty hair dryer, lamp or toaster.

5 AUTOMATE AS MUCH AS POSSIBLE

Electricians know that devices like programmable thermostats, lighting timers/motion sensors and electronic door-locking systems (including those that are smart/Wi-Fi enabled) offer much more than convenience. They also offer a sense of security and save money and energy. For example, a programmable thermostat can potentially reduce heating

and cooling costs by up to 10%, according to the U.S. Department of Energy.

Lights with timers and motion sensors allow you to make sure lights are not left on unnecessarily. McKusker says he sometimes installs motion sensor lights in kids' rooms, because kids are notorious for leaving lights on. That's bound to cut your monthly power bill.

Motion sensors and timed lighting also offer a sense of security. You'll know your outdoor lighting will come on, for example, if someone is creeping around in your yard late at night. Automatic/smart door locks let you unlock your door from your driveway, and some can even monitor the arrival and departure of family members.

"Once people use this type of technology, they generally don't go back," says Mock.

6 USE THE CORRECT LIGHTBULBS

When the bulb in your favorite lamp or fixture burns out, don't just grab the first replacement bulb you can find. "Make sure you put the correct wattage bulb into the fixture," says McKusker.

If you use a 100-watt bulb in a light fixture that's designed for 40 watts, McKusker says you will essentially "cook" the fixture. This will degrade the wires and create a fire hazard. The extra light output is not worth the risk! On the other hand, a bulb with wattage that's too low is likely to leave you sitting in a room that's darker than you want. Your lamp or fixture should have a sticker or printed text telling you how many watts are required.

7 CHECK CARBON MONOXIDE AND SMOKE DETECTORS REGULARLY

You're probably aware that you're supposed to check the batteries in your smoke and carbon monoxide detectors regularly. But do you actually do it? "Most people don't test them until they start chirping," says McKusker. Electricians, however, are good about keeping up with this task, because they know the stakes are high if they put it off. Namely, you might sleep through a fire or fail to recognize a carbon monoxide leak. The rules, which apply to all smoke and CO detectors (even those that are hard-wired into your home's electrical system), are straightforward:

■ Check your smoke detector and CO detector batteries once a month.

■ Replace the batteries once a year, even if they still seem to be working.
■ Replace the entire unit every 10 years because the devices are designed to last only a decade.

8 USE OUTLETS WITH INTERNAL USB PORTS

If you're like us, you probably have USB power adapters to charge your phone, tablet and other devices cluttering the electrical outlets all over your house. Not only do these adapters take up valuable outlet space, they're also easy to misplace.

Electricians know the secret to avoiding the hassle—they install electrical outlets with the USB ports built right in. This means you don't have to choose between charging your device and turning on a lamp, and you won't have to worry about finding an adapter. "All you have to have is the cord to plug it in," says McKusker.

9 RESPECT ELECTRICITY

Finally, and most importantly, electricians understand that electricity is powerful, so they treat it with respect. This means always following code and safety guidelines, Haas says, and understanding that shortcuts are never an option. Shortcuts, he says, can quickly lead to injury.

As a homeowner, you can respect electricity by checking and double-checking to make sure the power is off before you start working with your electrical system. And don't even attempt electrical projects unless you are 100% confident in your knowledge and skills. If there's any doubt, call a pro.

FIRE-BLOCKING BASICS

///

HOLES AND GAPS IN CEILING AND WALL CAVITIES ALLOW A FIRE TO SPREAD RAPIDLY. HOLES ALSO ALLOW AIRFLOW, WHICH FEEDS A FIRE. SEALING THESE GAPS SLOWS OR MAY EVEN STOP THE SPREAD OF FLAMES, SMOKE AND GASES.

Fire blocking aims to prevent or at least slow the vertical movement of flames, smoke and gases by sealing off concealed spaces like stud cavities and soffits. Smoke and gases readily travel horizontally as well, so preventing horizontal air movement, such as within a dropped ceiling, has its own name: draft stopping.

Code requirements for adding fire blocking and draft stopping apply mainly to new construction. But if you're planning on finishing a basement, putting on an addition, remodeling a room, or just running pipes or wires through a plate, you'll need to include fire blocking.

Here we will show you the most common fire blocking applications so you can apply the principles to your project.

AIRFLOW

AIRFLOW

MEET THE EXPERT

Don Sivigny, with decades of experience as a construction manager, contractor, inspector and code educator, has seen his fair share of framing errors and code violations.

THE PROBLEM
Flames spread easily through holes and gaps in wall or ceiling cavities. The airflow through the gaps adds more oxygen to feed the fire.

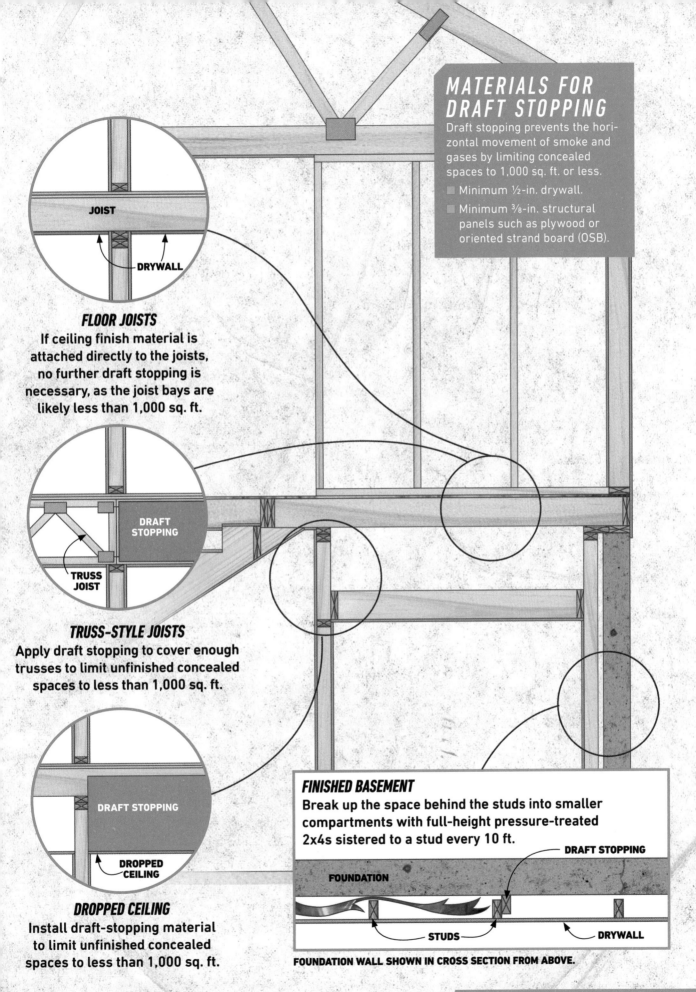

JOIST

DRYWALL

FLOOR JOISTS
If ceiling finish material is attached directly to the joists, no further draft stopping is necessary, as the joist bays are likely less than 1,000 sq. ft.

DRAFT STOPPING

TRUSS JOIST

TRUSS-STYLE JOISTS
Apply draft stopping to cover enough trusses to limit unfinished concealed spaces to less than 1,000 sq. ft.

DRAFT STOPPING

DROPPED CEILING

DROPPED CEILING
Install draft-stopping material to limit unfinished concealed spaces to less than 1,000 sq. ft.

MATERIALS FOR DRAFT STOPPING
Draft stopping prevents the horizontal movement of smoke and gases by limiting concealed spaces to 1,000 sq. ft. or less.

- Minimum ½-in. drywall.
- Minimum ⅜-in. structural panels such as plywood or oriented strand board (OSB).

FINISHED BASEMENT
Break up the space behind the studs into smaller compartments with full-height pressure-treated 2x4s sistered to a stud every 10 ft.

DRAFT STOPPING

FOUNDATION

STUDS

DRYWALL

FOUNDATION WALL SHOWN IN CROSS SECTION FROM ABOVE.

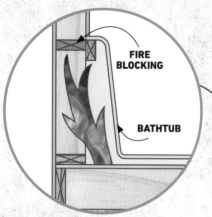

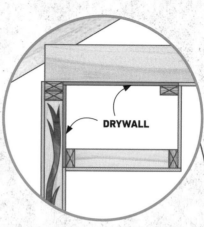

SOFFITS

Soffits provide an easy path to floor and ceiling joist bays if they're not fire blocked. Without a soffit, the top plate provides fire blocking.

DROP-IN TUBS

If the wall behind a drop-in bathtub is finished, no blocking is required. If the wall isn't finished, install 2-by material between the studs, flush with the top of the tub. Insulation batting in the wall extending at least 16 in. above the tub is also sufficient.

SOFFIT WITH A FINISHED BACK

If the wall and ceiling were drywalled before the soffit was put in, no further fire blocking is needed.

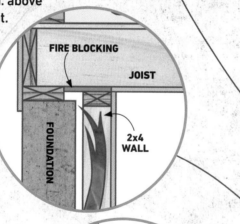

BASEMENT WALLS

The gap behind a 2x4 wall has to be sealed off from the joist bays above the wall.

LANDING

Install blocking in stud cavities above a landing over an unfinished space.

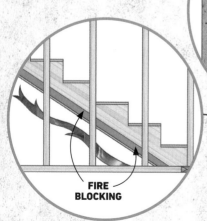

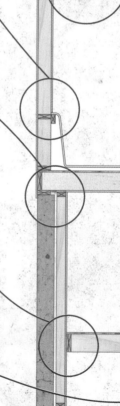

STAIRS ABOVE UNFINISHED SPACE

Angle-cut 2-by fire blocking to fit between the studs on the outside of the stair stringers.

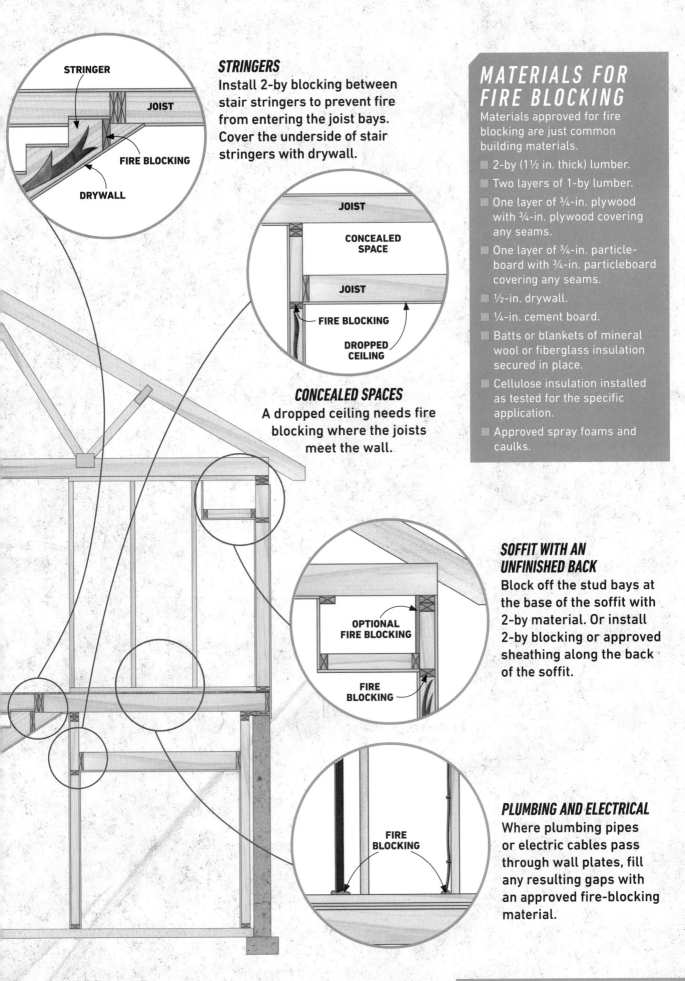

STRINGERS

Install 2-by blocking between stair stringers to prevent fire from entering the joist bays. Cover the underside of stair stringers with drywall.

STRINGER

JOIST

FIRE BLOCKING

DRYWALL

CONCEALED SPACES

A dropped ceiling needs fire blocking where the joists meet the wall.

JOIST

CONCEALED SPACE

JOIST

FIRE BLOCKING

DROPPED CEILING

MATERIALS FOR FIRE BLOCKING

Materials approved for fire blocking are just common building materials.

▪ 2-by (1½ in. thick) lumber.

▪ Two layers of 1-by lumber.

▪ One layer of ¾-in. plywood with ¾-in. plywood covering any seams.

▪ One layer of ¾-in. particleboard with ¾-in. particleboard covering any seams.

▪ ½-in. drywall.

▪ ¼-in. cement board.

▪ Batts or blankets of mineral wool or fiberglass insulation secured in place.

▪ Cellulose insulation installed as tested for the specific application.

▪ Approved spray foams and caulks.

SOFFIT WITH AN UNFINISHED BACK

Block off the stud bays at the base of the soffit with 2-by material. Or install 2-by blocking or approved sheathing along the back of the soffit.

OPTIONAL FIRE BLOCKING

FIRE BLOCKING

PLUMBING AND ELECTRICAL

Where plumbing pipes or electric cables pass through wall plates, fill any resulting gaps with an approved fire-blocking material.

FIRE BLOCKING

PREVENT FIRES & CUT YOUR ENERGY BILL!

SIMPLE STEPS TO CORRECT DRYER VENT PROBLEMS

On any top 10 list of home fire causes, you'll find "clothes dryer." But it would be more accurate to categorize these disasters as "lint fires." Lint buildup, plus the heating system inside a dryer, is a recipe for fire.

One cause of lint buildup is neglect. A dryer and its vent need to be cleaned out regularly (experts recommend cleaning every year). Another cause of lint buildup is a bad vent. A good vent allows the dryer's exhaust (and lint!) to flow outside easily. A bad vent traps lint. A bad vent also costs you time and money. By restricting airflow, it slows down drying, forces the dryer to work harder and drives up your energy bill. This article will help you recognize and correct problems with your dryer vent. In most situations, the materials cost for a completely new vent system is quite inexpensive.

1 FLEXIBLE VINYL
If you have this type of duct, replace it. The ridges inside impede airflow and trap lint. Worst of all, vinyl is flammable. Some vinyl ducts have a silver coating to imitate metal foil. Don't be fooled.

2 FLEXIBLE FOIL
Like vinyl ducts, these ducts impede airflow and trap lint. Aluminum foil won't burn, of course, but it will quickly disintegrate in a fire. Dryer manufacturers don't recommend foil ducts, and neither do we.

3 SEMI-RIGID METAL
If you need flexible duct, this is the best choice. It has smaller ridges inside for better airflow and less lint buildup. It also withstands fire better than other flexible duct.

4 RIGID METAL
With its smooth, straight walls, "pipe" provides maximum airflow and minimal lint traps. Most pros prefer aluminum; it's easier to cut and never rusts. It also has a smoother surface that catches less lint, according to some experts. But some pros prefer galvanized steel because it's stiffer and available in longer sections at some stores.

TIPS FOR A BETTER DRYER VENT

NEVER USE SCREWS

Join sections of duct with clamps or tape—never screws. Screw tips poking into the duct catch lint.

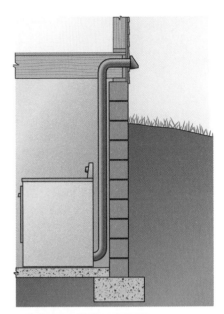

CHECK THE DUCT LENGTH

Longer ducts means more resistance to airflow, and most dryer manufacturers call for a total length of 35 ft. or less (check the owner's manual). But remember this: Each 90-degree elbow counts as 5 ft. So if you need two elbows, for example, the rest of the duct can total only 25 ft. If you need to go longer, install a special dryer booster fan (available online).

USE FOIL TAPE

Duct tape often falls off after months or years. Aluminum foil tape seals perfectly and stays put forever.

PUT SEAMS AT THE TOP

When you start up your dryer, moisture condensation forms inside the cool duct. If the seam on rigid duct faces down, that water will leak out and drip onto whatever is below. But if the seam faces up, the water will stay in the duct and evaporate as the duct heats up.

KEEP "FLEX" RUNS SHORT

Even the best flexible vent material reduces airflow and catches lint. So use rigid metal wherever you can and keep flex lengths to a minimum. Some inspectors and dryer manufacturers allow up to 8 ft. of flex—some less.

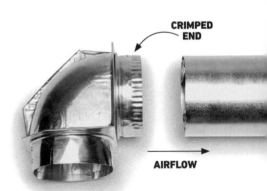

POINT CRIMPED ENDS TOWARD THE AIRFLOW

When you're building your duct system, make sure the crimped ends point toward the airflow direction and the uncrimped ends point toward the dryer. If you get this backward, lint is more likely to build up at joints.

CHAPTER 6

EXTERIOR, LAWN & PAVING

Better Than Wood!.. 200
5 Solutions for a Shabby Deck............................. 205
Build a Low-Upkeep Deck 210
Setting Fence Posts with Expanding Foam 214
Roof Tear-Off 216
Install an Irrigation System.................................... 221
Repair a Buried Cable.. 226
Cures for Top 5 Lawn Problems 228
Working with Bagged Concrete 234
Pour a Perfect Slab.. 238

BETTER THAN WOOD!

MANUFACTURED EXTERIOR TRIM BEATS WOOD IN EVERY WAY

Wood is a troublesome material for exterior trim. It shrinks and swells, rots, warps, and feeds insects. Years ago, builders used wood because that was their only option. But today, you have better choices. So skip the real wood—along with all the headaches—and go for something that looks just as good!

WOOD MOVES, PAINT PEELS

Wood trim expands and contracts with changes in humidity. Paint can flex with that movement for a while. But, eventually, tiny cracks develop. Those cracks let in moisture, which causes more movement, which leads to larger cracks and peeling and rot...you get the idea.

One of the big advantages of manufactured products is that they remain stable when exposed to moisture. That means the paint lasts longer. As all materials do, they move with temperature changes, but that movement is less extreme and easier on the paint than moisture movement. A related advantage of manufactured products is that they don't warp or split like wood. So you don't have to hunt for straight, good-looking boards.

THE BUCKET TEST

We soaked five types of trim in a bucket of water for about a month. That's not a scientific simulation of real-world conditions, and most of these products aren't intended for that kind of punishment. Still, we think the results are worth sharing.

- Cellular PVC and poly ash were completely unaffected—just what you'd expect from products rated for ground contact.
- Composite swelled near the edges but didn't blister or blow apart.
- Engineered wood also swelled a little bit but didn't blister or blow apart.

- Fiber cement seemed unaffected by the water, which surprised us because it's not approved for ground contact. But don't try this at home! Again, this isn't a fair test. But we were very impressed by how well all five products held up. Bottom line, any of these five trim options is likely a great choice for your home as long as you carefully follow the manufacturers' installation instructions, which are available on their websites.

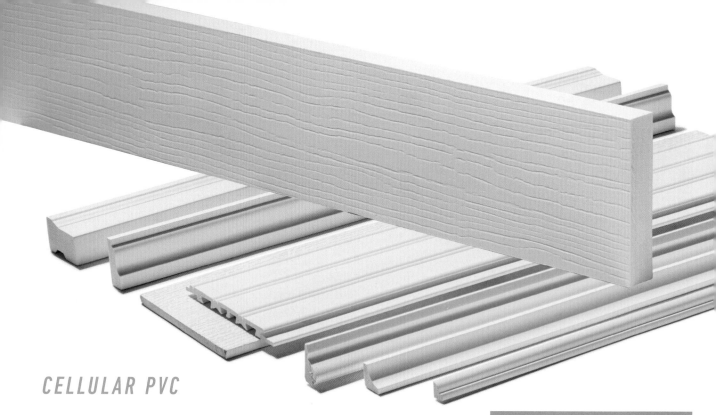

CELLULAR PVC

Because it's plastic, cellular PVC trim will probably last longer than the rest of your house. It is rot- and insect-proof and doesn't absorb water, which makes it a great option for trim that'll get wet a lot. But it's also the most expensive—about twice as much as other manufactured options.

Cellular PVC looks and cuts just like wood and comes in traditional thicknesses and widths. You can work it with regular power tools, blades and router bits. It expands quite a bit along its length when it's hot out or the sun hits it, so it's important to fasten it well with nails or screws, being sure to drive them through the sheathing and into framing members. You'll need to leave ⅛ in. of space for heat expansion per 18 ft. of trim (skip this if it's already hot outside).

Dark paint colors absorb heat and can make expansion problems worse. Some manufacturers recommend using paint with a light reflective value (LRV) of 55 or higher to minimize expansion of the trim when the sun hits it. Detailed installation guides are available on manufacturers' websites.

VOICE OF EXPERIENCE, FORMER ASSOCIATE EDITOR JASON WHITE: I replaced a lot of rotted wood trim on my house a few years ago with cellular PVC. It cuts and routs just like wood—I even replicated some moldings with it using my router table. It smells bad when you cut or rout it, and the shavings stick to your skin. The edges are a bit rough after you rout profiles but smooth easily with hand-sanding. Really long lengths get floppy and are hard to move around. I didn't experience a lot of the expansion problems others have reported, most likely because I used lots of screws. Because it's white, you don't have to paint it if you use white hole filler, but I think it looks much better painted. Scuff-sanding the trim with fine-grit sandpaper helps paint stick better.

HANDYMAN RECOMMENDS: If maintenance-free sounds good to you, especially if you'd like to avoid painting, spend the extra money and go with cellular PVC.

COMPOSITE

This kind of trim looks like medium-density fiberboard (MDF), but it's made to handle weather extremes. It's basically wood fibers mixed with resins with chemicals added for insect and rot resistance. You can cut and rout it just like wood. It comes primed and holds paint very well.

VOICE OF EXPERIENCE, FORMER EDITOR-IN-CHIEF GARY WENTZ: Over a decade ago I replaced my trim with MiraTEC. It has held the paint remarkably well and looks almost as good as new. There's just one trouble spot: Some sloppy flashing work allowed water to puddle against the MiraTEC, which swelled and blistered. Since I was the sloppy flashing installer, I guess I can't complain.

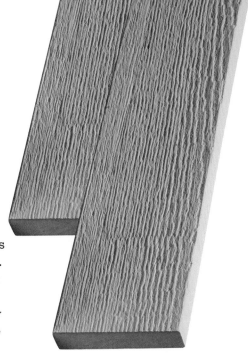

HANDYMAN RECOMMENDS:
If you're looking for affordable trim that'll look great for years, MiraTEC is hard to beat.

WHAT IT TAKES

COST:
A 1x4 costs about $2 per foot at supply stores.

PROS:
Inexpensive. Rot and insect resistant. Minimal expansion in humid conditions.

CONS:
Can be damaged by water; must be protected by paint and caulk. Not recommended for ground contact.

WORKING WITH IT:
Cuts and routs with regular woodworking tools. Prime cut edges before installation.

BRANDS:
MiraTEC

PERFORMANCE:
Holds paint well. Can swell and blister when in direct contact with water for too long.

AVAILABLE AS:
Trim boards. Primed and prefinished, smooth on one side, textured on the other.

ENGINEERED WOOD

This trim looks much like oriented strand board (OSB) on the back side but has far better weather resistance. It's basically compressed wood fibers and resins with a textured shell, giving it the appearance of solid wood. It comes primed, and the boards stay nice and straight during and after installation. It's treated for rot and termite resistance.

VOICE OF EXPERIENCE, FORMER ASSOCIATE EDITOR JEFF GORTON: As good-quality, paintable wood for exterior use has gotten harder to find and super expensive, I've switched to engineered wood for exterior trim. All the boards are long and of consistent quality. No more searching for a straight board with a good-looking face. They're all straight with a surface perfect for painting.

HANDYMAN RECOMMENDS:
If you like being able to find manufactured trim at home centers and not having to pay too much for a good-looking, long-lasting product, this is a great choice.

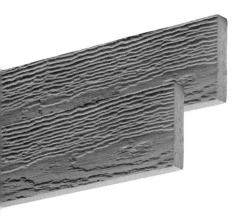

WHAT IT TAKES

COST:
A 1x4 costs less than $2 per foot at home centers.

PROS:
Rot and insect resistant. Nice, straight boards.

CONS:
Mitering of corner and edges is not recommended. Can't rout profiles in it.

WORKING WITH IT:
Install a minimum of 6 in. above grade and 1 in. above rooflines and decks. Cut ends and edges must be primed and painted.

BRANDS:
LP SmartSide

PERFORMANCE:
Minimal expansion and contraction with changes in humidity. Engineered wood takes and holds paint well.

AVAILABLE AS:
Trim and fascia boards, cedar shakes, lap siding, soffit and panels

FIBER CEMENT

This is a masonry-like product containing mostly cement, cellulose fibers and sand. Unlike wood, it resists cracking, splitting, rotting and swelling. It doesn't expand and contract a lot, so paint jobs can last for decades. You can't rout it, however, and dust collection is highly recommended when cutting it. You can cut it with regular carbide blades, but they will dull quickly because fiber cement is very abrasive. Use blades made for fiber cement instead. Hot-dipped galvanized or stainless steel nails are recommended and must be set flush. Field-cut edges must be painted. You can get fiber cement trim primed or prefinished in many colors. You won't find this trim in stock at every home center, but you can special-order it.

VOICE OF EXPERIENCE, FIELD EDITOR TOM DVORAK: Fiber cement trim is relatively easy to work with. The boards cut easily with a regular circular saw blade, but fiber cement blades last longer. Cutting fiber cement is very dusty, so I always do it outside and use a cheap circular saw because it will eventually ruin the saw—at least in my experience. Be sure to blow off all the dust before caulking or painting.

HANDYMAN RECOMMENDS: If you want moderately priced trim that won't need a new paint job for many years, fiber cement is a terrific option.

POLY ASH

This is an interesting product because it's made from coal ash left behind by power plants. Referred to as "poly ash" because it's made of polymers mixed with ash, this trim doesn't expand or contract with changes in humidity or in hot weather, and it's suitable for ground contact. Cut and rout it with regular blades and router bits and install it just like wood. It's rot resistant, and you can even nail near the board's end and not split it. You don't have to prime the cut ends before installing, and you can paint it any color without worrying about heat expansion issues.

VOICE OF EXPERIENCE, NATHAN CHRISTENSON, CO-OWNER OF DOVETAIL RENOVATION INC: We used Boral trim when we needed something that could withstand splashing water. Unlike PVC, it doesn't expand and contract a lot in hot weather, so you can paint it any color. Trim nails and screws work great without blowout, and you can cut curves with a jigsaw and get a clean edge. Long lengths can be a bit floppy if you're moving them around on the flat, so support them to keep them from snapping in two.

HANDYMAN RECOMMENDS: If you like using building materials that contain recycled products and want trim that'll last a lifetime, poly ash might be the answer.

5 SOLUTIONS FOR A SHABBY DECK

//

PICK THE FIX THAT'S BEST FOR YOU

Nothing beats the natural appeal of a real wood deck. But after just a few years of weather and foot traffic, that same wood deck can become an eyesore. To revive it, there are five main paths you can take, and we will guide you through each one.

This article will also help you decide whether to refinish your old decking or step up to an overlay option so you can spend more time enjoying your deck and spend less time taking care of it.

COST: About $400 total for tools, materials and pressure washer rental

LIFE SPAN: Lasts 1 to 6 years

PROS:
- Refinishing makes an old deck look almost like new.
- It is much less expensive than most other options.
- It is far less work than tearing off your old deck boards and replacing them.
- It maintains the natural beauty of real wood.

CONS:
- You'll have to refinish your deck every few years.
- You'll have to scrape or blast off any old flaking finish, and you might be left with a little sanding to do.
- You'll need to replace any rotted wood before refinishing.
- You'll still have to deal with bigger problems such as rot or worn, damaged wood.

OTHER CONSIDERATIONS:
- You'll need to do the job on a cool, dry day.
- Be prepared to spend a couple of weekends refinishing your deck.

SOLUTION 1: CLEAN & REFINISH

The basics of refinishing a deck are pretty straightforward: Strip, clean, stain ... repeat! It's a tough chore that might take you several days to complete, and one you'll have to do every few years to keep your deck looking great. But all that hard work has a huge payoff! When you're finished, your all-wood deck will look almost as good as it did the day it was built. Here are some things to think about before tackling the job.

PRESSURE WASHERS MAKE THE JOB EASIER

A pressure washer does a great job of cleaning your deck and stripping old finishes. Available at home centers in gas or electric models, they can vary widely in price—from about $70 to $1,000—or they're on hand to rent. You can get the job done without a pressure washer, but using one saves a lot of time and labor. For more information on choosing and using pressure washers, search for "outdoor cleaning pressure washers" at *familyhandyman.com*.

SOLUTION 2: DECK RESTORATION COATINGS

Deck restoration coatings are acrylic based and go on like thick paint in two coats. Once dry, the coating is similar in appearance to composite decking (as shown in the above left image where the Rust-Oleum brand was used).

A word of caution about these products: We found many online complaints and even some reports of lawsuits related to peeling of deck coating products not long after application. It's very important to follow preparation instructions from the manufacturer, which might include power washing and application of a prime coat. Bottom line: Read the manufacturer's instructions before use and contact the company directly if you have questions or concerns about whether it'll work for your particular situation.

COST: About $55 per gallon, which covers up to 75 sq. ft. in two coats

LIFE SPAN: Some manufacturers claim 12 years or more; customers say more like five years.

PROS:
- The coating fills in small holes and cracks.
- It is textured for slip resistance.
- It provides excellent UV protection.
- Lots of color (tintable) options are available.
- It goes on easily with a roller and paintbrush.

- It is much cheaper than replacing all your old decking.
- It can be recoated if you follow manufacturer's prep instructions carefully.

CONS:
- Wood can look like plastic after coating.
- Lots of careful prep is involved.
- Two coats are required.
- It is susceptible to scratches from pets, furniture, etc.
- It is prone to peeling if you don't carefully follow prep instructions.
- If it starts peeling, you'll have lots of scraping to do.

SOLUTION 3: REPLACE THE DECK BOARDS

It's not the easiest option, but replacing your wooden deck boards with synthetic decking (composite or PVC) might be your best investment, in both time and money. In just a few weekends and with basic carpentry tools, you can have a stunning deck that looks brand new and will look great for many years.

Costs vary widely for synthetic decking, but expect to pay anywhere from $5 to $10 per square foot. Be warned, however, that synthetic decking requires closer spacing of joists and stair stringers (maximum 16 in. apart), so you might have lots of framing to do.

COST: Varies widely, but generally about $5 to $10 per sq. ft.

LIFE SPAN: Can easily last 20 years or more

PROS:
- Low maintenance—it just needs occasional cleaning.
- It stands up well to heavy traffic.
- It lasts for decades.
- You can install it with screws or hidden fasteners.
- Wood grain patterns are available with many brands.
- Lots of color choices are available.

CONS:
- You'll have to tear off the old decking first—a huge job.
- It's expensive.
- It gets very hot when the sun hits it (especially dark colors and dense boards).
- It doesn't look like real wood (but some brands come close).
- It can be slippery when wet.

OTHER CONSIDERATIONS:
- You'll need a building permit and inspection.
- It's a lot of work to install.
- You'll need a dumpster for all the old material.

SYNTHETIC DECKING OPTIONS

There are three types:
- **Composite.** Lowest cost but the surface isn't as tough or stain resistant.
- **Capped composite.** Composite capped in hard plastic for extra durability. Stain and fade resistant.
- **Solid PVC.** Lighter weight than composite, making it easier to handle. Good for wet areas like docks because there's no organic content that could promote mold. Most expensive option.

COMPOSITE

CAPPED COMPOSITE

SOLID PVC

LIFE SPAN: Decades, depending on material selected

PROS:
- Tiles are super easy to install.
- No fasteners are required.
- Tiles snap together in any direction, allowing you to be creative with patterns and layout.

CONS:
- It will create height changes with steps and at door thresholds.
- You may see old decking in the gaps of the new deck tiles.

SOLUTION 4: DECK TILES

Think of this option as a slipcover for your deck. Instead of ripping out or recoating old deck boards, place new wood or synthetic decking right over an old deck. Several companies, such as HandyDeck (product shown above), make tiles out of composite or exotic woods like ipe that you just lay down and snap together. Plastic grids underneath the tiles allow for airflow, which helps prevent wood rot.

COST: Varies depending on manufacturer and material, but generally $5 to $15 per 12 x 12-in. tile

SOLUTION 5: EXTERIOR FLOOR COVERING

DeckRite is a sheet material that comes on a roll, much like sheet vinyl flooring. It basically turns your old deck into an outdoor floor with no gaps in it and creates a watertight roof for the area beneath your deck. As long as your old deck boards are at least 5/4 thick and structurally sound, you can screw ½-in. pressure-treated plywood right over it and stick the flooring membrane on top. If the deck is really big, it might require multiple sheets, and you'll need to rent a hot air welder from DeckRite to deal with overlapped seams. The cost for all the materials you'll need is similar to that of other solutions listed. Visit *deckrite.com* for more information.

BOB

RANDY

MATT

MEET THE EXPERTS

We asked Randy Moe from Decks Unlimited and Bob Januik and Matt Norden from Precision Decks for some tips on working with low-maintenance deck materials. Altogether, these guys have built more than 1,000 decks, using every material imaginable. Over 10 years ago about half their jobs were wood. Today they install low-maintenance materials on three out of four decks.

BUILD A LOW-UPKEEP DECK

TIPS FOR USING LOW-MAINTENANCE MATERIALS

Your deck should be a place to relax, not a painful reminder of those looming weekends you're going to spend sanding, painting and staining it to keep it looking healthy. So if you are in the planning stages for a new deck, considering alternatives to wood may be a good idea.

You can build yourself a low-maintenance deck with the same tools as you would a wood deck, and using similar techniques. But there are differences between low-maintenance and wood products. We asked our pros for some tips to help DIYers avoid expensive mistakes.

1 BEWARE OF DARK COLORS

Boards with dark colors can get blistering hot when the sun is beating down on them. If you like to go barefoot, consider a lighter color.

2 FLATTEN THE JOISTS TO AVOID A WAVY DECK

Most PVC and composite products aren't as rigid as wood, so they don't bridge imperfections in the framing as well. If some of your joists are higher than others, you might end up with a wavy surface. Our pros stretch a string across the deck joists to detect high spots and then plane them down with a power hand planer. This might seem like a pain, but it takes less than an hour and pays off with a better-looking deck.

3 HIDE THE ENDS

Many PVC and composite decking products are not the same color all the way through, so you'll want to cover the ends. One solution is to "picture frame" the deck by installing deck boards around the perimeter. A picture frame creates a professional look but does require some additional framing. One way to support the perimeter boards is to add an extra joist 5½ in. away from the outside joist and then install a 2x6 on its side between the two joists.

4 PROTECT JOISTS FROM ROT

Pressure-treated lumber is rot-resistant, not rot-proof. Two places our pros often see deterioration are along the top edge, where the decking traps moisture, and in between two joists that have been sandwiched together. Rolling butyl tape over the top of the joists will add years to your deck's framing. Choose a dark-colored tape; shiny silver and white are noticeable between the gaps. A 4-in. x 75-ft. roll will cost you about $30 at a home center.

5 CHECK YOUR JOIST SPACING

If you're planning to replace old wood decking with PVC or composite, measure the joist spacing first. Most deck joists are centered 16 in. apart, which is the maximum span for most low-maintenance decking. If you plan to install your decking at a 45-degree angle, your joists may need to be 12 in. apart. You may also have to install more stair stringers. Check your product specs, and talk to your local building official before you buy.

6 AVOID RANDOM SPLICES

If your deck is 24 ft. long, don't use random-length boards and butt-joint them together. Install a splice board to create two 12 x 12-ft. spaces instead. Your deck will look better and you'll avoid the frustration of trying to splice the decking over joists. A splice board will also require extra framing. Do it the same way you would for the perimeter boards (one extra joist and a 2x6 on its side between the outside joist and the extra joist).

SPLICE BOARD

7A

7B

7 MAKE STAIR RAILS SIMPLE

Stair railings are one of the trickiest parts of any deck project. Some aluminum manufacturers offer a pre-assembled railing that racks to whatever angle you need. Just measure the distance between the posts, transfer the proper angle and cut to length. If your rails fit into a sleeve, you can cut them with a hacksaw, recip saw or circular saw. If your rail ends will be exposed, you may want to invest in an aluminum blade for your chop saw. Either way, clean up the ends with a file so you don't scratch things up during installation.

8 HIDE THE SCREWS

When it comes to fastening PVC or composite decking, our three pros like the Cortex concealed fastening system. Just countersink the screws

PLUG

using the special bit included with the kit, and hammer in a plug made of the exact same material as the decking. Screw holes virtually disappear, and damaged boards are easy to remove if needed.

9 MIX AND MATCH

You don't have to stick with one type of product or one look for the entire deck. Our pros mix and match all the time: composite posts with aluminum rails, composite rails with aluminum spindles. And don't be afraid to think outside the box when it comes to color. You can install perimeter boards the same color as the railing. Choose a post color that's different from the railing. Have the spindles be a different color than the posts and rails. The possibilities are endless.

10 FIT RAILINGS EASIER WITH CONNECTORS

Creating a tight fit between a composite post and a rail is difficult—even pros struggle with it. Railing connectors make it easy. This connector, made by Deckorator, is screwed onto the end of the rail before being attached to the post. It comes in five colors. You can buy these connectors from the same place you get your decking, or order them at amazon.com for less than $10 a pair.

11 DRESS UP AN UGLY POST

If your deck is more than a couple of feet off the ground, wrap the posts in PVC to match the rest of the deck. You'll need two 1x6s and two 1x8s for each post. Our pros avoid material thinner than ¾ in. because PVC expands and contracts more than wood, and it's hard to keep the seams together using thinner material. Pin the boards in place with a trim gun before screwing them together.

12 DARK, ROUND SPINDLES IMPROVE YOUR VIEW

Do you know why horse fences are usually white? It's because dark ones are harder for horses to see. The same principle applies to deck railings and people (as shown in **Photos 12A** and **12B** with options from Decks Unlimited). If you want an unobstructed view, choose dark spindles. And round is better than square. A ¾-in.-diameter round spindle stays ¾ in. no matter what direction it's viewed from, but a ¾-in. square spindle grows to more than an inch when you view it at an angle.

10

RAILING CONNECTOR

11

12A

12B

The use of expanding foam to set fence posts is a recent innovation. We asked two experts how foam compares with concrete for strength and usability.

SETTING FENCE POSTS WITH EXPANDING FOAM

///

ENSURE STRONG POSTS FOR A STURDY FENCE BY BACKFILLING POSTHOLES WITH A DENSE, HARD MATERIAL OTHER THAN DIRT

While a lot can be said for using well-draining gravel to set fence posts, the material of choice has long been concrete mix. It's available in 50-lb. bags at any home center, and you usually need two bags per post. For a 100-ft. fence with 10 posts, that means lugging half a ton or more of concrete mix to the site, mixing it with water and shoveling it into the holes.

If a lightweight alternative to concrete performed just as well, many fence builders would choose it just to save their backs. Foam offers promise, but is it just as good as concrete? We asked two experts who set posts with foam: Alex Capozzolo, co-founder of Brotherly Love Real Estate in Philadelphia, and Forrest McCall, co-owner of the home improvement blog "Mama Needs a Project."

EXPANDING FOAM VS. CONCRETE

Post-setting foam is a two-part product, and before use, the parts must be mixed, which is done right in the bag. It's far lighter than concrete mix. Each bag contains enough material for a single post and weighs only 2 or 3 lbs.

Note: Unlike spray foam in an aerosol can, post-setting foam is a closed-cell formulation without air bubbles, making it more rigid. Most insulating foam is open cell.

BRACING IS KEY

Whether you backfill with concrete or foam, you dig the same size postholes to the same depth, which should be one-third the length of the entire post for stability.

Backfilling is more difficult with foam. Because the foam expands when it sets, McCall says the post tends to move if not braced properly. Capozzolo adds that there's little time to fix leveling errors. Bracing is also recommended with concrete, but it isn't as critical because concrete sets more slowly and provides plenty of time for readjustment.

FOAM SAVES TIME

Post-setting foam hardens in minutes (15, according to Capozzolo) and cures fully in about two hours, much faster than concrete. This means you could backfill all your posts in the morning and continue building the fence in the afternoon—instead of waiting until the next day as you would with concrete.

FOAM COSTS MORE

A single bag of Sika foam costs about $16, at one bag per posthole. A bag of concrete mix costs about $6, at two bags per posthole.

FOAM ISN'T TEMPERATURE DEPENDENT

Unlike concrete, post-setting foam sets just as quickly in low temperatures as it does in higher ones. McCall also claims you can use foam in wet weather. Concrete also sets in wet weather, but rainwater in the mixture can weaken it. That won't happen with foam because it isn't water soluble.

CONCRETE IS STRONGER

Capozzolo and McCall agree foam isn't as strong as concrete. "For lightweight fences or locations that aren't subject to high winds, the expanded foam would be the ideal choice," Capozzolo says. "But if structural strength is a concern, then I'd recommend concrete."

Part of the problem is that foam contracts slightly during curing. That creates gaps between the foam and the post as well as the sides of the hole. You can strengthen loose posts by adding more foam and covering it with dirt to force the foam into gaps as it expands. But all in all, you're probably better off choosing concrete when you need strength.

MISTAKES TO AVOID

Post-setting foam is relatively new on the market, and it's important to follow the instructions on the packaging. The mixing time differs for each product and is usually very short—15 to 30 seconds. Once mixed, you must be ready to use everything in the bag. Here are some common mistakes made by first-time users:

■ Undersizing the hole: A bag of foam fills a hole 8 in. in diameter by 36 in. deep. If the hole is too small, the foam will expand above ground and harden. You can trim it to ground level with a reciprocating saw, but don't pour part of a bag into an undersized hole unless you have a plan for disposing of the rest (maybe letting it expand inside a bucket). If it keeps flowing onto the ground, it'll be a messy cleanup.

■ Not being prepared: In our experience setting 4 x 4 posts at a depth of 3 ft., it takes about a bag and a half per hole. Always have at least two holes ready.

■ Failing to cut the bag open after mixing: Every bag has a warning about this. If the foam can't get out, the bag will explode, showering everyone and everything in the vicinity with sticky foam. You do not want this stuff on your skin or clothes!

■ Touching liquid foam with bare hands: Like spray foam, post-setting foam is extremely difficult to remove from skin. Always wear gloves, long pants and long sleeves. Know that you will very likely get foam on your work clothes, and it will never come off.

BEST FOAM FOR SETTING POSTS

Some manufacturers call their product "expanding concrete" or "expanding composite," and some formulations are stronger (and more expensive) than others.

Sika PostFix (about $16) sets in three minutes, cures in two hours and can be used with all types of posts, including wood, metal and vinyl.

At about $25, Fast 2K Fence Post Mix and Concrete Alternative comes in a 32.8-oz. bag that replaces 80 to 100 lbs. of concrete mix. It sets in 15 minutes in temperatures down to minus 20.

The two parts of the Secure Set 10-Post Kit (about $90) come in separate containers, giving you the option of mixing smaller quantities. The cost per post is about $7 cheaper than Sika.

ROOF TEAR-OFF

////////////////////////////////
SIMPLIFY AN UGLY JOB

If you're a roofer, you have your routine perfected already. But for the rest of us—who tear off asphalt shingles only occasionally—here's a primer on how to do it quickly, safely and right.

ROOF SAFETY IS ESSENTIAL!
Working on a roof is dangerous, so take precautions.
- Set roof jacks and a 2x10 about 3 ft. up from the roof edge **(Photo 1)**.
- Be sure to wear a safety harness **(Photo 2)**, which you can buy at safety equipment stores and at some roofing suppliers and home centers.
- Wear soft rubber-soled shoes for traction, long pants, work gloves and safety glasses.

PREP FOR THE TEAR-OFF

Doing a little prep work on the ground will keep nails and other debris out of the grass and flower beds, reduce cleanup time and preserve the landscaping. Place plywood over the air conditioner (be sure the power to it is turned off) and over doors or windows near the spot where you'll be tossing the debris off the roof. Then cover plants, shrubs, grass and other areas around the house with tarps to vastly simplify cleanup.

Rent a trash container (a 20-cu.-yd. size will handle most roofs). If possible, have it dropped next to the house so you can easily throw old shingles directly into it from the roof.

For safety and better footing, nail the roof jacks below the area you intend to strip first **(Photo 1)**. Buy the adjustable type designed to hold a 2x10 board. Space the jacks no more than 4 ft. apart. Fasten each with at least three 16d nails driven through the roof sheathing into a rafter.

STRIP THE ROOF

Start the tear-off at the section farthest from the trash container. Standing at the peak, use a garden fork or a notched roofing shovel to tear away the ridge caps and the top courses of shingles **(Photo 3)**. Forks and roofing shovels are available at roofing and home centers. Some roofers prefer forks because they don't get caught on nails, making it easier and faster to remove the shingles. Others like the shovels because they pull out more nails with the shingles.

Work the fork under the ridge caps, prying them loose. As they come loose, allow them to slide down to the roof jacks. Or, if they don't slide down the roof, carry them to the edge of the roof and throw them into the trash container.

Once the ridge caps are gone, slide the fork under the shingles and felt paper and pry the shingles up. Some nails will come up with the shingles. Others won't. Ignore them for now.

Remove shingles in a 2-to-3-ft.-wide section as you work down the roof **(Photo 4)**. The shingles will roll up like a ball in front of the fork. Push the shingles down to the roof jacks. Continue tearing off the shingles and underlayment until you reach the roof jacks, then start over at the top of the roof.

PUT INTO THE TRASH

As the old roofing material piles up at the roof jacks, carry it to the edge of the roof and toss it into the trash container below **(Photo 5)**. If you couldn't

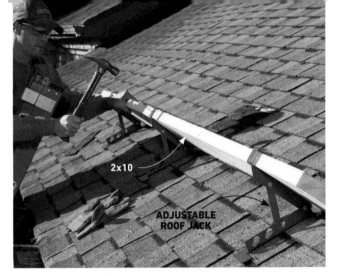

1 START WITH ROOF JACKS
Nail roof jacks to the rafters and then nail on a 2x10 to prevent you—and the shingles—from sliding off the roof.

2 HARNESS UP!
Use a safety harness system to prevent falls. Wear boots or shoes with soft rubber soles for a good grip and long pants to protect against the skin-scraping shingles.

3 ATTACK THE RIDGE FIRST
Tear off the ridge caps so you can work the fork under the shingles near the peak.

4 ROLL DOWNHILL

Work from the peak down, tearing off shingles in easy-to-carry sections. Tear off a section all the way down to the roof jacks before returning to the peak.

5 HANDLE OLD SHINGLES JUST ONCE

Throw old shingles directly into the trash container as they pile up at the roof jacks. Dispose of the shingles before the pile gets too large and they slide off the roof.

USE CARE AT ROOF PENETRATIONS

Slow down and work carefully near chimneys, skylights, dormers or an exterior wall. While it's usually best to replace metal flashing, sometimes it's better to reuse difficult-to-replace types if they're in good shape. But if you see rust and cracks in the metal, replace it. Damaged metal won't last as long as your new roof.

If you're keeping the old metal flashing, remove nails and bend it upward off the shingles with a pry bar (Photo 6). Be careful not to damage the flashing. Once it's out of the way, pull any nails and remove any shingles and underlayment that are underneath. Do the same with the step flashing (the flashing interwoven with the shingles) where the roof abuts a wall (Photo 7).

TEAR OFF SHINGLES ALONG THE EDGE

After stripping the shingles down to the roof jacks, remove the jacks. Work the remaining courses loose with a fork or shovel, but don't pry them completely free or they'll slide off the roof (Photo 8).

Loosen the shingles all along the eaves. Then pull off the shingles with your hands, carry them across the roof to the trash container location and throw them in.

Some roofs have a self-stick ice and water barrier installed along the edge. This asphalt membrane usually pulls up with a fork or shovel but may require

6 SAVE SPECIAL FLASHINGS

Pull nails carefully around flashings you plan to reuse. Skylight and chimney flashings are often worth saving if they're in good condition.

get the trash container close to the house, throw the shingles onto a tarp on the ground. Make the pile in a flat area away from flowers and shrubs.

Shingles are heavy. They usually come off in clumps. If you're peeling off two or more layers of shingles, even a small section will be heavy. You may have to pull the shingles apart to make them light enough to carry. Rolling the shingles and underlayment into a ball will also make them easier to handle.

7 GO GENTLE ON STEP FLASHING
Pull nails from any step flashing you want to save, bend it up slightly and pull out the shingles from underneath.

8 FINISH UP THE EAVES
Remove the roof jacks and work the shingles loose along the roof edge with a fork. Then pull them off by hand.

some scraping. If it refuses to come loose, simply leave it and install your new underlayment over it.

If you don't have time before dark to clean the roof and apply underlayment, nail down tarps for the night.

TOSS OLD VALLEY AND VENT FLASHING
Pry up the flashing in valleys and over plumbing vents last. This flashing usually has the same life span as the shingles, so plan to replace it.

Starting at the top of the valley, slip the fork or a flat bar under the flashing and pry the metal edges loose. Continue working down the valley, lifting up the flashing **(Photo 9)**. Pry up and toss out old vent flashing as well **(Photo 10)**.

CLEAN THE DECK
Once a section has been stripped, go back and pull out protruding nails. Then use a large broom to sweep the roof deck clean **(Photo 11)**. Walk carefully. The shingle granules make the sheathing slippery.

When the roof is clean and bare, inspect the sheathing for damage. Rotted areas and broken boards are the most common problems. Cut out and replace damaged sections as needed. Use new sheathing that's the same thickness as the

9 TRASH THE VALLEY FLASHING
Pry up the old flashing in the valleys using a fork. Valley flashing is never worth reusing.

old. When you remove a damaged section, center the cuts over the rafters so you can nail the new sheathing to the rafters. Also keep an eye out for loose roof sheathing that needs renailing.

"BUTTON UP" THE ROOF

This is the final prep step before shingling. It consists of installing ice and water barrier and underlayment. The underlayment acts as a temporary weather barrier to keep rain out. But it won't stop heavy rain and wind, so once you start a section, always try to flash and shingle it by the end of the day.

Ice and water barrier is used at roof edges and other vulnerable areas. To install it, snap a chalk line 36 in. from the edge of the eaves. If you have gutters, you'll want the ice and water barrier to cover all the gutter flashing that's on the roof **(Photo 12)**.

Starting at the rake edge of the roof, align the ice and water barrier with the chalk line. Tack it at the top with staples every few feet. Once the entire section is tacked along the chalk line, lift up the bottom part, peel off the backing, then let it fall back into place. The ice and water barrier will immediately stick to the roof.

Flip the top part of the ice and water barrier back over the bottom section (the staples will easily pop out), peel off the backing, then set it back into place on the roof. Work carefully to avoid wrinkles. They're hard to get out. Move on to the next section of roof edge, overlapping the vertical seams of the ice and water barrier by 6 in.

Add a second course above the first, if required, overlapping the first by 4 in. Also lay the ice and water barrier in valleys and around chimneys, skylights and other roof penetrations.

Then unroll and staple down underlayment over the rest of the roof. Use plenty of staples (5/16 in.) to make the underlayment safer to walk on and to keep it from blowing off. This is where a hammer-type stapler pays off. You can drive a dozen staples in seconds.

CLEAN UP THE AREA

Before climbing off the roof, clean any debris out of the gutters. You don't want nails and shingle granules pouring out of your downspouts the next time it rains.

Run a broom magnet over the yard to pick up stray nails. You can rent one at tool rental stores. Make several passes in different directions. Even if you were careful, nails have a way of ending up in the lawn and you don't want someone to step on one.

RUINED SEAL

PLUMBING FLASHING

10 *POP OFF VENT FLASHING*
Pry flashing loose around vent pipes. Use a pry bar rather than a fork to avoid damaging the pipes. Never reuse vent flashing.

11 *SWEEP AND INSPECT*
Sweep the roof clean to avoid slips and falls. Watch for any nails you missed earlier and pull them.

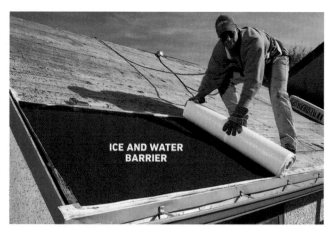

ICE AND WATER BARRIER

12 *BUTTON UP*
Cover the roof right away to protect against rain. Cover the lower end with self-stick ice and water barrier. Then staple down underlayment to protect the rest of the roof.

MEET THE EXPERT

Brian Larson is the owner of Northway Irrigation in Ham Lake, Minnesota. Northway has been installing residential and commercial irrigation systems for more than 30 years.

INSTALL AN IRRIGATION SYSTEM

PROVIDE AN EFFICIENT DRINK FOR A LAWN AND AVOID WASTING WATER

Installing an irrigation system is a great way to keep a lawn green through the doggiest days of summer. We spent a day with pro installers who taught us how to pull pipe, make solid connections faster and get it done safely. The result: a well designed irriga-tion system that sips water instead of guzzling it.

However, we don't show how to connect an irrigation system to a home's water supply or how to install a vacuum breaker/backflow preventer. Our crew hired a licensed plumber for those steps.

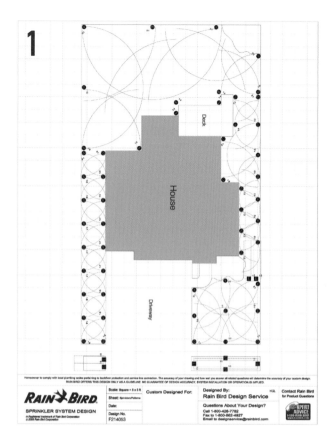

1 DESIGN A GOOD PLAN TO SAVE WATER

It takes a lot of know-how to figure out how many zones to install and which sprinkler head goes where. A poorly designed system will waste water—a lot of it! Luckily, irrigation product manufacturers such as Hunter, Toro and Rain Bird have extensive literature online to help. Rain Bird will even design your layout for you if you send in the measurements of the property.

2 REMOVE SOD FIRST

Slice off the sod before you dig a hole so it can be put back into place. If you do it right, the yard should show very few signs of your labor— besides the greener grass, of course.

3 PULL THE PIPES WITH A VIBRATORY PLOW

Pulling polyethylene pipe through the ground is faster and easier than digging trenches, and it doesn't create a huge mess. Here are some things to consider when pulling pipes:

■ Avoid tree roots. (To get an idea of how far they extend from the trunk, consider that the root structure is often the same size as the canopy.)

■ Shoot for a depth of about 10 in.

■ Avoid pulling pipes that are spliced (they could come apart underground).

■ Feed the pipe into the hole as you pull.

■ If you're renting a plow, pull all the pipes right away and return the machine. This may allow you to rent for only a half day and save money.

■ A vibratory plow may not work in super-compacted soil. You may need a trencher instead. A local rental center should know what types of soil you are likely to encounter.

■ Caution: Always call 811 to have the utilities located before you dig!

4 HAND-DIG AROUND UTILITIES

No matter how deep you think a utility pipe or wire is buried, always hand-dig over and around those areas.

BORING ROD

DRILL HEAD

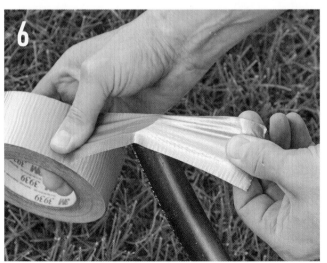

5 BORE UNDER OBSTRUCTIONS

Some vibratory plows/trenchers are capable of horizontal boring as well. If you plan to rent a plow and have to dig under a sidewalk or driveway, you might as well rent the boring rods and the drill head at the same time.

6 KEEP PIPES CLEAN

Dirt and other debris that get into the pipes will plug the heads. Keep all that out by covering the ends with duct tape. Besides dirt and rocks, these pros have found the occasional snake and frog clogging up the works... surprise! If you know you've kicked dirt down in the pipe, flush the line before installing the head.

7 DON'T CUT PIPES WITH A SAW

Cutting pipes with a saw can leave behind plastic shavings that could clog the sprinkler heads. Instead, an inexpensive poly pipe cutter works well. If you have the option, pick a bright-colored one that will be easier to spot in the grass. A pipe cutter like this one costs less than $20 at home centers.

7

SWING PIPE

8 INSTALL HEADS WITH SWING PIPE

Install a section of "swing pipe," often called "funny pipe," between the end of the poly pipe and the sprinkler head. Because funny pipe is flexible, you can much more easily position the head exactly where it needs to be. Funny pipe also allows the head to move in case it's run over by a vehicle or pushed around by frozen ground. When a head is connected directly to the rigid poly pipe, any movement could crack the fitting that connects them.

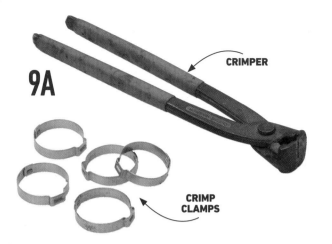

9A

CRIMPER

CRIMP CLAMPS

9 DOUBLE-CLAMP MAIN LINES

You can secure pipes to fittings quickly and easily with crimp clamps, but sometimes they can ever so slightly squish the pipe into an oval shape, creating a less-than-perfect connection. Main lines (the lines leading to the zone valves) are always pressurized, so install two crimp rings on each side of each fitting connection for extra protection against leaks. Stagger the ears on the two clamps to offset any pipe distortions.

10 CUT OUT KINKS

A kink in poly pipe creates a weak spot. Don't try to straighten the pipe. Instead cut out the kink and splice two pipes together with a coupler. If you must pull a pipe that has been spliced, add a couple of extra clamps to the fitting and hook up the longest of the spliced sections to the plow.

11 LEAVE ROOM FOR THE PIPES

Overcut the access holes in the valve box to provide extra room for the pipes. If the pipes fit snugly, they could be crushed if the box is run over by a lawn tractor or other vehicle when the ground is soft or saturated.

STAGGERED EARS

9B

10

COUPLER

OVERCUT ACCESS HOLES

11

12

SELF-
TAPPING
FITTING

13

RAIN BIRD

12 USE SELF-TAPPING FITTINGS

When you pull pipes instead of trenching, traditional tee fittings can be difficult to install. Instead install self-tapping fittings (saddles). Just snap the saddle onto the pipe and screw in the spike, which taps directly into the pipe. Hook up your funny pipe to the saddle and you're good to go.

13 SAVE WATER WITH SMART CONTROLLERS

The EPA states that U.S. residential outdoor water use accounts for nearly 9 billion gallons per day. Experts estimate that as much as 50% of this water is wasted through overwatering caused by inefficiencies in irrigation methods and systems. Controllers and sensors are now available that can track temperatures, sunlight and seasonal conditions, and adjust the watering schedule accordingly. Such a controller, along with a well-planned design, can save a couple hundred gallons of water per day! The Rain Bird model shown here connects to Wi-Fi, allowing the owner to have control or get updated on a smartphone.

14 PROTECT WIRES FROM THE ELEMENTS

The wire connections in the valve box require connectors approved for direct burial, which are basically tubes filled with dielectric grease. The connectors shown here are made by NorthStar Industries.

14A

14B

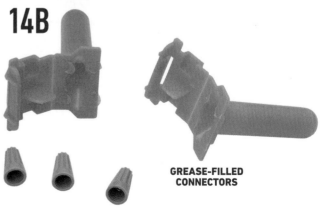

GREASE-FILLED
CONNECTORS

REPAIR A BURIED CABLE

SPLICE KITS MAKE FIXING DAMAGED UNDERGROUND WIRES GOOF-PROOF

If you're digging holes in your backyard, you should always call 811 a few days beforehand to mark all the underground utilities. Unfortunately, privately owned wiring will not be marked, so it's still possible to strike an electrical cable. It's especially likely if you're digging between the house and a freestanding garage, shed or yard light. If you do cut a power line, though, it's easy to fix. Here's how.

ASSESS THE DAMAGE

Turn off the circuit breaker to the cut cable and double-check at the damaged area with a voltage sniffer to be sure it's really off. Then enlarge the hole to a 2-ft. diameter. If the cable is cut cleanly, you can just splice it back together with a single underground splice kit. But if it's cut or nicked in several places, you'll have to remove the damaged section and splice in a "jumper" piece of UF (underground feeder) cable using two splice kits.

CHOOSE A SPLICE KIT

Underground AC splice kits come in two varieties: heat-shrinkable tubing and gel-filled shield. Both use a brass splicing block to connect the wires. But they differ in how they protect the splice.

The most common type of kit protects the splice with an 8-in. length of heat-shrinkable tubing filled with watertight hot-melt adhesive. (The Gardner Bender HST-1300, about $18, is shown above left.) Slide the tubing over the cable before you connect the wires to the splice block. Then slide the tubing over the connector and shrink it with a heat gun (best bet) or a torch (very gently!). The other type is a corrugated plastic shield filled with an encapsulating gel. (Shown above right and in **Photos 1-5** is the Tyco Electronics PowerGel Wrap around UF Splice Kit, about $30). It's more expensive, but it installs much faster, is goof-proof and is very long lasting.

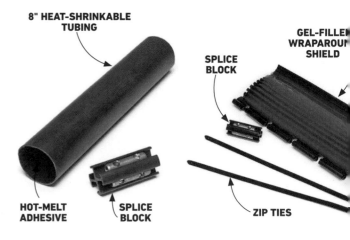

8" HEAT-SHRINKABLE TUBING — GEL-FILLED WRAPAROUND SHIELD — SPLICE BLOCK — HOT-MELT ADHESIVE — SPLICE BLOCK — ZIP TIES

TWO SPLICE KITS
On the left, one with heat-shrinkable tubing. On the right, one with gel. For both, the wires are connected in a splice block.

TEAR DOWN THE CENTER

UNDERGROUND FEEDER (UF) CABLE

1 TWIST AND PULL TO SEPARATE
Start by cutting out damaged sections. Then grab each of the side conductors with pliers. Twist your hands in opposite directions to start the tear. Pull the conductors 180 degrees away from each other to separate and expose a 1½-in. length. Strip ¾ in. of insulation off black and white wires.

SPLICE LOW-VOLTAGE CABLE

Besides underground power cable, it's also possible to slice through low-voltage lighting, irrigation and telephone cable, and coaxial cable. Since they're low voltage, you may be tempted to just twist the wires and wrap the splice with electrical tape. Instead, get a couple of low-voltage connectors for direct burial. They rely on gel to encapsulate the splice to prevent water intrusion and corrosion.

2 MATCH THE COLORS AND SPLICE
Slide the black wires into opposite ends of the brass barrel and tighten the screws. Then do the same for the white and bare copper wires.

3 POSITION THE SPLICE ON THE SHIELD
Place the splice block dead-center over the gel-filled shield. Clean off any debris that may have fallen into the gel. Then press the splice into the gel.

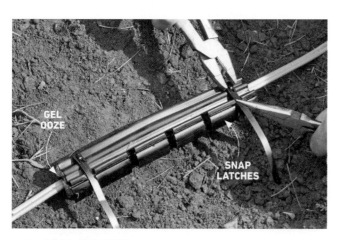

4 ROLL AND SNAP
Roll shield around the splice; align and snap the plastic latches, starting at the center and working to the edges. Install the zip ties and tighten with pliers. Repower circuit to make sure it works.

5 MARK THE LOCATION
Tie bright-colored surveyor's tape around the splice and fill the hole with soil. Replace the grass and trim the tape at soil level so you can find it again.

For solid irrigation and telephone wire, shove the wires in an insulation-piercing gel-filled connector and snap it closed. For low-voltage stranded cable, as you might find on lighting, use the wire nut/gel-filled capsule style. Twist on the wire nut, plunge the connector into the capsule until the gel oozes out the top, then snap the lid.

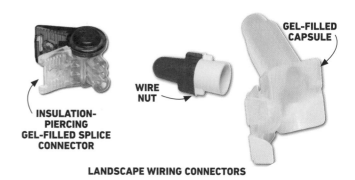

LANDSCAPE WIRING CONNECTORS

PRO TIP
When you're watering new seed, moisten the soil daily and keep it damp—but don't soak it. Over-watering is a common mistake.

CURES FOR TOP 5 LAWN PROBLEMS

EVEN THE BEST LAWNS COULD USE A LITTLE THERAPEUTIC ATTENTION NOW AND AGAIN

area, the urine is diluted and the nitrogen spreads, causing the grass surrounding the spot to grow faster and turn greener.

Remedy: You have to replant your grass; it won't come back on its own. But first you have to dilute or remove the caustic urine from the soil **(Photo 1)**. Thoroughly soak the area with lots of water. Let the hose run for at least three minutes. Then you can start the replanting process **(Photo 2)**. Add half an inch of new soil to help absorb any remaining urine **(Photo 3)**. Then you can spread new seed, or use a commercial yard patch mixture (available at most nurseries or home centers) or even sod. The secret of good germination is keeping the seed moist. Keep the area moist until the new grass is about 3 in. high.

Recovery time: Four to six weeks.

AN OUNCE OF PREVENTION

- Soak your pet's favorite areas in your lawn to get the salts out of the root zone before they kill the grass.
- Fertilize your lawn in the spring to boost the overall color and mask the darker green dog spots.
- Train your pet to urinate in a designated area. Replace or repair the grass in this area annually or cover it with mulch.
- Keep your pet well hydrated to make its urine less concentrated.

PROBLEM: DOG SPOTS ON GRASS

Symptoms: Dog spots are round patches about 4 to 8 in. in diameter with dead grass in the middle, encircled by dark green grass. They are most apparent in the early spring when dormant grass begins to turn green again.

Cause: Dog urine contains high concentrations of acids, salts and nitrogen, which burn (dry out) the grass roots and kill them. As rain washes the

1 Soak the patch until the grass is sopping wet in order to dilute the urine acids and salts and to wash them deeper into the soil, beyond the grass roots.

2 Scrape up the dead grass with a hand rake and remove it. Rough up the area to loosen the soil ½ in. deep. Seeds germinate better in soft soil.

3 Sprinkle on a ½-in.-thick layer of topsoil, then pepper it with grass seed. Cover with a thin layer of new soil. Keep the area moist until the new grass is about 3 in. high.

PROBLEM: THATCH

Symptoms: If your grass feels soft and spongy when you walk on it, your lawn may have a thatch buildup. Thatch (shown above) is a fibrous mat of dead stalks and roots that settles between the lawn's green leaves and the soil. When this mat becomes greater than ¾ in. thick, it can cause your lawn to suffer from heat and drought. Affected lawns will rapidly wilt and turn blue-green, indicating they're hot and dry.

Cause: Cutting off too much at each mowing (letting the grass get too long) and cutting too low will both produce more dead grass tissue than microbes and earthworms can recycle. Thatch can develop in any soil but is most often associated with high clay content. Other causes are overfertilization and frequent, light watering, which encourage a shallow root system.

Remedy: Slice open a section of your lawn **(Photo 1)**.

If your grass shows ¾ in. or more of thatch, it's time to rent an aerator. An aerator is a heavy machine that opens the soil by pulling up finger-sized soil cores to help the lawn absorb more oxygen and water, which will encourage healthy microbe growth and give worms some wiggle room.

Aerate in the spring or fall when the grass is growing but the weather is not too hot to stress the plants **(Photo 2)**. If the machine isn't pulling plugs, your lawn may be too dry. To avoid this, water thoroughly the day before you aerate. You can also rake in topsoil **(Photo 3)** to increase the healthy microorganisms that aid thatch's natural decomposition. Topsoil is available at garden centers.

Recovery time: You can expect the thatch layer to decrease by about ¼ in. per year, about the same rate at which it forms.

AN OUNCE OF PREVENTION

- Mow often and cut no more than one-third of the grass height.
- Water your lawn less often but for longer periods to prevent shallow root systems.
- Reduce the amount of fertilizer you spread at any one time.
- Reduce the use of pesticides. This will help keep the worm and microorganism populations healthy.
- Aerate at least once every year if your lawn is prone to thatch.

CAUTION:
Call your local utility provider or 811 to mark your underground utility lines before you aerate.

1 Slice the turf grass with a shovel and pry it back. If the thatch depth measures more than ¾ in., aerate at least 3 in. deep.

2 Make two or three passes with an aerator until you've made 3-in.-deep holes 2 in. apart throughout your yard.

3 Spread ¼ in. of topsoil on the yard's most thatchy areas and then rake vigorously to fill the holes with loose soil.

PROBLEM: FAIRY RINGS

Symptoms: Fairy rings are circles approximately 3 to 8 ft. wide that consist of a dark green and fast-growing area of grass surrounding an inner area of partially dead or thin grass. Some rings also produce mushrooms.

Cause: Fairy rings are caused by fungi that live in the soil. As the fungi feed on organic matter, they release nitrogen, causing the grass to turn dark green. As the colony grows, it disturbs the flow of needed water to the turf roots, creating thin or dead spots. Fairy rings often begin with the decomposition of organic matter, such as an old tree stump buried under the lawn.

Remedy: By bringing up the color in the rest of your lawn with a nitrogen fertilizer, you can mask much of the overgreening of the fairy ring **(Photo 1)**. Hand-aerating the ring will break up the fungus and allow the flow of water and other nutrients to the grass roots **(Photo 2)**.

Recovery time: Generally fairy rings can be masked with the application of fertilizer, with results in 10 to 14 days. The grass within the ring will thicken up with aeration in about two to three weeks.

AN OUNCE OF PREVENTION

Aeration will help with fairy rings, but maintaining a healthy lawn with a balanced fertilization program is essential. Apply three doses:

- Apply ½ lb. per 1,000 sq. ft. in late April or early May to give the overwintering grass roots a bit of a boost.
- Add no more than ½ lb. per 1,000 sq. ft. at the end of June or in early July when temperatures are not at their peak. Stimulating growth during a heat wave will stress the plants.
- Spread 1 lb. per 1,000 sq. ft. at the end of October. The best root growth takes place when the soil temps are between 58 and 65 degrees F. The roots store energy over the winter, making the entire lawn healthier the following spring.

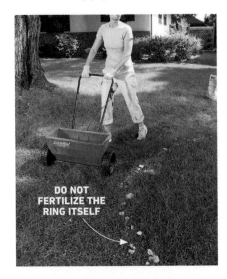

DO NOT FERTILIZE THE RING ITSELF

1 Spread ½ lb. of nitrogen fertilizer per 1,000 sq. ft. to green up your lawn, but skip the fairy ring zone. This will mask the lush green of the fairy ring by blending it into the rest of your yard.

CORE PLUGS

2 Break up the fungi with a hand aerator (available at home centers and garden stores). Punch holes every 2 to 4 in. throughout the ring and 2 ft. beyond.

DECAYING WOOD

3 If you see no improvement in three weeks, go treasure hunting to dig out rotting stumps, roots, construction debris or other organic materials under your lawn.

PROBLEM: GRUBS

Symptoms: Grub-chewed turf has patchy areas that wilt and die. You can easily pull up the affected turf if you tug on it. Another indicator of grubs may be increased raccoon, bird or mole activity. They like to dig up and eat the grubs at night. While this may sound good, the moles will kill the grass as they forage for grubs.

Cause: Lawn grubs are the larval stage of moths and beetles. The grubs eat the roots of grass, setting the roots up to die by dehydration.

Remedy: Be vigilant. Are beetles swarming around your porch light? In the next month, keep an eye out for patches of grass that wilt or are blue-green on hot days. They may be larvae infested. Turn over some turf (**Photo 1**). If you count 6 to 10 grubs (white wormlike larvae with black heads) under a 1-sq.-ft. area of sod, consider using a grub insecticide (available at home centers and nurseries). Or talk to a professional (search online for "grass service") about treating your yard. An expert will be familiar with the grub problems in your region and the most suitable treatment methods.

If you spot the grubs but your count is lower than six per square foot, baby your lawn to strengthen its natural defenses. Mow on a higher blade setting and water thoroughly but infrequently to encourage the grass to grow new, deep roots. Do not cut off more than one-third of the grass height at each mowing to avoid stressing the plant.

AN OUNCE OF PREVENTION

Inspect your turf periodically by pulling on patches that look unhealthy, or have a professional inspect your lawn if you suspect a problem.

1 Pierce the lawn with a shovel, making a U shape. Peel back the lawn (as though rolling up a rug) and count the white grubs in a 1-sq.-ft. area.

2 Treat your lawn with an insecticide if the count is 6 to 10 grubs in a square foot. Follow the manufacturer's directions carefully. Or consult with a yard service.

PROBLEM: SHADE

Symptoms: Shaded grass will look thin and patchy. Some types of grass actually produce wider blades as the plant attempts to catch more rays. But they also produce far fewer blades, lending a spindly appearance to the lawn. The cold truth is, if your lawn gets less than six to eight hours of sun daily, you are unlikely to sustain lush grass.

Cause: Trees, buildings and bushes.

Remedy: You can increase the sunlight as much as possible by trimming trees and shrubs. Also, try starting areas in shade with sod instead of seed. The sod will adjust to the lower level of light. Although all seed varieties have their shade limitations, try overseeding your thin area with a shady grass mix.

Or throw in the towel, grab your trowel and plant a shade-tolerant ground cover. Many will thrive where your turf withered. Lamium (dead nettle) and ajuga (bugleweed) collaborate nicely in providing lovely blooms and an enthusiastic, but not invasive, carpet. This pair fares well, with a hearty tolerance spanning zones 3 to 8, and can be planted right up to your grass. They are fairly low growers and won't get more than a few nicks from a lawn mower.

Also, mulching between the ground cover plants will help retain moisture. This is especially wise if your new "shade garden" is on a slope; mulch will help prevent your fledgling plants from washing out in a hard rain.

Recovery time: The plants and mulch will immediately boost the appearance of an area that was once thin grass. It'll take a couple of seasons for the ground cover to become fully established.

AN OUNCE OF PREVENTION

Avoid the frustration of sun-starved grass by starting a shade garden or ground cover in any area that doesn't receive six to eight hours of good light per day.

Using a garden hoe, work up the shaded area to remove any struggling grass. Plant ground cover or a shade garden.

WORKING WITH BAGGED CONCRETE

///

GET THE MOST FROM THIS AFFORDABLE, DIY-FRIENDLY PRODUCT

Large jobs that require several yards of concrete—like patios and driveways—always call for ready-mixed concrete trucked to your site. But if you need just a few cubic feet of concrete for a stoop, deck stair landing or fence-post setting, you will use bagged concrete mix. We'll show you the proper mixing technique plus a few pointers to help you work more efficiently.

1 MAKE MIXING EASY

Stab the bag in the center with a shovel. Then open the bag like a clamshell and dump it into a wheelbarrow or plastic mortar pan.

2 DON'T ADD TOO MUCH WATER!

Read the directions on the bag for the proper amount of water to add. Use that exact amount and resist the temptation to pour in more. Too much water makes for weaker concrete.

3 MIX FROM BOTH DIRECTIONS

Use a hoe to pull portions of the dry mix through the water. When you've moved all the concrete to one end, start over from the other direction. Keep reversing direction until no more dry powder remains.

4 TEST THE CONSISTENCY

When concrete is properly mixed, it looks surprisingly dry and crumbly. You can tell whether it has enough water by patting it with the flat part of the hoe. If you pack it a half-dozen times and the surface becomes creamy, you'll know it's just right.

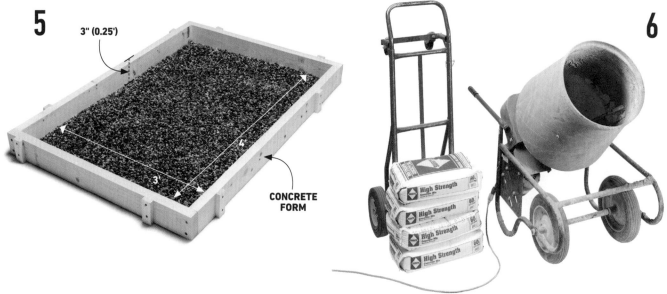

5

3" (0.25')

CONCRETE FORM

6

7

5 BUY THE RIGHT AMOUNT

When you mix up a 60-lb. bag of concrete, you'll have a volume of 0.5 cu. ft.; an 80-lb. bag yields 0.66 cu. ft. (The volume is listed on each bag.) To determine how many bags you need, measure the length, width and depth of the form. Then go on-line and find a "concrete calculator." One example is at *sakrete.com/concrete-calculator/slab-pour/*.

6 RENT A MIXER FOR BIG BATCHES

Hand-mixing a few bags is one thing. Mixing 20 bags will wear you out. Plus, you'll have a much stronger chunk of concrete if all of it is mixed and placed as quickly as possible. Don't hesitate to rent a mixer. You can find small electric ones that fit in the back of your hatchback and cost you about $55 per day. For a bit more, you can get a much larger electric or gas unit that you tow home.

7 DON'T FORGET SPECIALTY MIXES

There are several mixes formulated for special purposes. Two of our favorites are fast-setting and countertop mixes.

Fast-setting mix, from a brand such as Sakrete **(Photo 7)**, is great because there's no mixing involved. You just pour water into the hole and add the mix.

If you'd like to cast custom concrete countertops, tabletops or bench tops, choose countertop mix. It's formulated for high strength and low shrinkage. This mix also has special additives and aggregates to make it flow well. Best of all, you can polish it. But if you use melamine forms, it'll be very smooth and need little polishing.

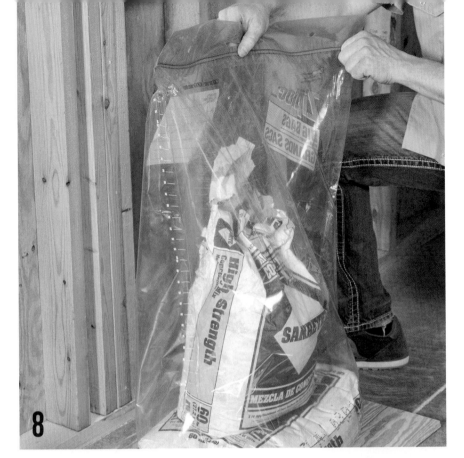

8 KEEP IT DRY

Bags of concrete will absorb moisture from damp concrete floors and the air. And before long you'll have rock-hard bags out in the garage. Never store bags on concrete surfaces, and for long-term storage, keep them in giant sealed bags.

9 ADD SOME COLOR

You'll find several earth-tone dyes at the home center. So if you'd like a terra cotta, buff or other color besides basic gray, it's simple. But don't throw the dye into the mix and start working it in or you'll have uneven color distribution. Instead, stir the dye into the water before you add the water to the dry concrete.

DYE

POUR A PERFECT SLAB

FOLLOW THESE SIMPLE STEPS FOR A FLAWLESS, LONG-LASTING CONCRETE DRIVEWAY

A concrete driveway makes a beautiful gateway to your home that can last for decades if it's installed correctly. But if you don't follow the proper procedures, it could turn into a pile of rubble in half the time. The good news: Installing it the right way doesn't take extra time or money. We tagged along with a longtime professional mason for an actual pour. Glenn Anderson showed us the best ways to prevent water from pooling and to stop unsightly cracking, spalling and scaling. For great tips on prepping the ground before the pour, search for "concrete slab prep" at *familyhandyman.com.*

1 PROTECT ADJOINING CONCRETE

Our expert uses duct tape to protect adjacent slabs and sidewalks. Concrete can splash when it runs from the chute onto the ground, so you'll also want to lay plastic over doors, siding, brick, windows or anything else you want to keep clean. Smearing wet concrete into porous surfaces creates an even bigger mess, so if you do get a couple of globs where you don't want them, wait till they dry and then scrape them off.

CHAIR

CONCRETE PLACER

3 POUR THE CONCRETE IN SMALL SECTIONS

Spread the concrete by moving the chute back and forth and having the driver pull forward as you go.

CHAIR

Once the truck reaches the end of a section, spread the concrete evenly, a touch higher than the form, with a concrete placer/rake. Don't fill the whole form or giant sections—the extra concrete you'll drag with the screed board will get too heavy.

This rebar grid is sitting on chairs, keeping it suspended at the proper height. You won't be able to use chairs if you have to distribute the concrete with a wheelbarrow. If that's the case, use the hook on the edge of the concrete placer to pull the rebar into the center of the concrete as you pour. Place the rebar near the slab's center for maximum strength, not near the ground or the surface.

TRUCK HOSE

2 DAMPEN THE BASE TO LENGTHEN FINISH TIME

To extend your finish time on hot, sunny days, spray bone-dry ground with water to keep the base from sucking the water out of the concrete. A water spray also slows down curing, which makes for a stronger slab. If there's no hose bib nearby, you can use the water and hose that are onboard the truck. If you don't have water on site, also use the truck hose to fill a couple of buckets with water for cleaning tools after the truck leaves.

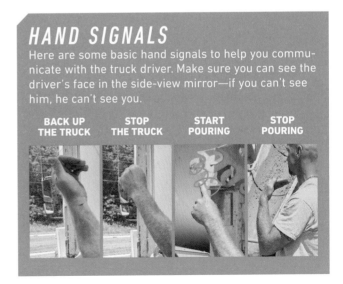

HAND SIGNALS

Here are some basic hand signals to help you communicate with the truck driver. Make sure you can see the driver's face in the side-view mirror—if you can't see him, he can't see you.

| BACK UP THE TRUCK | STOP THE TRUCK | START POURING | STOP POURING |

MUCKER

NICE GUY! (DRIVERS USUALLY DON'T HELP)

SCREED BOARD

4 SLIDE THE SCREED BOARD BACK AND FORTH AS YOU PULL

Pull back the excess concrete with the screed board. As you pull, slide the screed board back and forth to help you prevent voids in the surface. Have a mucker (that's what they are really called) pull the excess back and fill in low spots during the screeding process.

5 FACE SCREED BOARD WITH CROWN SIDE UP

A slight crown (bow) in the screed board is not only OK; it's preferred. Just make sure the crown side is facing up. That will create a slight hump down the middle of the slab, so water will drain off. If the crown faces down, you'll end up creating a trough in the slab where water can pool.

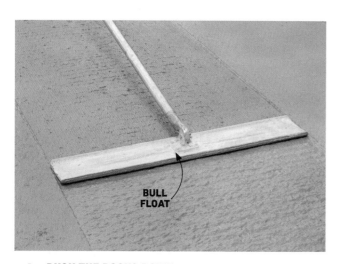

BULL FLOAT

6 PUSH THE ROCKS DOWN

Larger aggregate (chunks of gravel) near the surface may cause spalling (chipping). Our expert pushes the larger rocks deeper into the mix. He does this by making small stabbing motions with the float on the first return pass. Start floating the slab immediately after the pour is complete.

7 START FLOATING RIGHT AWAY

In addition to pushing the aggregate down under the surface, a bull float helps level the slab, so start floating right after you screed, while the concrete is still wet enough to shape.

Whenever possible, run the bull float perpendicular to the direction you pulled the concrete with the screed board (this slab was too long to do that). That will help to smooth out the ridges, troughs and valleys created by screeding. Our expert likes to float in both directions when he can.

FRESNO
TROWEL

9 DON'T OVER-TROWEL CONCRETE

Actually, exterior concrete surfaces don't need to be troweled at all. But if you want to use a trowel to knock down the ridges left by the bull float, make as few passes as possible and wait until all the surface "bleed water" is gone. Overworking and troweling wet concrete can trap water just under the surface, making it weak and more prone to spalling and scaling (pitting and peeling), especially on slabs poured in cold climates.

10 MAKE LONG STROKES WITH THE EDGER

The concrete should be firm before you start edging. If the edger is leaving behind large wet grooves, wait a while before you continue. Longer strokes will result in straighter lines.

8 CLEAN YOUR TOOLS AS YOU GO

Don't wait until the end of the day to clean your tools. Clean each one immediately after use.

BE PREPARED!

Concrete doesn't care if you are not organized or don't have time to finish all the edging—it will start setting up right away regardless. Make sure all your tools are ready to go and there are at least three people on hand, one to muck and two to screed. Sometimes the truck driver will help, but don't count on that happening.

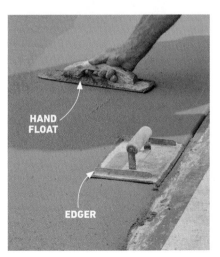

HAND
FLOAT

EDGER

11 KEEP A HAND FLOAT NEARBY WHEN EDGING

Run a hand float over the ridges left behind by the edger. A hand float is also a good tool for dragging small amounts of material or moisture (cream) into voids or dry spots near the edge.

HOW TO ORDER

Calculate the volume you need in cubic yards. Multiply the length by the width by the depth, and divide that number by 27 (the number of cubic feet in a cubic yard). Then add 10% to allow for spillage and slab depth variations. If you're not sure which slump (consistency) or psi (strength) to order, ask your concrete supplier to suggest the proper mix for your slab's intended use.

12 CUT IN CONTROL JOINTS

A 100-ft. run of concrete can shrink as much as ½ in. as it hardens. Shrinking causes cracks. You can't stop your slab from cracking, but you can control where it cracks. Cut in control joints to create individual sections no larger than 8 x 8 ft. for a 3½-in.-thick slab, and no larger than 10 x 10 ft. for a 5½-in.-thick slab. Cut the control joints at least one-fourth the depth of the concrete. You could use a groover like this one, which works similar to an edger, but many pros prefer to cut the control joints with a diamond blade saw the day after pouring.

GROOVER

13 CREATE TRACTION WITH A BROOM

A broom finish creates a nonslip surface when wet. Make it rough enough for traction but not so rough that it hurts to walk on barefoot. If the broom starts to bounce, lower the angle. Wavy lines are more hidden if perpendicular to the direction that the slab is most visible.

SPRAY ON A SEALER

Concrete will become significantly weaker if the water in the mix evaporates before the chemical curing process is complete. Spray down the slab with water every day for at least a week to slow down the curing process. Another option is to spray on an acrylic cure and seal product. Sealing the surface also protects the concrete from scaling and spalling in cold climates. Apply the sealer right after you broom.

15 FINISH UP

The slab can be walked on and the forms pulled in 24 hours. Wait at least 10 days to drive on it, and avoid spreading any ice-melting chemicals for the first two years. Before you pour, ask your neighbors to keep an eye on their pets, and use caution tape around the area to warn curious neighbor kids.

CHAPTER 7

GARAGE & AUTOMOTIVE

Garage Door Makeover 246
8 Garage Door Maintenance Tips 250
Space-Saving Garage Storage 252
10 Tips to Save Gas 260
What to Do If 262
Change Your Engine Coolant 266
How to Buy a Reliable Used Car 268

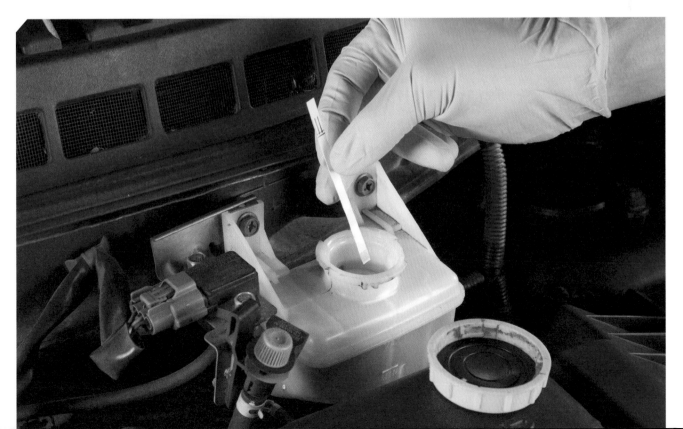

220

GARAGE DOOR MAKEOVER

AMAZING CURB APPEAL—IN JUST ONE WEEKEND!

Former contributing editor Spike Carlsen's Greek Revival house stood garageless for the first 150 years of its life. He knew when it came time to add one, it had to honor the character of the old home. Unfortunately, he had a bad case of sticker shock after shopping for a carriage house–style overhead door. Wood doors of the style started at $2,800 and climbed to four times that amount. So he did what any self-respecting do-it-yourselfer would do: He built his own. And he did it using inexpensive hardboard, cedar boards and tongue-and-groove paneling.

You can use these techniques to customize a new door or update an old one. Note: The design shown on the following pages isn't exactly like the door shown above. Spike changed some details, especially about the arch.

MEET THE EXPERT

Spike Carlsen, a former *Family Handyman* editor, is an author whose books include *A Splintered History of Wood*, *Ridiculously Simple Furniture Projects* and *Woodworking FAQ*.

TOOLS AND MATERIALS

Since most "off the shelf" doors are metal or fiber-glass, you may have to special-order hardboard door panels through a home center, lumberyard or garage door dealer. Do your homework: Spike had quotes as high as more than twice what he actually paid.

Purchase cedar boards, rough sawn on one face and smooth on the other, for the rails and stiles, and ¼-in. x 4-in. x 8-ft. cedar tongue-and-groove material—often used for wainscoting or closet lining—for the recessed slats. Choose material that's straight with a minimum of knots. Cedar is ideal because it's lightweight and naturally rot resistant.

Use a pneumatic finish nailer to work twice as fast as hand nailing, and since the nail heads leave only tiny dents, the primer and paint will fill them, saving you hours of nail setting, puttying and sanding. The nails are important, but it's the adhesive that holds the boards flat and secure for the long haul. Spike used heavy-duty "subfloor" adhesive for that task. The caulk is equally important since it keeps moisture from getting between the boards and the door. He used white silicone caulk—itself a tenacious adhesive—for that job. Some silicone caulk isn't paintable—and it's usually available in a limited number of colors. If you can't find a silicone caulk that matches the paint color of your door, buy a "paintable" version.

To ensure accurate cuts, a power miter saw is the tool to use.

STRUCTURAL AND SAFETY NOTES

Keep these factors in mind before diving in:

1. When you modify a door, you'll most likely void the manufacturer's warranty, so take pains to create watertight seals wherever you can.
2. Since you're adding ¾ in. of thickness to the door, the vertical garage door tracks will need to be set back from the opening an extra ¾ in. You may need oversize jamb brackets for the job.
3. Your door will be 40 to 60 lbs. heavier once the wood overlay is added. Figure out the total weight of your door and install springs and a garage door opener rated for that weight.
4. Make certain each of the four hardboard door panels has a heavy-duty horizontal reinforcement bar along the back to prevent bowing. Those bars are installed when the door is hung.
5. If working with an existing door, make certain it's in good shape. Remove loose or flaking paint so the glue and caulk have a surface to adhere to.

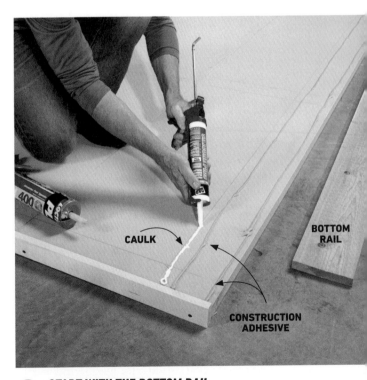

CHALK LINES INDICATE EDGES OF RAILS AND STILES

CLEAT

CAULK

BOTTOM RAIL

CONSTRUCTION ADHESIVE

1 MARK THE LAYOUT

Lock the panels together with 1x3 cleats and drywall screws. Snap chalk lines to indicate the edges of the rails and stiles. The four "openings" between the stiles should be of equal width.

2 START WITH THE BOTTOM RAIL

Run two beads of construction adhesive and one bead of caulk before nailing on the rails and stiles. Caulk locks out moisture along the edges while adhesive provides long-term holding power.

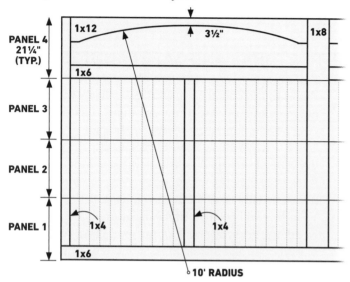

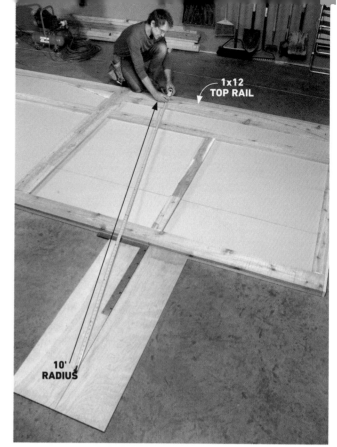

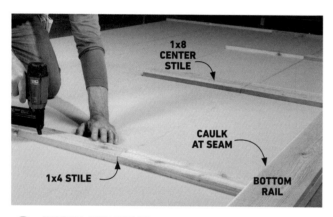

INSTALL THE STILES

3 Apply silicone caulk to the ends of the stiles before butting them against the rails. Use nails sparingly; just enough to hold the parts in place until the construction adhesive cures.

Hanging a garage door is tricky—and potentially dangerous—work. Have the door hung by a pro who knows how to install the door, the track and the opener safely. Talk BEFORE you start, to get additional input.

A GAME PLAN AND A SKETCH

Spike designed the 16-ft.-wide door to resemble a pair of carriage house doors, but you could come up with other designs. First, measure the height and width of each door panel, as well as the total height and width of the assembled garage door. Sketch it on graph paper. Draw in the rails and stiles to make a game plan.

Position your four garage panels on the floor in the proper order (if they're new, they'll be marked top, middle, middle, bottom), and make sure the edge

MARK ARCHES ON THE TOP RAILS

4 Center a scrap of plywood below the door and drive in a screw to act as a pivot point. Hook on your tape measure, hold your pencil at the desired radius and "swing" an arch across the 1x12 top rail. In this case, the 10-ft. mark on the tape provided the perfect radius. Cut the arch with a jigsaw.

grooves overlap properly. Temporarily secure them to one another using 1x3 cleats and drywall screws **(Photo 1)**. Transfer the measurements from your graph paper to the door, then snap chalk lines to indicate the edges of all the rails and stiles.

First snap lines for the horizontal rails, then the lines for the two 1x4 outer stiles and the 1x8 center stile. Measure between the edge stiles and the center stile to find that center point, then snap lines for the intermediate stiles. When done, the four spaces between the stiles should be identical in width.

RAILS, STILES AND SLATS

Apply construction adhesive and silicone caulk to secure the bottom rail **(Photo 2)**. Just "kiss" the chalk line with caulk so it spreads to create a watertight seal at the board's top. Set the bottom rail in place, rough side up, and secure it with nails every 12 inches.

Next install the edge, center and intermediate stiles **(Photo 3)** even with the door panel seams. Lay beads of adhesive and caulk along the chalk lines prior to

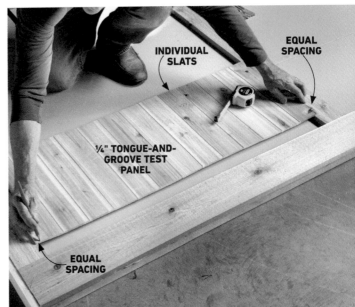

5 GET IDENTICAL LENGTHS WITHOUT MEASURING
Determine the exact length of the slats for each panel, then clamp down a bump block to cut them to identical lengths.

BUMP BLOCK

INDIVIDUAL SLATS

EQUAL SPACING

¼" TONGUE-AND-GROOVE TEST PANEL

EQUAL SPACING

6 LAY OUT SLATS FOR SYMMETRY
Fit slats together as a "test panel" and center it. Mark the two end slats, then cut to width.

installation. Run caulk at the outer edges to create a good seal. Install 1x6 rails at the top of panel 3.

Draw arches onto top rails using a screw and a tape measure **(Photo 4)**. Cut them using a jigsaw, smooth the edges, and install arches with adhesive and caulk.

Measure the height for the tongue-and-groove slats for panel 1. Mark one slat to length, position it on the miter saw, then install a "bump block" so all the slats you cut for panel 1 will be identical lengths **(Photo 5)**.

Nest precut pieces side by side to create the test panel **(Photo 6)**. Center it in the opening, then mark the two end slats so the slats will be centered during installation. Rip the first end slat to width, then install it with the tongue facing out. Continue installing the other pieces **(Photo 7)**. Rip the last piece to the exact width so it butts tightly to the other stile. Install all the pieces in panel 1, then move to panel 2. The "starters" in each panel's section should be identical.

FINISHING UP
Once all the slats are installed, apply caulk where they butt to the stiles and rails **(Photo 8)**. Remove the 1x3 cleats holding the panels together, place the panels on sawhorses, and prime any exposed edges and surfaces with a thick coat of stain-blocking exterior primer to prevent moisture from wicking in. Once the primer has dried, apply two coats of good exterior paint, paying special attention to exposed ends.

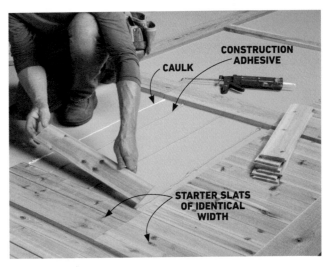

CONSTRUCTION ADHESIVE

CAULK

STARTER SLATS OF IDENTICAL WIDTH

7 INSTALL THE SLATS
Run triple beads of adhesive and a single bead of caulk, then nail slats into place one by one.

CAULK

8 CAULK THE SLATS
Apply additional caulk where the slats butt into the rails and stiles.

8 GARAGE DOOR MAINTENANCE TIPS

//

KEEP YOUR GARAGE DOOR RUNNING SMOOTHLY WITH REGULAR UPKEEP

An overhead garage door is the largest moving object in the typical home, and as such, it merits regular maintenance. It gets heavy use, has a lot of moving parts and is expensive to replace. The typical price range for a 16 x 7-ft. garage door is $1,000 to $5,000.

Here's how to prolong your garage door's life and keep it running smoothly.

1 TEST THE AUTO REVERSE

This safety feature forces the garage door to quickly reverse if it detects an obstacle, such as a car, animal or child. It's activated by a pressure sensor or photocells on each side of the door.

Test your auto reverse monthly by placing a 1½-in. block on the floor under the door. The door should reverse within two seconds after striking the block. To test the photoelectric system sensors, which are mounted 4 to 6 in. above the floor on each side of the garage door frame, start your door downward and move a board in the door's path. The door should reverse and move up.

If the auto reverse fails, disconnect the opener and call a pro to fix it. Older garage door openers without this basic feature—now mandated by building code in many areas—should be replaced.

2 LUBRICATE

Twice a year, spray lubricant on the rollers and hinges, then wipe off excess. Lubricating the rollers and other moving parts reduces stress on the rollers and opener.

"Dust collects and builds up on parts, creating noise," says Dave Krzyzak of Palm Valley Garage Doors in Goodyear, Arizona. "The original version

of WD-40 breaks down gunk and prevents rust and corrosion. In my 20 years in the industry, I've found WD-40 works best."

3 CLEAR TRACKS & TIGHTEN HARDWARE

Remove rust and debris from the tracks on both sides of the garage door. Check the brackets that hold the tracks to the wall and ceiling, as well as the fasteners that secure the garage door opener unit. Door vibration can loosen hardware, so use a socket wrench to tighten loose bolts.

"With garage doors, you should not touch anything that requires special tools," says Krzyzak. "Also, I see customers who have fiddled with red nuts and bolts on garage doors. Some of them end up in a hospital—the red is a danger warning."

4 LIMIT USE

Many homeowners with an attached garage enter and exit their home almost exclusively through the garage door. If that's you, it would be smart to break that habit.

"Go through your house doors more often," says Krzyzak. "I tell customers to use their house key, and some of them smile and say, 'What's a house key?'

"The garage door typically has five to 10 up-down cycles a day," Krzyzak says. "At 10 cycles daily, you may have to replace the springs every 2½ years. But if it's two cycles a day, spring replacement may be every seven or eight years."

5 TEST THE DOOR BALANCE

Springs balance the garage door so it opens and closes smoothly. An unbalanced garage door makes the opener work harder, shortening its life span.

Here's how to test the balance: Close the garage door and pull the release handle, which disengages the automatic opener. Then manually lift the door until it's about halfway open. The door should not go up or down more than a foot, and then remain in place without help.

If it creeps up or down, the door is not balanced or the springs are worn. Call a professional to have it repaired.

6 SCHEDULE INSPECTIONS

"People tend to overlook their garage door until there is a major problem that's costly to fix," says Krzyzak. "They don't think twice about scheduling an oil change for their car, and they should do the same for their garage door." Inspect your doors twice a year to check the panels, hinges, pulleys, rollers, cables and springs. It's helpful to periodically book an inspection with a garage door specialist.

7 CLEAN & PAINT

Protect and preserve your garage door, which often takes a beating from the sun and the weather. Sand, prime and paint rust spots on steel garage doors. Wash fiberglass doors with an all-purpose cleaner. For wood doors, which are subject to warping and water damage, remove chipped and peeling paint before sanding and painting.

"Here in Arizona's sun and heat, you have to regularly treat garage doors," says Krzyzak. "You may install a new high-end, $10,000 cedar overlay door, and within six months without treatment it can look like it's 15 years old."

8 REPLACE WEATHERSTRIPPING

The rubber weatherstripping keeps out cold, water and debris. Sold at hardware stores and home centers, it has a flange that slides into a groove in the bottom of the garage door.

Weatherstripping for wood garage doors is usually nailed in place. If the bottom weatherstripping is torn, replace it. Reattach loose weatherstripping along the sides of the door, or replace it if it's badly worn or damaged.

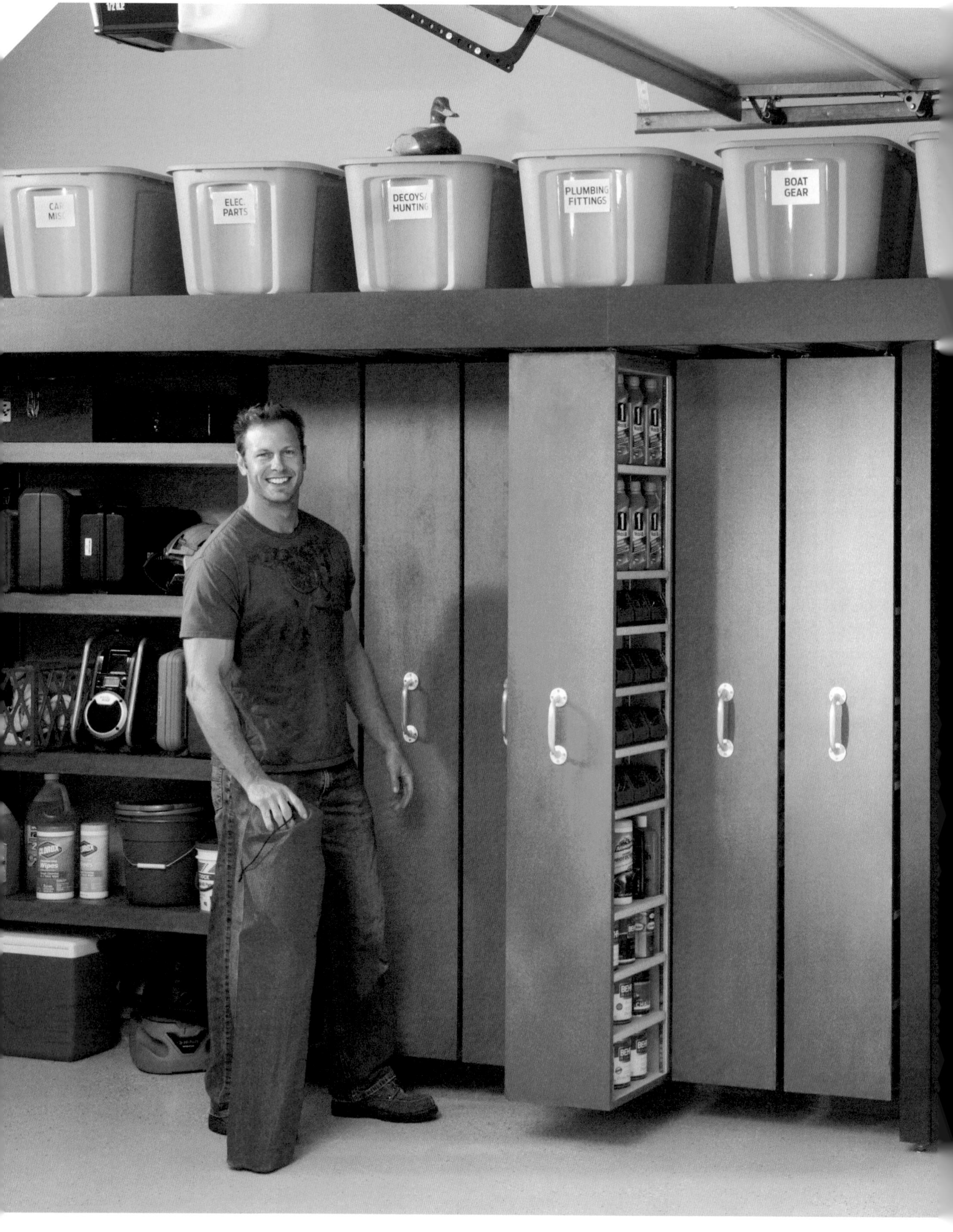
ELEC.
PARTS
DECOYS/
HUNTING
PLUMBING
FITTINGS
BOAT
GEAR

SPACE-SAVING GARAGE STORAGE

//

CREATE A SPOT FOR ALL YOUR STUFF—SLIDING SHELF UNITS FOR SMALLER ITEMS AND A GIANT AREA OVERHEAD FOR EVERYTHING ELSE

Let's face it. No matter how big your garage is, there never seems to be enough room to store everything. But this storage project can help by making ultra-efficient use of the narrow area on the sidewall of your garage.

The heart of the system is a series of double-sided rollout shelves that allow easy access to everything that can be stored in a narrow space. With these rollouts, you don't have to store your paint cans, nails, screws and other stuff four layers deep and then shuffle everything around to find what you're looking for. When the shelves are pulled out, everything is in full view and easily accessible. Plus, the garage looks neat and tidy when the shelves are pushed back in.

Don't worry if you've also got some large items to store. The 16-ft.-long top shelf is 32 in. deep to hold big storage containers, and there's a 3-ft.-wide section of 16-in.-deep shelves for medium-size items. The storage unit in total measures 16 ft. long, 84 in. tall and 16 in. deep.

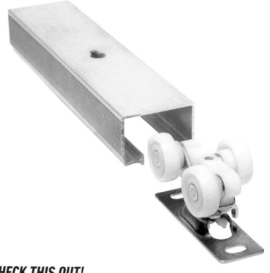

SLIDING STORAGE = MORE CONVENIENCE, MORE SPACE

The rollout shelves provide better access and make small stuff easier to find. The rollouts are versatile too. You can set the divider wherever you want to create different-depth shelves.

The bypass unit adds 50% more storage for long-handled tools and all sorts of items that take up too much wall space. You simply slide it to either side to access the stuff behind.

If you want to save some money and don't require as much narrow storage space, just reduce the number of rollout shelves. Each rollout, including hardware, costs about $100.

Expect to spend three or four days building this

CHECK THIS OUT!

This bypass door hardware is the key to smooth-gliding rollouts.

project. It's not complicated or difficult, but there are a lot of parts to cut out and assemble. For the most part, we used standard carpentry tools, but we did use a table saw to cut the particleboard, and a biscuit joiner and pocket screw jig to assemble the rollouts and bypass unit. The latter tools are optional, though. You can cut parts with a circular saw, but it'll take longer and won't be as accurate. And you can substitute screws and glue for the biscuit joints. You can also nail through the face of the cabinets to secure the divider rather than using pocket screws.

1 MARK THE WALL
Make a level line to indicate the bottom edge of the top shelf, and then mark the location of all four columns. Draw plumb lines to mark the edges of the 2x2 cleats.

2 ASSEMBLE THE COLUMNS
Wood glue creates a strong bond on particleboard and makes a strong assembly. Use brads to hold the parts together until the glue sets.

3 INSTALL LEG LEVELERS
Garage floors tend to be damp and unlevel. Adjustable leg levelers on the bottom of each column keep the columns dry and adjust to sloping floors.

The particleboard and framing lumber you'll need are available from home centers and most lumberyards. The bypass door track and three-wheel rollers we used to support the shelves may be hard to find locally, but you can order them online at *johnsonhardware.com*. You can also buy the shelf standards and leg levelers online at *wwhardware.com*.

MAP IT OUT ON THE WALL

Mark the locations of the top shelf and columns on the wall before you start building **(Photo 1)**. This allows you to check for obstructions and double-check the height of the columns. Start by deciding where the endpoints for the 16-ft. storage unit will be. If you have leeway, you could adjust the position so the end columns land over wall studs, but it's not necessary.

Next, use a level to see if the garage floor slopes. Measure 81 in. up from the highest point on the floor and mark the wall. Draw a 16-ft. level line across the wall from this point. We used a laser level to establish level reference points on each end of a 16-ft. line and measured up from these points to mark the endpoint of the horizontal layout line. Then we snapped a chalk line between these points to indicate the bottom edge of the shelf and the top of the columns. You could also use a line level or step a 4-ft. level across the wall to mark the level line.

If your garage floor slopes more than 1½ in. from one end of the unit to the other, you'll have to build some of the columns a little taller. Check this by measuring down from the level line at each end. Finally, using **Figure B** (p. 259) as a guide, carefully mark the location of the wall cleats that anchor each column, and draw plumb lines down from each mark **(Photo 1)**. Now you're ready to build the columns and wide shelf.

ASSEMBLE THE COLUMNS AND SHELF

Cut out the parts according to the Cutting List on p. 259. Then build the columns. **Photo 2** shows how to assemble the columns using wood glue and finish nails. Let the glue set. Then install the leg levelers **(Photo 3)**. Mount the cleats on the wall at each of the column locations. Use toggle-type hollow wall anchors to anchor the cleats if there aren't any studs to screw into. We used Toggler Snaptoggle anchors, which are easier and faster to install than standard toggle bolts.

Mount the columns by slipping them over the cleats and driving screws through the sides into the cleats **(Photo 4)**. We had to notch the bottoms of

2x2 MOUNTED ON WALL

COLUMN

INSTALL THE COLUMNS
Slip the columns over cleats mounted to the wall. It's easy to adjust the height and plumb the face of each column before screwing it to the cleat.

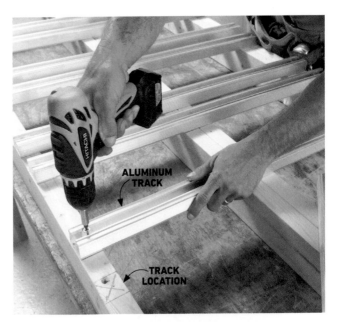

ALUMINUM TRACK

TRACK LOCATION

ATTACH THE TRACKS TO THE SHELF FRAME
To avoid working overhead later, screw the tracks to the shelf before you install it. Use the dimensions in **Figure B**, p. 259, to lay out the track locations.

6 SET THE TOP SHELF FRAME ON THE COLUMNS
Align the ends of the shelf with the outside edges of the columns and screw it to the studs.

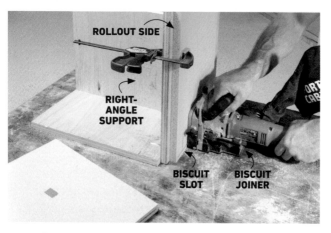

7 CUT BISCUIT SLOTS IN THE ROLLOUT PARTS
Cut three biscuit slots on the faces of the sides and matching slots on the ends of the top and bottom. The right angle support allowed us to use the workbench top to support the biscuit joiner.

8 ASSEMBLE THE ROLLOUTS
Join the sides to the top and bottom of the rollouts with biscuits and wood glue. Clamp the parts together until the glue sets.

the columns to fit around the protruding foundation block. If you have a similar situation and the block is more than 6 in. above the floor, make sure to either shorten the rollout shelves or make them narrower so they don't run into the protruding foundation.

Adjust the leg levelers until the tops of the columns are even with the horizontal line. Then set a level against the front edge to make sure the column is plumb. You can slide narrow shims between the wall and the back edge of the column if necessary to plumb the column. When the column is plumb and the top is even with the level line, drive screws through the side and into the cleats. The next step is to build and install the horizontal shelf.

Screw 2x4s together to make the top shelf using **Figure B** as a guide. It's easier to attach the aluminum tracks to the shelf before you lift it onto the columns **(Photo 5)**. Use **Figure B** as a guide for marking the track locations. Cut the tracks to 32 in. with a hacksaw. Then drill holes for the mounting screws. Attach the tracks with 2-in. pan-head or washer-head screws.

Mark the stud locations on the wall. Then lift the shelf onto the columns and screw it to the studs with 4-in. structural screws or lag screws **(Photo 6)**. Screw ¾-in. particleboard to the top of the shelf frame. Check with a framing square to make sure the columns are at a right angle to the wall before you toe-screw the front of the columns to the shelf frame.

BUILD THE ROLLOUT SHELVES AND BYPASS

Photo 7 shows how we used a biscuit joiner to slot the sides of the rollouts. For more information on this "bench reference" biscuit joining method, go to *familyhandyman.com* and enter "biscuit joints" in the search box. Mark the orientation of the parts by putting a piece of masking tape on the side facing you. When you assemble the parts, face the tape to the inside of the rollout. Glue and clamp the sides to the top and bottom **(Photo 8)**. Glue a second layer of particleboard to the top for extra strength and to allow for the 1½-in. roller mounting screws. **Photo 9** shows how to support the center divider with spacers while you attach it with pocket screws. If you don't have a pocket screw jig, just drive finish nails through the front and back of the rollout to secure the divider. You can adjust the position of the divider to accommodate your items. We moved one off-center to allow for 7-in.-deep shelves and built another unit with full-depth shelves. Use the same method to build the large bypass unit.

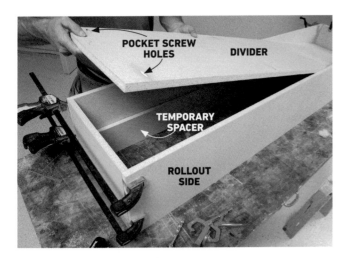

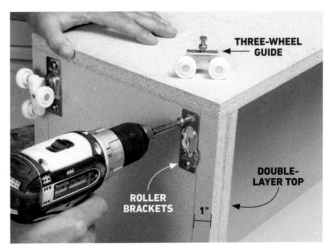

9   INSTALL THE ROLLOUT DIVIDER

Use spacers to support the divider while you screw or nail it to the sides of the shelf. Vary the size of the spacers to create different-width shelves.

10   MOUNT THE ROLLERS

Adjustable rollers allow you to fine-tune the rollout shelves after they're installed. Each pair of rollers is rated for 125 lbs., for a total weight limit of 250 lbs. per rollout.

Finish the rollouts by attaching the roller mounting brackets (**Photo 10**) and the metal shelf standards. Draw lines 1 in. from the edge as guides for the brackets. Drill pilot holes and attach the brackets with 1½-in. screws. Position the shelf standards about ⅜ in. from the front and back of the cabinet. We used ½-in. No. 4 flat-head screws to attach the standards, but you can also use the small nails usually included.

MOUNT THE ROLLOUTS AND BYPASS

We used different techniques to hang the rollout shelves and the bypass unit. For the rollouts, it's simpler to connect the rollers to the top of the shelf first and then slide the wheels into the tracks (**Photo 11**). For the bypass unit, install the rollers in the track before you mount it, and then hang the bypass by sliding the rollers into the mounting brackets.

To prevent the rollers on the rollout shelves from bumping into the face trim, screw 1½-in.-square blocks of particleboard to the outside end of each of the rollout shelf tracks. After all the rollouts are hung, adjust the rollers until the spaces between rollouts are even and the faces are flush when they're pushed in. Use the small wrench included with the rollers to turn the adjusting bolt located just below the rollers.

11   INSTALL THE ROLLOUTS ON THE TRACKS

Slide the rollers into the tracks to hang each rollout shelf. It's easy if you pile up some scraps to support the heavy rollout while you align the rollers.

FINISH WITH TRIM BOARDS

Complete the project by nailing strips of particleboard trim to the faces of the columns and the top shelf (**Photo 12**). Two 8-ft. trim pieces will just cover

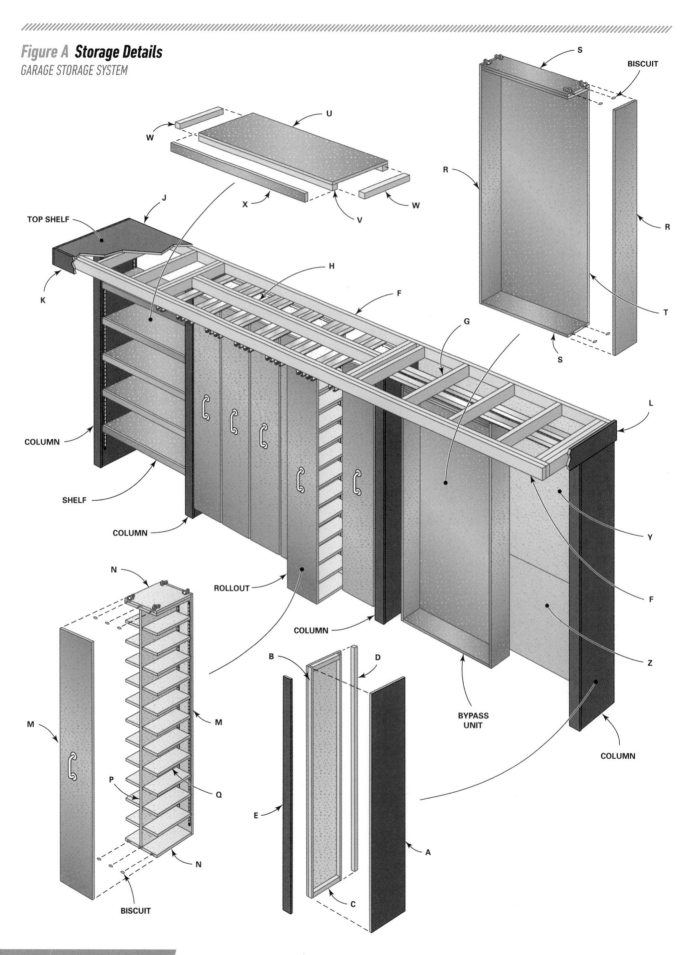

TOP SHELF

BISCUIT

COLUMN

SHELF

COLUMN

ROLLOUT

COLUMN

BYPASS
UNIT

COLUMN

BISCUIT

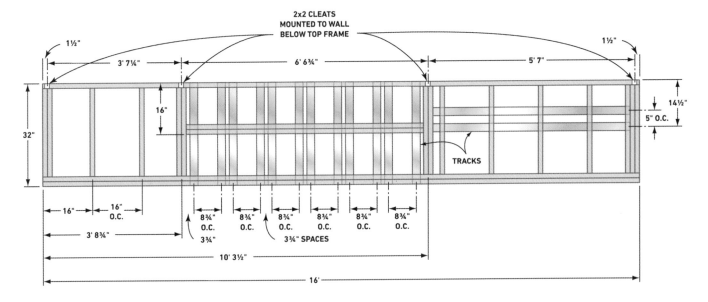

CUTTING LIST

KEY	QTY.	PART
A	8	15¼" x 80" x ¾" particleboard sides
B	8	1½" x 80" x ¾" particleboard spacers
C	8	1½" x 1½" x 12¼" spf (spruce, pine, fir)
D	4	1½" x 1½" x 80" spf
E	4	3⅛" x 80" x ¾" particleboard face trim
Top shelf		
F	3	2x4 x 16' spf
G	15	2x4 x 27½" spf
H	2	2x4 x 75¾" spf
J	2	32" x 96" x ¾" particleboard top
K	2	5¾" x 96" x ¾" particleboard face trim
L	2	5¾" x 32¾" x ¾" particleboard end trim
Rollouts (all particleboard)		
M	12	11¾" x 74½" x ¾" sides
N	18	11¾" x 14½" x ¾" tops and bottoms
P	6	14½" x 72¼" x ¾" divider
Q	132*	5½" x 14" x ¾" shelves

* Adjust to your needs. This includes 22 shelves for each rollout.

Bypass unit (all particleboard)		
R	2	8" x 74½" x ¾" sides
S	3	8" x 30½" x ¾" tops and bottoms
T	1	30½" x 72¼" x ¾" back shelves
U	5	14½" x 39¾" x ¾" particleboard tops
V	10	1½" x 1½" x 39¾" spf top and back frame
W	10	1½" x 1½" x 11½" spf side frames
X	5	2¼" x 39¾" x ¾" particleboard face trim
Y	1	64" x 48" x ¾" particleboard
Z	1	64" x 48" x ¾" particleboard

MATERIALS LIST

ITEM	QTY.
2x2 x 8' spf (spruce, pine, fir)	9
2x2 x 10' spf	1
2x4 x 16' spf	6
4' x 8' x ¾" particleboard	15
Johnson No. 1120 three-wheel hanger* (part of No. 1500 pocket door hardware set)	52
Johnson No. 100-0096 96" track*	4
Johnson No. 100-0072 72" track*	2

* Parts numbers for *johnsonhardware.com*

KV0255 ZC 72 shelf standards**	28
KV0256 ZC shelf supports**	548
SC4X12F ZC No. 4 x ½" flat head screws**	200
SCT3816 T-Nut**	4
LA38 212 Leg Leveler**	4

** Parts numbers for *wwhardware.com*

Wood glue	
No. 20 biscuit	72
1¼" pocket screws	56
4" structural screws or lag screws	24
3" screws (to toe-screw columns to frames)	4
1½" finish nails or nail gun pins	
Handles	

the front edge. Then overlap the side pieces at each end. We also screwed sheets of particleboard to the wall behind the bypass unit to provide an attachment surface for hooks and other hanging hardware. We stained the columns and trim black, and the faces of the rollouts and the bypass unit with Cabot Early American stain. When the stain was dry,

we brushed two coats of Minwax Oil-Modified Polyurethane finish over the whole unit to provide a little sheen and extra protection. If you plan to stain and finish the storage unit, consider doing it before you assemble the parts. It'll save you a lot of time and effort.

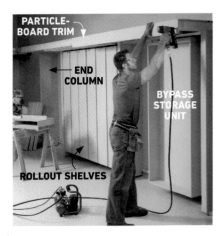

12 ADD THE FINISHING TOUCHES

Finish by nailing strips of particleboard over the front edge of the top shelf and the faces of the columns. You can stain or paint the particleboard or just brush a coat or two of polyurethane over it.

10 TIPS TO SAVE GAS

MANY THINGS CAN LOWER YOUR MPG AND END UP COSTING YOU MORE IN GAS, SO WHY NOT KEEP YOUR CAR IN TOP SHAPE AND POCKET THE MONEY YOU'D OTHERWISE WASTE ON FILLING UP? WE'LL HELP YOU GET STARTED.

1 KEEP YOUR TIRES AT THE RIGHT PRESSURE

Surveys show that 50% of drivers are driving on under-inflated tires. You can't eyeball tire pressure, and you shouldn't rely on the low tire pressure warning light—it doesn't light up until your tires are at least 25% underinflated, when you've already been wasting gas. Instead, check them monthly with a tire pressure gauge (less than $10).

Underinflated tires have higher rolling resistance, causing your engine to work harder and waste about $450 a year in gas. (The savings given for each tip assume you drive 20,000 miles a year and gas is $2.50 a gallon.) Low air pressure also wears out your tires twice as fast, costing you about $150 a year. The recommended air pressure for your vehicle's tires is on the driver's door or pillar.

2 CHANGE YOUR SPARK PLUGS AHEAD OF TIME

Most drivers think their spark plugs will last well over 100,000 miles. That's not true for all engines. Refer to your car's maintenance guide for the recommended interval for your engine. Regardless, it's never a good idea to squeeze the last drop of life out of your spark plugs.

Here's why. If your 100,000-mile spark plugs have 80,000 miles on them, they're 80% worn. Misfires and incomplete combustion will occur more often, costing you about $350 in wasted fuel. You have to replace them anyway, so do it early and pocket the savings. Even if you have to replace the plugs one extra time over the life of your car, you'll come out way ahead.

3 ALIGN YOUR WHEELS

If your tires are bowed out of alignment by just 0.017 in., it's the equivalent of dragging your tire sideways for 102 miles for every 20,000 you drive. That'll cost you about $100 a year in wasted gas. It will also wear your tires faster, costing you about $70 more a year.

Here's an easy way to check your alignment without taking your car to the shop. Buy a tread depth gauge (about $2) and measure the tread depth on both edges of a tire (rear tires too). If one side of the tire is worn more than the other, your car needs to be aligned. A front-end alignment costs about $80, so you'll save about $90 the first year alone.

4 REPLACE A FAILING THERMOSTAT

A thermostat that opens too quickly or stays open can dramatically lower the coolant temperature and put a damper on your gas mileage. If you have an infrared thermometer (see tip 6), simply aim it at the thermostat housing. If your engine is warmed up and the thermometer reads less than 160 degrees F, you're wasting gas and it's time to replace the thermostat. (To reduce reflection errors, spray the thermostat housing with black paint before testing.) A new thermostat costs about $10.

5 TAKE IT EASY: A LEAD FOOT = A LIGHT WALLET

Hard acceleration in stop-and-go driving costs you 20% in gas mileage. If you live your life in rush-hour traffic and like to put the pedal to the metal, you may want to spend your extra time at the next stoplight figuring out how you could have used the $450 a year you're wasting.

6 CHECK FOR BRAKE DRAG

Brake calipers have a habit of rusting and binding and really depressing your gas mileage. But how can you tell if you have "brake drag" without getting your brakes checked at a shop? Easy! Buy a noncontact infrared laser thermometer (about $30 at any home center), remove the wheel cover (if equipped) and aim the laser at the wheel hub after a drive. Compare the readings from the right and left sides. If they vary by more than 20%, you've probably got a dragging brake or a wheel-bearing problem, so take your vehicle in for repair.

7 ADD THAT MISSING SPOILER

The plastic air dam (aka "spoiler") that's broken or missing wasn't just for looks. It actually serves a purpose: It forces air up and over the hood to help your car cut through the air with less drag. Similarly, under-engine splashguards help reduce aerodynamic drag by keeping the air flowing smoothly under your car instead of producing turbulence that causes drag. Contact a junkyard to find a replacement air dam and engine splashguards.

8 AVOID SPEEDING

Aerodynamic drag is a minor concern in city driving, but it really kills mileage at speeds over 55 mph. In fact, increasing your speed from 55 to 65 increases drag by 36%! If you do a lot of highway driving, getting to your destination a few minutes early could cost you an extra $375 a year. Keep it closer to 55 mph and use cruise control.

9 PAY ATTENTION TO YOUR WARNING LIGHTS

A glowing check engine light means you have an emissions problem, which is almost always caused by an incomplete burn. That means you're wasting gas, and worse, that gas goes into your catalytic converter, causing it to fail early. Replacing the converter can cost over $1,000, and then you still have to fix the problem that activated the engine light. It's likely a bum sensor or a vacuum leak. Replacing a sensor or fixing a vacuum leak can significantly cut your fuel costs.

10 REFRESH YOUR CABIN AIR FILTER

A clogged cabin air filter dramatically lowers cooling efficiency. Your A/C compressor will run longer and harder, which drags down your mpg. It also causes your blower motor to run longer and hotter and fail early. A filter costs about $15. Replace it before summer, and save more in gas than the cost of the filter.

WHAT TO DO IF ...

BE PREPARED IF SOMETHING GOES WRONG, AND LEARN HOW TO AVOID IT

In a quick survey of co-workers and friends, we at *Family Handyman* discovered that many people really don't know what to do when a warning light appears on their dash. And they're just as confused when it comes to which maintenance services are really important. So we've put together these tip lists for warning lights, maintenance services and emergency kits. We guarantee you will find something here to help you be a safer, smarter driver and car owner.

WHAT TO DO WHEN WARNING LIGHTS COME ON

You're driving down the road and your "HOT" light comes on. If your first thought is, "You're hot? I'm sweatin' bullets in here," you've failed to understand the seriousness of the situation. Those warning lights aren't a joke. If you ignore them and keep driving, you're setting yourself up for major repair bills. Here's what the lights mean and what you should do if any of them come on when you're driving.

TPS (TIRE PRESSURE SENSOR)

At least one tire is low on air pressure. Fill it as soon as possible. Driving on an underinflated tire can cause a blowout, possibly resulting in an "at-fault" accident. Air is free (or cheap). But a new tire can be more than $125, and an accident will cost you your deductible and increased premiums.

OIL

The oil pressure is too low to keep driving. Pull over to a safe spot immediately. Check the oil level. If it's low and you have oil on hand, add it and see if the light goes out. If you don't have oil, call a tow truck or ask a friend to make a roadside delivery. It's better to spend $150 on a tow than $5,000 to replace a seized engine.

HOT

The engine is overheated. Pull over to a safe spot immediately. Open the hood, then call a tow truck (about $150 for a tow to the nearest shop). If you keep driving, you can warp the cylinder head (a more than $1,000 repair bill) or completely destroy your engine.

BATTERY LIGHT

Something is wrong with the battery or charging system. Turn off all high-load electrical accessories such as the air conditioning, heater fan and rear window defogger, and drive to the nearest shop.

FLASHING "CHECK ENGINE" LIGHT

The computer has detected a misfire serious enough to damage your catalytic converter. Pull over or drive to the nearest exit and call a tow truck. Get the underlying misfire problem fixed right away—a new catalytic converter can cost about $2,000.

STEADY-ON "CHECK ENGINE" LIGHT

The computer has detected a problem with the engine or the emissions system. If the vehicle is running fine, you don't have to rush in for service. But if it's running rough, stalls, hesitates on acceleration or gets poor gas mileage, make an appointment to get it checked out sooner rather than later.

WHAT TO DO TO KEEP YOUR ENGINE RUNNING

Shops recommend 30,000-, 60,000- and 90,000-mile services that can easily cost hundreds of dollars. The majority of the items on those lists are inspections. Sure, they're important, but the "replace" items are the most important. Here are the top five items you must replace in order to avoid major repair bills later.

1 TRANSMISSION FLUID

If you put on 200,000 miles during the life of the car, you'll spend about $800 on fluid changes. If you skip the fluid changes, you'll have only $800 to put toward the more than $2,000 cost for a transmission rebuild. Did you buy an extended warranty? Well, you just voided that too. It never pays to skip this service.

2 COOLANT

If you change the newer long-life coolants twice over a 200,000-mile period, you'll spend $300. If you don't change your coolant, plan on spending about $1,800 on a new radiator, heater core and water pump. Kiss the extended warranty goodbye too. For best results, always use genuine factory coolant.

3 OIL FILTER

You already know how important oil changes and synthetic oil are to the life of your engine. But an extended-life oil filter is just as important. They cost less than $20 but are rated to last up to 10,000 miles. Economy filters start to clog and self-destruct after about 4,000 miles. Once the filter media disintegrates, it can spew debris into critical parts and cause thousands in repair bills.

4 SPARK PLUGS

Newer-style platinum/iridium spark plugs are rated for 100,000 miles. But they start misfiring at about 80,000 miles. Misfires damage spark plug wires, ignition coils, ignition modules and sometimes even your catalytic converter. If you don't change the plugs, you can count on a minimum of $400 in ignition system–related repairs.

5 TIMING BELT

A broken timing belt will leave you stranded. If you're lucky, you'll have to pay just $150 for a tow and then $700 (parts and labor) for the new belt. But if you have a certain type of engine (called an "interference" engine) and the belt breaks while you're driving, it'll destroy your engine, costing you about $5,000.

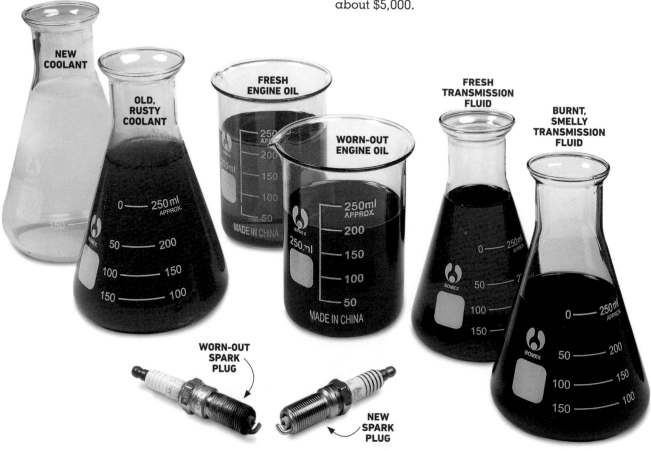

NEW COOLANT

OLD, RUSTY COOLANT

FRESH ENGINE OIL

WORN-OUT ENGINE OIL

FRESH TRANSMISSION FLUID

BURNT, SMELLY TRANSMISSION FLUID

WORN-OUT SPARK PLUG

NEW SPARK PLUG

WHAT TO DO TO PREPARE FOR AN EMERGENCY

Most people don't think clearly in an emergency. So clip this section and stuff it in your glove box. Follow the steps and you'll improve your chances of getting out safely.

AN EMERGENCY KIT

If you follow every expert's advice on what to carry in the event of an emergency, you'd have a trunk full of supplies (especially candy bars). We're not disputing the value of carrying all those items, but we don't know anyone who does. So we've assembled a list of "must-have" items that take up very little space and can really help you in an emergency situation.

- Pad/pencil for accident information
- Jumper cables to get you going again and right to a service station
- Duct tape to use as a handyman bandage or to reattach vehicle parts after an accident
- Cellphone charger to keep your cellphone running until help arrives

- LED headlight so you can use both hands while you fix a flat tire, add oil, etc.
- Oil to refill your engine if it's critically low from leaks or excessive consumption
- Air compressor to inflate your spare tire
- A can of Fix-a-Flat (about $15) to fix a flat tire when the wheel is rusted in place and won't come off.

COLD WEATHER GEAR

If you've ever changed a tire in the dead of winter, you know how quickly your hands can get numb from working with subzero tools. And winter winds can freeze your ears in seconds, making you unable to even finish the job. Frostbite is a serious risk. If you pack nothing else in your winter emergency kit, make sure you at least have warm gloves and a hat that covers your ears.

CHANGE YOUR ENGINE COOLANT

THE RIGHT TOOLS AND MATERIALS MAKE ALL THE DIFFERENCE

Over time, engine coolant loses its anticorrosive properties and lubricating ability. Some car manufacturers recommend changing the coolant every 30,000 miles. The recommended change intervals vary widely, however, so check the maintenance schedule in your owner's manual.

You can change a car's coolant yourself in about an hour. You'll need to invest in an air-powered refilling tool to remove air pockets from the cooling system as you fill. You'll save about $50 on your first coolant change and about $100 on each change after that.

This procedure works for any cooling system that's not contaminated with rust or oil. We'll show you how to check your coolant and then how to change it.

HERE'S WHAT YOU'LL NEED:
■ Coolant (2 gallons; about $60)
■ Air-powered refill tool (about $105)
■ Air compressor
■ Hose removal tool (about $13)
■ Repair manual to locate block drain plugs
■ Drain pan and paper towels
■ Wrenches and screwdrivers

To begin, check the condition of your coolant when the engine is cool. Remove the radiator or coolant reservoir cap and examine the coolant. If it looks rusty (don't confuse orange coolant with rust), has crud or oil floating on the top, or looks like chocolate milk, call it quits and take it to a pro. You have problems that this procedure won't solve.

If the coolant looks clean, start the job by jacking up the vehicle and supporting it with jack stands. Next, place a large drain pan under the radiator. Loosen the lower radiator hose clamp with pliers (spring-type clamp) or a screwdriver (worm-drive clamp), and remove the hose **(Photo 1)**. If the hose won't budge, use a hose removal tool (one choice is Tool Aid No. SGT13860, about $13 online) to break the hose loose **(Photo 1)**. Let the radiator and water pump drain completely. Then reattach the lower radiator hose and clamp.

Next, locate and remove the block drain plugs (they're not in the same spot on every engine, so refer to a repair manual for the location of yours). Reinstall the block drain plugs and move on to the refilling step.

1 REMOVE THE LOWER HOSE
Slip the pointed end of the removal tool all the way into the end of the hose. Pull the tool around the radiator neck to break the hose loose. Then pull it off quickly and immediately direct the coolant into the drain pan.

2 VACUUM-FILL THE COOLING SYSTEM
Insert the fill tube into the coolant bottle. Then open the valve and let the vacuum suck fresh coolant into the system. Repeat the procedure until the system is full.

REFILL WITH FRESH COOLANT
Insert the air-powered refilling tool (we used the UView 550500 AirLift II Economy Cooling System Refiller, about $105 online) into the radiator neck or overflow bottle. Connect the exhaust hose and compressed air line, and route the open end of the tool's exhaust hose into an empty gallon jug or pail. Then open the valve and let the vacuum rise until the needle reaches the edge of the red zone on the gauge. Then fill with coolant **(Photo 2)**. The vacuum sucks out any air pockets as it refills the system. When it's full, just reinstall the radiator or overflow tank caps, remove the jack stands and go for a spin.

BUY THE RIGHT COOLANT
Most DIYers buy coolant at the auto parts store, which carries a product labeled "universal," meaning it works in all cars. Carmakers disagree. Over the past several years, they've issued service bulletins warning that "universal" coolants are often incompatible with the newer metal alloys and gaskets and seals used in their vehicles. The carmakers aren't saying that just to increase sales of their proprietary coolants. They're seeing real (and expensive) damage caused by these coolants.

If you use the wrong coolant, you won't see the damage for a few years. But when you do, it'll cost you a bundle. So heed the manufacturer's warnings and buy coolant right from the dealer. It'll cost about $10 to $15 more per gallon (and most vehicles need 2 gallons), but the peace of mind is worth it.

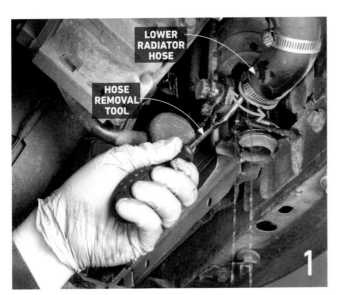

HOW TO BUY A
RELIABLE USED CAR

DO RESEARCH AND PERFORM INSPECTIONS TO AVOID PROBLEMATIC VEHICLES

Cars and trucks have changed a lot over the last 10 to 15 years. These days, almost every mechanical system is controlled by electronics. In fact, a typical 10-year-old vehicle has more than 100 microprocessors, 50 electronic control units and 5 miles of wiring. If you think you can thoroughly check out a late-model vehicle by taking it for a short spin and kicking the tires, think again.

Finding a reliable used vehicle works best as a three-step process that involves online research,

a thorough initial inspection, and a final physical and computerized inspection performed by a mechanic. We'll give you some tips on handling the first two steps yourself so you can weed out the clunkers before spending money for your mechanic to do a final check. But trust us: If you skip the final mechanic's inspection, it could cost you dearly. So if you have your heart set on a particular make and model, start with Step 1 before you go shopping.

STEP 1:

CHECK OUT VEHICLE RELIABILITY

Some makes, models, engines and transmissions are known for their high failure rates, which you want to know before you start shopping. Some of the following sources charge a fee but may also be available for free at your local public library. Here's where to look:

■ Consumer Reports (digital, about $40 per year)— Vehicle system reliability info based on actual readers' experiences.

■ *Truedelta.com* (about $10 for 90 days)—Vehicle system reliability information along with actual repair costs incurred by owners.

■ *Alldatadiy.com* (about $60 per year) or *eautorepair .net* (about $40 per year)—Up-to-date lists of technical service bulletins from carmakers disclosing known failures, updated parts and repair procedures, and software fixes.

STEP 2:

DO YOUR OWN INSPECTION OF ALL THE FEATURES

Once you've selected a particular make and model and you want to check out actual cars, here are simple, quick things you can check to eliminate possible problems. Test every vehicle feature to check for proper operation: power windows and locks, power sliding door and hatch, sunroof, power seat, heated seats, power mirrors, cruise control, all climate control settings, backup camera and sensors, keyless entry and remote start, and exterior/interior lights.

1 ASSEMBLE A CAR INSPECTION TOOLBOX
Before you check out a vehicle, go to the auto parts store and buy a tread depth gauge, brake test strips and a digital volt ohm meter. You'll also need a kitchen thermometer and a flashlight. Then go through the inspection steps on your own car so you know what you're doing when you conduct a real inspection on a prospective purchase.

2 DO A BULB CHECK
Turn the key to the On position but don't start the vehicle. All the warning lights (icons) should illuminate to prove the bulbs work. Consult the owner's manual to see which warning lights are installed on that vehicle. The most common is the "Check Engine" or "Service Engine Soon" light. But also check for ABS, Brake, SRS (airbag), TPMS (tire pressure), OIL, HOT (or gauge), ESP/TCS (traction/stability), and Battery/Charging lights. Then start the engine. All warning lights should turn off. If not, there's a problem.

3 CHECK THE DIPSTICK
Pull the engine oil dipstick and examine the color. A honey color is an indication of fresh oil— light brown is slightly used oil (both good signs). But a chocolate milk color is a bad sign that may indicate a leaking head gasket—easily a $1,500-plus repair.

4 CHECK TIRE TREAD DEPTH
Using a tread depth gauge, measure each tire at the center and both edges. The three tread depth readings on each tire should be within $1/32$ in. of each other. A greater difference indicates an alignment, inflation or suspension problem. All four tires should be within $2/32$ in. of one another. A greater difference indicates lack of proper tire rotation. Tires with a tread depth of $4/32$ in. or less should be replaced (factor the cost of new tires into your offer).

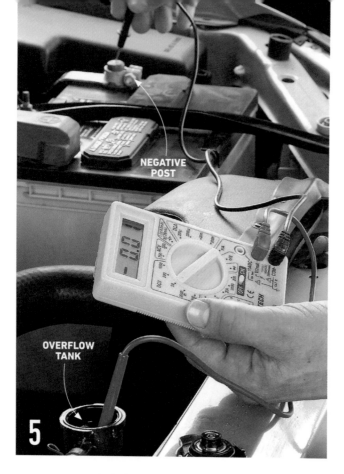

NEGATIVE POST

OVERFLOW TANK

5

5 CHECK ENGINE COOLANT FOR ELECTROLYSIS

On a cool engine, remove the radiator or over-flow tank cap. Using a digital volt ohm meter, set the dial to the 2-volt DC scale. Touch the negative meter lead to the negative battery post. Dip the positive lead directly into the coolant in the tank. The reading should be less than 0.300 volts. If it's not, the coolant is worn and there's a good chance corrosion is already eating away at cooling system components.

If the reading is below 0.300 volts, turn off all electrical accessories, start the engine and rev it to 2,000 rpm, and repeat the test. If the reading rises, the vehicle has an electrical grounding problem that must be addressed. Wipe the meter probes before storing.

6A

BRAKE FLUID RESERVOIR

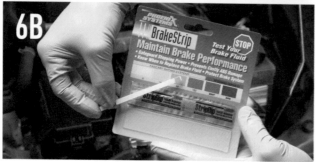

6B

6 CHECK BRAKE FLUID CONDITION

When brake fluid wears out, internal corrosion sets in and corrodes brake parts from the inside out. The corrosion process leaches copper into the brake fluid. Test for the presence of copper by dipping a test strip (such as BrakeStrip, about $75 online for 100 test strips) into the brake fluid reservoir and comparing the color with the package's chart. A high reading indicates owner neglect as well as a high possibility of internal brake system corrosion damage.

7 CHECK FOR RUST AND PAINT BLISTERS

Check along the edges of the hood and trunk lid, rocker panels, bottom edges of doors and around wheel wells for rough or raised areas that can indicate the start of rust issues. Sellers may mask rust problems with touch-up paint, so look carefully.

8 TEST A/C PERFORMANCE

Close the windows and doors and set the A/C to "Max" and "Recirculate." Insert a kitchen thermometer into the center air duct. Start the engine and rev to 1,500 rpm for several minutes. The temperature should slowly drop into the 40s (unless it's a very hot day with high humidity). If the temperature doesn't fall below the high 50s, the A/C system requires service.

7

8

9 CHECK FOR LEAKING CV BOOTS

Turn the wheels full left or right. Shine your flashlight at the CV boots on each end of the axle. If you see tears or grease, you're looking at a repair costing several hundred dollars.

10 TEST-DRIVE THE VEHICLE

The vehicle should start right up and idle smoothly. Acceleration and all shifts should be smooth; jerky acceleration or harsh shifts are trouble signs. Apply the brakes at highway speed and check for brake pedal pulsation, steering wheel shake or pulling to one side.

Also, drive the vehicle to a secluded area with flat pavement and drive for a short distance with your hands off the wheel. The vehicle should not pull or wander. If it does, that could be a sign of tire, suspension or steering issues.

11 NEGOTIATE A PRICE CONTINGENT ON A MECHANIC'S APPROVAL

Consult *nada.com*, *kbb.com*, *edmunds.com* and *truecar.com* to find what buyers in your area are paying for the same vehicle. Then subtract the cost of any required repairs discovered during your inspection. You can't blame a private seller for asking full retail car-lot price for a used car. But a fair market value for a used car from a private seller is halfway between trade-in and retail. So that's where you should start your negotiations—at that halfway point. Then subtract the cost of discovered repairs. Once you and the seller settle on a price, make the deal contingent on receiving a clean bill of health (no more than $300 in additional repairs) from your mechanic.

12 BEWARE OF SELLER'S CLAIMS

The most common buyer mistake is to trust the seller's claim that "the car just needs this small fix." The truth is, if the problem were really that small, the seller would have fixed it already. What the seller most likely means is: "I was hoping the transmission needed only a fluid change. Then the shop told me it was going to cost $2,000. So I'm actually telling you what my first guess was and hoping you'll believe it." So when a seller says, "It just needs this small fix," RUN!

STEP 3:

GET A PROFESSIONAL INSPECTION

Expect a professional mechanic's inspection to run you about $125 to $300. A professional inspection can discover the early stages of problems way before they turn into costly failures. So it's worth it to pay for a full physical inspection and test drive along with a complete computer scan.

The computer scan can discover whether the seller recently cleared trouble codes to cover up a problem. A professional scan tool can also check whether the vehicle's software is up to date. Software updates are critical to the proper performance of your vehicle, and unlike free software updates for your home and business computers, updating vehicle software costs about $200.